Invisible Children: A Portrait of Migrant Education in the United States

A Final Report of the
National Commission on Migrant Education

September 23, 1992

The National Commission on Migrant Education was established in 1988 by the Hawkins-Stafford Act (Public Law 100-297) to study the issues related to the education of migrant children and report their findings to the Secretary of Education and Congress. The Commission's first report addressed the status of the Migrant Student Record Transfer System (MSRTS) and was released in 1991. This document is the Commission's second and final report. It responds to the mandates set forth in the legislation which authorized the Commission's formation.

For sale by the U.S. Government Printing Office
Superintendent of Documents, Mail Stop: SSOP, Washington, DC 20402-9328
ISBN 0-16-038063-4

National Commision on Migrant Education

Commissioners

Honorable Linda Chavez
Chairman
Manhatten Institute
New York, New York/Bethesda, Maryland

Honorable Thad Cochran
U.S. Senate (MS)

Honorable William D. Ford
U.S. House of Representatives (MI)

Honorable Donna G. Garner
High School English Teacher
Midway High School
Hewitt, Texas

Honorable William F. Goodling
U.S. House of Representatives (PA)

Dr. Patricia A. Hayes
St. Edward's University
Austin, Texas

Honorable Michael J. LaVelle
Diversified Research, Inc.
Irvington, New York

Carolina Mata-Woodruff
Department of Children and Family Services
Springfield, Illinois

Honorable Howard M. Metzenbaum
U.S. Senate (OH)

Carolyn P. Paseneaux, J.D.
Wyoming Wool Growers Association
Casper, Wyoming

Wendell N. Rollason
Redlands Christian Migrant Association
Immokalee, Florida

Honorable Robert G. Simmons, Jr.
Simmons, Olsen, Ediger, Selzer, & Ballew, P.C.
Scottsbluff, Nebraska

Staff

Carol Pendas Whitten
Staff Director
Bethesda, Maryland

Lisandra Carlos
Senior Policy Analyst
Bethesda, Maryland

Robert C. Suggs, Ph.D
Senior Policy Analyst
(Retired)

Elizabeth J. Skiles
Administrative Officer
Bethesda, Maryland

Colette D. Yost
Staff Assistant
Bethesda, Maryland

Margaret R. Hoppe, ED.D
Special Consultant to Staff

Bette Kindman-Koffler, ED.D
Editoral Consultant

We would also like to thank the following staff who previously worked for the Commission:

Vidal A. Rivera, Jr.

Nancy D. Watson

Interns:

Victoria Carreon

Lidia Espinoza

Lisa Rodriguez

Alma D. Velasquez

We would like to thank the following individuals and organizations for their help in the Commission's work:

Administrative Conference of the United States (ACUS)

Bornstein Associates

Burness Communications

Business Communication Group

Christine H. Rossell, PhD

G&G Associates

Maria V. Colon, Pennsylvania State University

Noel H. Klores, JD

David Martin, JD

Philip L. Martin, PhD

Pittelli & Associates

Richard A. Figueroa, PhD, University of California, Davis

Villarreal Analytical Management and Organizational Services (VAMOS)

William G. Durden, PhD, Center for Talented Youth, The Johns Hopkins University

William O'Hare, PhD, Urban Research Institute, University of Louisville

Special thanks goes to the following individuals for their continued assistance throughout the Commission's tenure:

Cheryl Birdsall

Doris Dixon

Kris Gilbert

Lynn Selmser

Chairman's Preface

The Final Report of the National Commission on Migrant Education represents three years of study and consultation toward improving migrant education. When the twelve members of this Commission began our journey on September 27, 1989, few people, including the Commissioners themselves, believed we would ultimately produce a consensus document. This Commission spans the political, ideological, and professional spectrum—with opinions so varied among its members that at times it seemed impossible we would reach agreement.

One issue, nonetheless, kept us united and focused. As we travelled the country, hearing from those who serve migrants as well as from migrant families, all of us developed a sincere admiration for this population and an appreciation for their struggles. Our mission then became how best to help migrant children. Once we could agree that our purpose was to analyze the programs designed to serve these children and to recommend ways to improve such programs, our task became much simpler.

Although it would be misleading to suggest that differences among the Commissioners disappeared in the writing of this report, it is fair to say that on most major issues we reached consensus of opinion. That sometimes meant compromise—but never over the basic principle that our duty was to help migrant children. What we have achieved, then, is a document that reflects a broad accord and that, we sincerely hope, will improve the opportunity for migrant children to receive a decent education in America.

I want to thank all of my fellow Commissioners, who were a delight to get to know and a pleasure to deal with, and to express my gratitude to a skillful and dedicated staff, without whom none of this could have been accomplished. Most of all, however, I want to thank all those persons who work with migrants to ensure that the people who help put food on our table can provide a better life for their own families.

LINDA CHAVEZ
Chairman

Executive Summary

problem

On Thanksgiving evening of 1960, Americans switched on their televisions to watch Edward R. Morrow's portrayal of migrant farmworkers, a program appropriately titled Harvest of Shame. The images captured in that program—hard-working, exploited, and desperately needy people—awoke the public to a sobering situation. Due to such increased awareness over the plight of the migrant farmworkers and the President's War on Poverty program, Congress created a series of special programs specifically targeted to assist migrant farmworkers. One of these programs, the Migrant Education Program (MEP), was established to address the unique educational needs of children of migrant farmworkers.

In trying to examine the efforts of MEP, the National Commission on Migrant Education began its task in 1988 by assessing the current status of migrant farmworkers' children and their families. Needless to say, many of today's migrant farmworkers evoke a similar sentiment to those of their predecessors. There is no doubt that migrant farmworkers continue to be one of the most industrious, yet under-rewarded populations found in this country. Their efforts to remain self-sufficient are heroic. As members of the working poor, migrant farmworkers continue to travel thousands of miles annually, often to work at below-minimum wages, to conduct menial and sometimes hazardous labor. Although the situation has improved in some places, migrant farmworkers continue to be alienated by the same communities who benefit financially from their hard work and perseverance.

Many critical concerns were brought to the attention of the Commission during its 3 years of hearings and communications with members of the public. Because many of these issues are complex, the Commission has chosen to discuss some of them in further detail in the body of this report. Therefore, the findings and recommendations presented below capture the essence of these concerns but do not specifically touch upon all the important issues affecting this population and the MEP community:

Findings

■ For 25 years MEP has provided essential instruction and support services to a population of children whose education is interrupted or otherwise limited. The characteristics of the children being served by MEP,

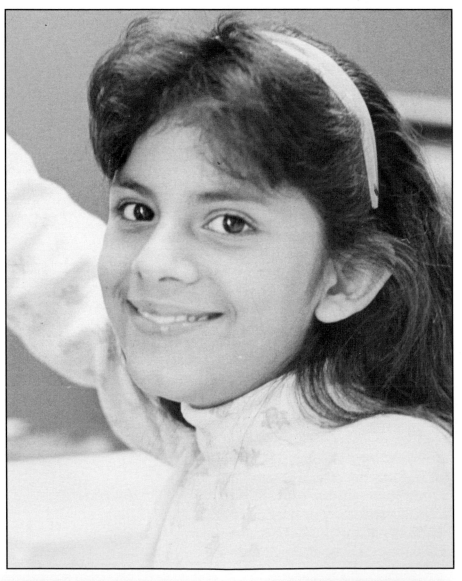

however, have changed dramatically during this period. When the program began in the mid-1960s, most MEP children were U.S.-born children of follow-the-crop agricultural workers, who accompanied their parents during the school year, thus interrupting their education. Today, most children in MEPs in many areas of the country do not currently migrate with their parents during the normal school year. Of those children who do migrate, most migrate between Mexico and the United States. MEP, therefore, has become a program that is increasingly serving a predominantly immigrant student population whose parents are or have recently been employed in agricultural work. The children themselves, however, may not necessarily conform to the common understanding of the term "migrant" that was used when the program was created.

■ Children served by MEP have multiple needs that are not adequately met by their families, employers, the communities in which they live, or the Federal Government. While the migratory lifestyle which many of these children share with their parents contributes to some of the health and education problems these children encounter, other factors play an important role as well. Among the most important of these are poverty, lack of English proficiency, and social isolation from the larger community in which they live. In addition, migrant farmworkers—whose educational attainment is among the lowest of any occupational group—have educational needs that affect the growth and development of their children; moreover, instruction in parenting skills and academic or job training opportunities are rare. These factors make it especially difficult for MEP children to become integrated into the social mainstream and to take full advantage of educational opportunities.

■ For these reasons, many of the children will drop out of school before completing high school, thereby limiting their own social and economic mobility and, likely, that of their children as well. The dropout rate of this population, while difficult to ascertain precisely, is estimated to be several times higher than the national average. High school credits are frequently lost when migrant youth move from one school to another. Utilization of high school equivalency programs and postsecondary education is limited.

■ Because of the changing demographic profile of the farmworker population, increasing numbers of new entrants are young immigrant males, many of whom are unaccompanied minors. This group is among the most overlooked of those qualifying for migrant assistance.

■ Since its inception, MEP has changed and expanded in scope, but appropriations have not increased proportionally. In 1991, funding was only 33.41 percent of the amount that would be generated by the formula as legislated.

Recommendations

Unless such children are provided with the necessary skills to be able to compete for jobs in an increasingly complex and technological society, they may become a social and economic burden to the nation. The National Commission on Migrant Education, therefore, makes the following recommendations based on its findings and 3 years of study and hearings:

■ The Congress, the Federal Government, and the states should recognize the changing profile of students served by MEP and take appropriate steps to allow enough flexibility to accommodate the programs that best serve this population's needs. Because so many of these students are the children of very poorly educated recent immigrants, their needs may be even greater than past generations of migrant students. Rather than shying away from acknowledging the differences between the students now served by MEP and those for whom the program was created some 25 years ago, these governmental entities should identify and implement changes in program design and emphasis necessary to serve the students actually now in the program.

■ The Congress and the President should make the funding of programs for these students a priority.

■ Federal programs serving migrant farmworkers and their families must be better integrated and coordinated. Changes are needed in legislation, administrative regulations, and Federal agencies to ensure that programs are not duplicative, that needy populations are not missed, and that needed services are provided. Among those specific steps that should be taken are to develop:

a. a common definition of migrant farmworkers to facilitate data collection across programs which serve this population;

b. a more streamlined (consistent) set of eligibility criteria for participation in programs which serve migrant farmworkers;

c. a mechanism for ensuring avoidance of duplication of effort and inefficiency in the delivery of services across programs; and

d. an executive order establishing an interagency council whose priority it is to coordinate services to migrant farmworkers and their families among Federal agencies.

■ MEP should serve as an advocate for migrant children in local communities. The program should be more aggressive in finding and serving migrant children and their families who need services from Federal, state, and other programs. In addition, the Department of Education should ensure that State Education Administrators not abrogate their decision-making responsibilities and authority over MEP local projects.

■ The allocation of MEP funds to state and local agencies should ensure that those students who are currently migrating during the school year are identified and served first, since these students are presumed to have the greatest needs. One of the options that should be explored is a funding allocation that would give greater weight to currently migrating students, which would give programs an economic incentive to identify and serve such students. However, given the changing demographics of the MEP population, the Commission understands that these children who no longer migrate and whose needs continue to be great should be counted and served.

■ MEP should ensure that migrant children get better access to all regular school programs funded by state and local sources. In addition, these children must have better access to those Federal education programs to which many of them are entitled, such as the Chapter 1 Basic Program and English-language acquisition programs. The latter is especially important given the fact that so many of these children are from non-English speaking immigrant families.

■ A more concerted effort should be made to assure that migrant children with special needs are identified and served, despite short enrollments, and to ensure better coordination between states and communities to assure appropriate services.

■ The Department of Education should reinforce the work of the National Secondary Credit Exchange and Accrual Project by collaborating with appropriate groups to foster agreement among the states about core courses or waivers, which will lead to the graduation of these students.

■ Given the limited funds available for migrant education, the Commission would urge state and local administrators to exercise restraint in relation to all administrative expenses including: travel, conferences, training, memberships, and subscriptions.

This report represents the culmination of a 3-year examination drawing from a wide array of resources including public testimony, prior research, commissioned studies and numerous discussions with members of the migrant community. The Commission is deeply indebted to all who contributed to this effort. The Commission is especially grateful for the time educators spent away from their classrooms to present their views to us. We hope this report will contribute to the efforts of all migrant educators.

Table of Contents

Demographics[1]

Migrant farmworkers, a fixture in American agriculture for many decades, are traditionally poor, hardworking people who travel great distances to live and work among strangers. Despite their instrumental role in agriculture, reliable statistical data accurately describing this population and their children are virtually nonexistent.[2]

The principal sources of available data which describe migrant farmworkers come from two independent sources: the National Agricultural Workers Survey, which describes a portion of the migrant population; and the Migrant Student Record Transfer System, which describes children who are identified as eligible to receive services provided by the Migrant Education Program. Neither source provides definitive data on migrant farmworkers and their families nor are the two sources comparable. Yet, each portrays a population

in need of educational, health, and social services. These data sources, although imperfect, provide insight into what the migrant workforce is like now and how it has changed over time; these sources also offer a glimpse of what the migrant workforce might look like in the year 2000.

Difficulties in Collecting Information

It is somewhat unusual that no reliable data exist for a group that receives substantial government assistance[3]. Although a number of studies and surveys have attempted to describe migrant farmworkers,[4] most of the profiles developed refer to only a portion of the population.[5] Part of the difficulty in collecting reliable information is that migrant farmworkers are not identified in the usual Federal data sources, are poorly educated, are often suspicious of interviewers asking questions, and are frequently lacking English lan-

NAWS is the only Federal demographic survey which collects data on migrant farmworkers. It was begun by the U.S. Department of Labor to determine whether 1986 immigration reforms (Immigration Reform and Control Act of 1986)[10] resulted in farm-labor shortages. In the course of finding that there were no farm-labor shortages, NAWS obtained demographic data on workers employed in most categories of crop agriculture. NAWS employs a multi-stage sampling procedure to select and interview "face-to-face" a sample of farmworkers and their employers in some, but not all, states. However, not all employers contacted nor all farmworkers contacted were willing to be interviewed. Little can be done to either estimate or eliminate bias caused by such omissions;[11] consequently, the reliability of the NAWS data has yet to been conclusively established.

guage skills. The group's high level of mobility and the fact that the population has been changing over time further intensify the problems of collecting data systematically.

Previous data-collection efforts have produced widely differing results. Depending on the definition of "migrant" and "migrancy" that was used to collect and analyze the data, the migrant farmworker could have a number of demographic profiles, could be distributed in a variety of patterns across states, and could represent different percentages of the total national farmworker population.[6]

Technical difficulties are further magnified when agencies use their own definitions to determine who qualifies as a migrant farmworker and who is eligible to receive services. Even the composite profile of the "average" migrant farmworker varies depending on how the data are collected and used by each program.

With such inconsistencies in defining who is a migrant, it is not surprising that estimates of the number and characteristics of migrant farmworkers vary considerably. A U.S. Department of Agriculture report indicated there were 159,000 migrant farmworkers in 1985, at the same time that Migrant Health estimated there were 4.2 million migrant and seasonal workers and their families. A U.S. Department of Labor study indicated that 80 percent of the crop farmworkers were Hispanic in 1989-90, but the 1987 Hired Farm Work Force study found that most U.S. farmworkers were non-Hispanic White and only 14 percent were Hispanic.[7] These variations have resulted from the methods used to collect data and the different

definitions of "migrant farmworker."[8]

The National Agricultural Workers Survey (NAWS) data are probably the most reliable demographic data available on 80 percent or 2 million of the nation's estimated 2.5 million hired farmworkers. These data can be used to develop a profile of the migrant population.

The National Agricultural Workers Survey[9]

NAWS annually collects data on farmworkers, of which migrant farmworkers are a subset, to measure changes in the composition and distribution of the seasonal agricultural workforce. It reflects only those farmworkers who are now employed in crop agriculture and who have traveled at least 75 miles in search of work. NAWS does not count individuals in other MEP-eligible occupations who migrate in search of work, i.e., agriculture-associated industries (processing and packing, for example), dairy or poultry farming, or those who at one time may have been employed in agriculture.[12]

The NAWS database is limited[13] in that it only describes one category of all agricultural workers, Seasonal Agricultural Services (SAS). However, it is the most useful of its kind since it does provide current information about a sample of seasonal farmworkers. For this reason, demographers are using NAWS data to make generalizations about migrant farmworkers.

The Migrant Population Identified by NAWS

Most Federal farmworker assistance programs that serve the Migrant and Seasonal Farmworker (MSFW)—a subset of those employed in agriculture—define seasonal workers as persons employed in agriculture for only part of the year. As a further distinction, migrant workers are characterized as those seasonal workers who cross a geographic boundary in order to do farm work. Although the criteria for defining "seasonal" and "migrant" are arbitrary,[14] such definitions are necessary in order to estimate who and how many people are migrant.

Based on the data collected by NAWS about the *general population* of Seasonal Agricultural Services[15] workers, 42 percent of the estimated 2 million U.S. crop farmworkers are migrants.[16] Of those, 60 percent are immigrants and 31 percent are parents accompanied by an average of approximately two children (about 587,000 children) during 1990.

According to NAWS, *migrant farmworkers within the general population of farmworkers* are predominantly male (82 percent), Hispanic (94 percent) born in Mexico (80 percent), and married (52 percent) with children. Fifty-nine percent do farm work unaccompanied by their families.[17] Almost half (378,000) are Seasonal Agricultural Workers (SAWs)[18] and almost one-quarter (185,000) are immigrants unauthorized to work in the United States. Most migrants (83 percent) "shuttle" between home bases abroad (usually Mexico or Central America) and U.S. farms or worksites and only 33 percent follow the crops within the United States—a ratio of 2.5 shuttle migrants for every migrant worker who follows the crops.[19]

The amount of time worked and the benefits available to or used by the SAW farmworkers[20] also vary. Most face extensive seasonal unemployment and have annual earnings below the poverty level. During the year, the average worker spends half the year doing SAS work for 1.7 farm employers for which he earns less than $5,000. On average, workers are unemployed for 10 weeks, spend 8 weeks doing non-agricultural work, and travel abroad for 8 weeks (although 40 percent spend an average of 19 weeks abroad). Less than one-half have unemployment insurance and workers compensation coverage, and less than one-quarter have off-the-job health insurance. Few participate in needs-based social service programs and other programs such as Food Stamps (16 percent) and Aid to Families with Dependent Children (3 percent).

The Industry of Agriculture

Agriculture, the industry employing all farmworkers, is a $170 billion industry which includes a number of products. Approximately one-sixth of annual agricultural sales come from Fruits, Vegetables, and Horticultural (FVH). FVH, i.e., vegetables, fruits, nuts, nursery, and horticultural specialties, was worth $28 billion in 1990. Most of the FVH sales are concentrated in a few states. For example, California produces one-third of FVH sales ($9 billion), which represents 75 percent of the state's total crop sales.

Although FVH is the smallest sector of agriculture according to sales figures, it employs the most seasonal farmworkers (90 percent),[21] who are often in seasonal "factories" that employ large crews of workers for tasks that last a few weeks. Those unable to find agricultural work either seek unemployment insurance or other assistance until farm jobs are available, they seek non-farm jobs, or emigrate from the United States.

Most farmworkers find jobs with growers or Farm Labor Contractors through leads from friends and relatives. About 75 percent of all workers interviewed for NAWS are employed directly by growers, presumably because they generally pay higher wages. The remainder are employed by Farm Labor Contractors who receive a commission for recruitment and supervision services.[22]

The vast majority of the farmworkers, especially those new to farm labor, are immigrants. The dominance of immigrants affects the structure and functioning of the farm-labor market, e.g., non-English speaking workers often require bilingual Farm Labor Contractors to help them find housing and social services. However, rather than hire U.S. citizens, some employers prefer to hire immigrants who will usually endure without question intermittent work schedules, low wages, and charges for housing, transportation, and food.[23]

Changes in the Agriculture Industry

The agriculture industry has changed substantially over the past four decades. Since the 1950s, fruit and vegetable production has been shifting to California and the Pacific Northwest from the East and Midwest. The shift, which made California the "garden" state, was caused by the need for a longer growing season and changes in the marketplace, such as an efficient transportation system, readily available labor, and an increased demand for fresh produce all year.

Today, other shifts are evident. Although Mexican immigrants have traditionally worked in southwestern agriculture, over the past two decades they have expanded their presence from California into Michigan, Florida, and New York. Almost 60 percent of California's farmworkers, who are mostly shuttle immigrants, are based in California.

Changes in production will influence the number of farmworkers needed and the type of work they will do. For example, production in Texas is decreasing while production in other states, i.e., North Carolina and Washington, is increasing. States such as New York and Michigan are switching to fresh production of fruits and vegetables, and even more migrants are now traveling to work in these states. Other vegetable-producing states to which migrants have traditionally traveled have either mechanized (e.g., Wisconsin) or will probably do so soon (e.g., Ohio).

Although harvest seasons have been lengthened through technological advances, FVH agriculture is still dominated by 3- to 10-week harvest jobs. To meet harvest requirements, hundreds of thousands of workers mobilize to fill millions of short-term jobs. Although the need for an efficient procedure to deploy workers is great, the process of matching people to jobs is haphazard at best. Thousands of individual farm foremen or Farm Labor Contractors recruit workers for their farms or crews. There is little communication among these recruiters, so each keeps workers "on-call" to guarantee a crew when work is available.

Mechanization has reduced employment in many commodities over the past 25 years, yet the production of other commodities has expanded enough to stabilize farm employment. For example, by 1990, mechanical tomato pickers reduced the number of farmworkers required to harvest three times more tomatoes for processing as in 1960. Although higher yields have increased production by almost 50 percent, much of the productivity increases are for fruits and vegetables which must be harvested by hand, not machine.[24] Yet, the number of cultivated acres of U.S. fruits and vegetables has remained stable since 1970.

The value of U.S. fruit and vegetable production has been rising much faster than the value of livestock and grain, assuring that the high-value FVH commodities will continue to maintain an important position in U.S. agriculture. The combination of increased production of hand-harvested fresh fruits and vegetables and various labor-intensive changes (e.g., packing produce for market in the fields rather than in a packing facility) virtually guaranteed the increased demand for labor in U.S. fruit and vegetable agriculture that occurred in the 1980s.

Over the years, the demand for labor increased within FVH agriculture. At the same time, FVH agriculture has come to depend on immigrant workers. This inter-relationship between rural Mexican workers and rural U.S. farmers has permitted labor-intensive agriculture to expand in the United States as the demand for fruits and vegetables has increased. With an almost inexhaustible labor supply, U.S. farmers are confident that seasonal workers will be available to hand-harvest crops when and where they are needed at what U.S. farmers deem to be reasonable wages.[25]

The demand for Mexican workers is especially dramatic in North Carolina. For example, in 1980, less than 10 percent of the state's farmworkers were from Mexico. Ten years later, the state's peak workforce was mostly Mexican. This "Mexicanization" came in the wake of U.S. citizens finding better nonfarm jobs and, as a result of IRCA, Farm Labor Contractors and Mexican workers are now forming networks to fill these farm jobs.[26]

The revolving door of the agriculture labor market provides opportunities for rural Mexican immigrants to enter the seasonal harvest workforce, to leave for better farm or nonfarm jobs, or to return to Mexico. Farm labor turns over fastest when nonfarm jobs are available. When unemployment in the nonfarm sector is high, farmworkers tend to stay in agriculture. Most farmworkers aspire to nonfarm jobs because they offer more stable employment, higher wages, better benefits, and more opportunities for advancement. However, some farmworkers who find nonfarm jobs or return to Mexico are likely to return to U.S. farm work when no other opportunities are available.

During the 1980s, U.S. economic conditions resulted in opportunities for immigrant farmworkers. U.S. farm wages stopped rising, especially in California, and benefits such as farmer-provided housing and health insurance often disappeared. Stagnation in farm wages and benefits, but rapid growth in service-sector jobs, attracted many U.S. farmworkers into year-round nonfarm jobs. The resulting vacuum in agriculture drew more rural Mexicans into the United States.[27] Unfortunately, there is no index which demonstrates neatly how the expansion of the industry increased the demand for Mexican workers in U.S. agriculture.[28]

Seasonal farmworkers generally stay in field work between 10 to 15 years, which means that an estimated 5 to 10 percent of U.S. citizens and immigrant farmworkers who are migrant seasonal farmworkers tend to leave farm work each year. In order to keep the farm workforce stable at 2 million, between 100,000 and 200,000 new entrants are needed annually.

The ongoing need for a farm workforce will remain great. U.S. FVH production will probably continue to grow in the 1990s both in response to a 1 percent rise in U.S. population annually and to the preferences of a more mature and increasingly health-conscious population. These circumstances should generate at least a 15 to 20 percent increase in fruit and vegetable consumption.[29] In addition, the Mexicanization of rural America and the revolving door of the harvest-labor market should continue to attract rural Mexicans into the United States in the 1990s. However, the rate of increase may be somewhat slower than that of the 1980s, since it is unclear whether FVH production will continue to expand at the same rate as in the past. The further Mexicanization of the farm workforce—at 50 to 60 percent of the workforce today—cannot continue indefinitely, and currently glutted nonfarm-labor markets may slow the departure of those wishing to leave agriculture. However, it appears that a significant need for rural Mexicans in U.S. agri-

culture will persist into the 1990s, virtually guaranteeing that the changes in the migrant workforce that started a few years ago will continue well into the decade.

Changing Characteristics of Migrant Farmworkers

The characteristics of the people who travel seeking employment in agriculture have changed since the inception of many of the programs designed to serve them. A dramatic illustration of the differences lies in Edward R. Murrow's television documentary, *Harvest of Shame*. In 1960, interviews of migrant farmworkers were conducted in English. If this documentary were to be replicated now, both the interviewers and the interviewed would most likely be speaking Spanish since most farmworkers entering the migrant stream today are immigrants who speak little or no English.[30]

During the first half of this century, two distinct groups of migrants were engaged in farm work. The first group was predominantly non-Hispanic White,[31] U.S. citizens traveling with their families to follow the crops northward, primarily from homes or home bases in the southern and western states.[32] The second major group entered the migrant stream in 1942 through a series of agreements between the governments of the United States and Mexico. The Bracero Program, as it became known, permitted 5 million Mexican farmworkers to enter the United States on a temporary basis. Although the program was terminated in 1964, it became the precursor of today's migrant assistance programs and marked the beginning of Mexico becoming the ongoing source

of migrant farm labor.

Before MEP and most migrant assistance programs began in the 1960s, migrant workers were ineligible for social services such as welfare since most states required a 6-month residency for eligibility. However, the Civil Rights movement and an awakened national consciousness prompted the creation of Federal programs to improve the condition of migrant farmworkers.

The new Federal programs provided much needed health, education, and social services to migrant families and their children who traveled from state to state to follow the crops. The focus of the programs was to help the poor non-Hispanic White and a smaller population of Black (who represented 25 percent of the 400,000 migrants)[33] migrants escape from the migrant stream. Hispanics were not counted separately until 1975 when they constituted one-fourth and Blacks one-eighth of the estimated 200,000 migrants.

While many thought mechanization might decrease the need for farmworkers during the 1970s, the reverse occurred. Growth states like California and Florida actually expanded the workforce needed to produce fruits and vegetables, even as they needed fewer workers to produce field crops such as cotton and sugar beets. Migrant farmworkers traveled to work in these states and then north as the crops became ready for harvest. By the early 1980s, interstate migration was changing migrant farmworker demographics. There were still considerable numbers of U.S. citizens (Blacks and non-Hispanic Whites) in the eastern stream and (Mexican Americans) from south Texas who migrated north and west. In addition, non-Hispanic White teenagers from the mid-west migrated to detassle corn, and families migrated within California and from California to the states of the Pacific Northwest.

At the same time, immigrant males willing to work for lower wages slowly started joining the ranks of farmworkers. Parallel growth in the manufacturing and service industries offered entry-level jobs that enticed U.S. farmworkers into manufacturing, hotel, restaurant, construction, janitorial, and other service jobs. Concurrently, farm work was becoming increasingly less desirable as the average fieldworker's wage slipped from 50 percent to 40 percent of the average manufacturing wage. The status of farm work was declining, farmworker unions were losing members as unionized farms closed, and farmworkers were losing fringe benefits such as health insurance and housing.

According to most current national estimates, fewer than 280,000 of the nation's 2 million crop farmworkers are today following the crops and only 40 percent of this group brings their families to the worksite. These estimates portray a vastly different population from 20 years ago when most were U.S. citizens traveling with their families in predictable patterns to follow the growing and harvesting cycles of the crops.

NAWS View of Migrant Farmworkers' Children

As the demographics of the migrant workforce changed, so did the demographics of their children. Previously, migrant farmworkers were predominantly non-Hispanic

White, U.S. citizens, who followed the crop harvesting cycle with their farmworker parents. Now, NAWS portrays migrant children as predominantly young Hispanic immigrants with limited-English proficiency, who may either remain at home with one parent or travel between one U.S. worksite and a home in Mexico or Central America. Over two-thirds come from households with incomes below the poverty level, yet they make little use of social services.

NAWS data indicate that approximately 587,000 currently migratory children are in the United States sometime during the year. Most travel with their families to do agricultural work but once here, most do not follow the crops:[34]

■ 382,000 (65 percent) age 21 or younger travel with or join migrant parents and do not do farm work;

■ 36,000 (6 percent) travel with their migrant parents and do farm work;

■ 169,000 (29 percent) travel on their own to do farm work.

NAWS found that instead of following the crops, as was the predominant pattern in the last decade, only an estimated 114,000 children or youths now follow the crops within the United States, while an estimated 378,000 annually cross the U.S. border to accompany their farmworker parents or to do farm work themselves. The border-crossing children "shuttle" between a school in Mexico and one in the United States at roughly the same rate (40 percent of the workers in each category are accompanied by dependents) as migrant children who follow the crops and shift between schools within the United States.[35]

A more difficult group to describe includes young migrant workers between the ages of 15 and 21.[36] There has always been a significant group of young farmworkers who travel on their own to do farm work. For example, the 1983 Current Population Survey (CPS) found that 35 percent of all farmworkers were 14 to 17 years of age[37] who, for example, migrated across county lines and stayed away from home overnight in order to detassle corn in the midwest or to harvest tobacco in the southeast.[39]

By contrast, the recent NAWS data estimated that approximately 17 percent were 21 or younger and that 60 percent of this group (202,000) migrate to, and, in some cases, around the United States without their families.[38] About one-third are unauthorized workers in the United States who have very little Mexican education[40] (and even less education than migrant farmworkers in the past).[41] They are predominantly Spanish-speaking males from Mexico,[42] mostly between the ages of 18 and 21 (80 percent); and about one-half do not live with their families. These youth, who are all potentially eligible for migrant education services, remain unidentified and unserved by MEP.

There is another group in the farmworker population composed of children and migrant youth who have not met the NAWS 75-mile criterion for migrancy but who would meet the MEP criterion of migrancy. They cross a school district, and they are the children of nonmigrating agricultural workers or fishermen who would be classified by MEP as formerly migratory. It is impossible to estimate the size of either of these

MSRTS collects and stores data on the children who recruiters locate and judge to be eligible for MEP. Consequently, the depth, scope, and reliability of MSRTS data depend on the ability of recruiters to identify all eligible children and then to log them accurately into MSRTS. A report recently issued by the National Commission on Migrant Education established that a considerable amount of MSRTS data were inaccurate and that substantial numbers of individual student records were incomplete.[44] Efforts are underway to improve the integrity of the MSRTS database; however, conclusions based on MSRTS should be made with caution since not all children who are eligible to receive services have been identified. Although MSRTS is still the major source of information about the children of migrant farmworkers, its records more closely reflect children who are identified as eligible to receive MEP services rather than those who did or who are now receiving services.

subpopulations, but their total may be in the tens of thousands. It is also impossible to determine how many of the migrant children counted through NAWS are also included in MSRTS. While the extent of overlap is not clear, it seems likely that some portion of this population is captured by both sources.

MSRTS View of Migrant Farmworkers' Children

In addition to NAWS, the Migrant Student Record Transfer System (MSRTS) provides nationwide information on the children of migratory farmworkers.[43]

As of March 1992, MSRTS had records for 628,150[45] migrant farmworkers' children ranging in ages from 3 to 21 who are now moving or have moved within the past 5 years so that family members could obtain temporary or seasonal work in agriculture or fishing.[46] About 53 percent of these children had not migrated in the preceding 12 months. The remaining 47 percent crossed school district lines within the past 12 months to accompany or join a parent or guardian who moved in search of agricultural or fishery employment, including 32 percent who crossed state lines.

Unlike NAWS, which portrays farmworkers on the basis of the characteristics of a sample of the population, MSRTS describes all children identified as eligible to receive MEP services. Unfortunately, MSRTS is not comprehensive since it lacks information on those children who might be eligible for MEP but who have not been identified.

While population characteristics of these children differ across states as well as geographic areas, national

MSRTS statistics indicate:

■ 95 percent are eligible for MEP because their families were or are involved in farmwork;[47]

■ slightly less than half are moving across district lines either during the regular and/or summer school term;[48]

■ over 65 percent were born in the United States and approximately 30 percent were born in Mexico;[49]

■ over half of the total MEP-eligible population are in three states—California, Texas, and Florida;[50]

■ even though identified children range in age from 3 through 21, and approximately 85 percent are between the ages of 6 and 16.[51]

The MSRTS database shows that the number of currently migrant children rose about 17 percent during the 1980s, while the number of formerly migrant children rose 42 percent over the same period.[52] Currently migratory refers to children whose families have moved within the past 12 months in search of temporary or seasonal work in agriculture or fishing industries. Formerly migratory refers to children who are not now migrating but who would have been considered currently migratory within the past 5 years.[53]

According to MSRTS data, the number of both currently and formerly migrant children increased faster in the second half of the 1980s than in the first half. The increases can be attributed, in large part, to an expansion of legislatively prescribed eligibility requirements that were modified in recognition of the economic, health, educational, and other needs of a large number of children not included among MEP's constituency as it was originally defined. *(Exhibit 1.1)*

Locations of the MEP Population.

By definition, children who are registered in MSRTS as currently migratory will be living in at least two locations during the year. Some states are considered by a large percentage of migrant families to be their "home base," or the place from which they start their migration and to which they return after completing seasonal work. The largest numbers live in California, Texas, and Florida during the regular school term.[54] Other states (e.g., Minnesota and Wyoming) have their largest number during the summer. Approximately a third of these children migrate annually, moving through—as well as to—states east, west, and north of their home base state. Still other states, because of their vast expanses (e.g., Alaska), have a sizeable number moving only within their state borders.

In states where agricultural/fishery work is only seasonal, the largest numbers of MEP children are present during the spring, summer, or fall. These states are known as "receiving states," since the bulk of their migrant population returns to their home base location after the agricultural or fishing season has ended.

Another group of states are viewed as having "settled-out" populations. Over time, many migrant families find stable employment and elect to exit the migratory stream. However, since these formerly migratory families can "settle out" in any state including "home base" and "receiving" states, a proportion of each state's eligible children includes those who are migrating and those who have not migrated in over 12

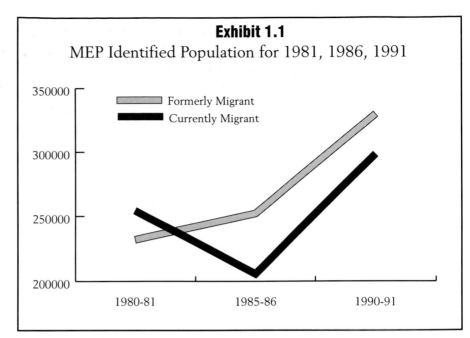

Exhibit 1.1
MEP Identified Population for 1981, 1986, 1991

Source MSRTS statistics - 3/31/92

months.

Migrant Streams.

Historically, migrant children have been portrayed as a population that moves seasonally across specific regions of the country, commonly referred to as streams. These streams represent three separate patterns of migration. One stream includes Texas and north to the central plains region; another stream consists of California to the northwest and the western states; and another includes Florida and north along the East Coast.

Demographic data and Commission testimony suggest that with changes in the population who do farmwork, the pattern of migration appears less distinct by stream. Nonetheless, regional migration patterns show that some children move in a defined path within a specific area. For example, children from Puerto Rico frequently travel to the northeastern and mid-Atlantic states; children from Mexico migrate to California and Texas; and children from Canada migrate into Maine. Since the migrant population in each state differs in size, length and time of residency, as well as pattern of migration,[55] migrant education programs must be flexible enough to adapt to these variations.

Of the migrant children included in MSRTS, roughly 68 percent

(intrastate and formerly migratory) presently remain in their home base states throughout the year.[56] The degree to which MSRTS enrolls currently migratory children has been a subject of considerable concern by the Commission. Although the Commission understands that needs created as a result of a migratory lifestyle continue after the children no longer migrate, it is assumed that currently migrating children will have greater needs. Since MEPs are need-based, the Commission supports the current legislation requiring that those children with the greatest needs be given priority in receiving services.

Racial/Ethnic Composition.

MSRTS portrays the children of migrant farmworkers as predominantly Hispanic, with a slightly higher proportion of Hispanics enrolled during the summer than during the regular school term.[57] Blacks, Asians, and Native Americans make up less than 4 percent each with a somewhat larger percentage of non-Hispanic Whites.

Exhibit 1.2 may not present the entire picture. The standard racial/ethnic reporting categories required by Federal programs tend to obscure the appearance of other racial/ethnic groups as migrants, i.e., indigenous Mexicans and Central Americans who do not speak Spanish. These relatively small groups are concentrated mainly in California and Florida; however, their numbers may be locally significant, e.g., 12,000 Mayan speakers are located in the Immokalee/Indian Town area of South Central Florida.

Health.
Although MSRTS records contain migrant student health information, the best sources of aggregate

Exhibit 1.2
Racial/Ethnic Profile of MEP-Eligible Population
1989-1990

Racial/Ethnic Category	MSRTS Regular Term	MSRTS Summer Term	RTI Regular Term	RTI Summer Term
American Indian/Alaskan Native	2%*	1%	1%	2%
Asian/Pacific Islander	3%	3%	3%	<1%
Black	5%	2%	3%	1%
Hispanic	79%	85%	74%	86%
Non-Hispanic White	11%	8%	20%	11%

*Rounded to the nearest percent

information on migrant health come from the Migrant Clinicians Network Survey. Studies conducted by this organization show that health conditions among migrant populations are similar to those in third-world nations. Among migrant children otitis media, upper respiratory infections, nutritional diseases, dental diseases, conjunctivitis, parasitic infections, and work-related injuries occur with a frequency much higher than in the U.S. national population.

Most surprising is the appearance of diabetes among females between 15- and 19-years old. By age 20, the diseases typical of children ages 1

The North American Free Trade Agreement (NAFTA)[64] represents an agreement between the United States, Mexico, and Canada to create a trading bloc even larger than the European Community. Some have speculated that, as a result of NAFTA, U.S. farmers will shift fruit and vegetable production to Mexico to take advantage of its lower labor costs and less stringent environmental regulations. Upon closer inspection, Mexico's costs may not be so low. Although Mexican farm wages are lower, Mexican farmers pay proportionately more for other associated costs such as housing. Production costs can also be high in Mexico, since Mexican yields are often half of U.S. yields and Mexican farmers have less equipment.

While Mexico will undoubtedly produce more fruits and vegetables for the U.S. market, FVH agriculture will probably expand in *both* countries as farmers take advantage of local climatic conditions. Mexico produces fruits and vegetables during the winter months, when California production ebbs but Florida production peaks. However, since three-fourths of U.S. fruits and vegetables are produced in the spring, summer, and fall seasons when Mexico is not producing, the United States will retain much of its fruit and vegetable industry as well as its need for farmworkers. By contrast, Mexico may have the advantage in processed fruits and vegetables. Some products are processed by freezing or canning, so while production can occur during one period, the product can be sold throughout the year.

Migrant Fishers

In 1974, Congress expanded MEP eligibility for services to children of migrant fishers. Since that time, the total number of children identified under this provision has risen significantly, particularly since 1980-81 when the total nearly doubled to 26,222. This growth mainly reflects increases in Alaska.

Some questions persist as to the migratory status of these children. Officials generally agree that fishers move frequently and far but that family members do not move. Exceptions were noted in the cases of Vietnamese fishers in the Gulf of Mexico whose families live aboard their boats.[67] In Alaska, with a state population of 524,000, the fishing industry is the largest source of private employment. Fishing and seafood processing employ approximately 41,000 people, half of whom are young, out-of-state males. MSRTS reports that Alaska has over 12,000 children of migrant fishers, a large number considering that Alaska only has about 165,000 children within the ages served by MEPs.

However, officials indicate that most fishing occurs in the summer and that in fishing districts the school year is adjusted to fit the seasonal fishing cycle. Although many males hold several fishing licenses and work in several fisheries each year, they almost always travel alone. Children accompany their parents usually for short trips or during summer vacation. Consequently, the children's education is virtually uninterrupted, and families do not migrate during the school year. Similar findings characterize the fishing industry in Massachusetts to which fishers from North Carolina and Cape Verde Islands travel.

Exceptions exist that indicate some groups of fishers do migrate with their families. In Louisiana, a small population of Vietnamese families live aboard the family boat. Shrimp fishers spend a few months in Florida and then migrate to follow the movement of shrimp.[68] In both cases, the children of these families attend more than one school during the school year.

Overall, the majority of fishing is done by unaccompanied males, mostly unmarried. The families of married fishers are almost totally sedentary and, for the most part, their children do not have problems associated with migrancy.

through 19 are replaced by environmentally caused problems and chronic diseases such as diabetes and gynecological problems for females and dermatitis, scarlet fever, dental disease, and genito-urinary disease for males. Also, an examination of records of migrant student deaths reported by MSRTS indicates that a relatively large number die as a result of work-related accidents, violence, and drowning.[60]

Education. Most adult migrant farmworkers have completed low levels of education. Over 90 percent primarily speak a language other than English, and 84 percent speak limited English or none at all.[61] These same problems burden their children. English proficiency appears to be decreasing based upon teachers' ratings of the child's oral-language skills. In 1977, approximately 65 percent of the migrant student population were judged to have oral-English skills at a level adequate for functioning in a classroom. By 1990, that percent fell to less than 40 percent.[62] Although these statistics are cause for concern, they should also be viewed with caution since they come from two noncomparable studies.

While the majority of the migrant workers represented in NAWS are Spanish-speaking Mexicans who immigrate on a seasonal basis, there are also about 65,000 Mexican and Central American agricultural workers who speak only indigenous Native American languages, rather than Spanish. The linguistic isolation of these workers and their children poses a special challenge for educators and other service providers.

Trends For the Year 2000

Although no one can predict with total accuracy future changes in the characteristics of the migrant farmworker, it seems that the trends already in evidence today will continue.[63] As the country moves closer to the year 2000, the United States will continue to have a labor-intensive agricultural industry. The demand for fresh fruits and vegetables has been growing by about 2 percent annually, or between 20 and 30 percent over the decade. Neither the North American Free Trade Agreement, IRCA provisions, nor mechanization are likely to reduce farmworker employment below current levels—2.5 million people who work in agriculture at some time during the year, with 2 million of those working in crops.

It appears that the major shift by the year 2000 will not be in the number of farmworkers, but rather in their distribution and characteristics. Several factors will play a pivotal role in determining the destination of migratory farmworkers. Uncontrollable factors, such as the natural phenomena of freezes, droughts, and storms, affect, if and for how long, work is available. Higher transportation costs may cause a shift in production closer to population areas. This is especially important since two-thirds of the population live on the East Coast yet two-thirds of the fruits and vegetables are grown elsewhere. Likewise, increased water costs might shift production to areas with more readily available but less-costly water supplies.

Possible shifts in production centers will produce a corresponding relocation of migrant farmworkers and require more flexibility in all the programs that serve migrants. This is an important consideration, since migrant farmworkers, especially those involved in entry-level harvest labor, will be increasingly disadvantaged relative to the average U.S. workforce. Of the 1.3 million applicants for the SAS program who said they did 90 days of farm work in 1985 and 1986, the median had a fifth-grade Mexican education; and most had not finished primary school in Mexico.[65]

A compounding problem is that the U.S. labor demands are shifting from entry-level industrial jobs to those requiring more education. Farmworkers who may want to move into nonfarm work may not be able to because they lack the skills needed in both the industry and service sectors jobs.[66]

Since the average migrant farmworker's career is less than 10 years, by the year 2000, migrant farmworkers and their children will have all the disadvantages normally associated with poorly educated immigrants who were employed in a seasonal industry which offered almost no career ladders and almost no fringe benefits. Their educational, health, and social services needs will continue to be great. Consequently, the migrant assistance and education programs will be targeting a much more needy population than ever before.

"…I was born in Jalpa, Zacatecas, Mexico. My father, an orphan since the age of 7, made his first move to the United States in 1961 at the age of 14. He spent several years working in the fields of southern California, migrating to and from Mexico…my father…married…my mother and [left to] follow the crops all the way to…a small town in northern California. Soon after my mother, my sister, and I joined him. At first we didn't have any place to go, nor any money with which to rent a home. We were taken in by an uncle who lived on a ranch. Our first stay in 'el norte' lasted for only a few months.

"Within a few months we discovered that even though it was very expensive to support a family in America on a farmer's income, it was easier than trying to make a living in our home town of Jalpa. Not only did we have luxuries like running water and electricity in America but the whole family could work to contribute to our family income. To us there was no such thing as child labor laws.

"…in the fields it is normal for children to be working at a very young age. Most migrant families are large and cannot survive on a single income. Many times even combined incomes do not bring enough money to support the family, much less pay for day care. Instead the whole family works together. I was 10 years old when I first started working. I picked fruit and vegetables along side my parents all season. Sometimes the income from picking berries was [only] enough…to buy the basic necessities. By the time I was in high school, I was employed at three different jobs at the same time…

"Even with a combined family income there were times when our family [of eight] was either in debt or very low on money. Every summer we would share a house with our relatives who also sought employment in the fields. With 14 people in the same house it was very difficult to make ends meet…"

—LIDIA ESPINOZA[69]

CHAPTER TWO

Administration and Governance

"...if you want to serve the migrant child, you have to serve the decision makers that impact and effect legislation of policy or educational curriculum..." —Dr. Tadeo Reyna[1]

Through literally hundreds of hours of meetings and thousands of pages of testimony, the National Commission on Migrant Education heard the eloquent and sometimes impassioned messages of administrators, teachers, parents, government officials, and even migrant youth. Although some carried their messages through translators, some in halting English, and others in the articulate mien of the truly educated, the message was similar—the Migrant Education Program (MEP) works, regardless of its shortcomings. Although a large measure of the program's success can be attributed to the enthusiasm and dedication of the individuals who "make it happen," many of the program's features and characteristics set forth in the legislation provide the backdrop that makes it possible.

Many supplementary programs and services for disadvantaged people were part of the War on Poverty programs created in the 1960s. At that time Congress enacted Title 1 of the Elementary and Secondary Education Act (ESEA) which authorized the creation of four programs: a Basic Grant Program to Local Education Agencies (LEAs) and three separate state grant programs. Each program focused on a distinct target population. The requirements for implementing all ESEA Title 1 programs remain today,[2] despite numerous reauthorizations and statutory revisions.

MEP originated as an amendment to ESEA Title 1 in 1966 [See Appendix C] when Congress acknowledged that children of migratory workers had certain needs that warranted a special program.

"The children of migratory agricultural workers present a unique problem for educators.

Requirements for all ESEA Title 1 programs:

■ eligible children must be assessed annually;

■ programs/services are based upon the assessed needs of eligible children;

■ children with the greatest needs receive priority for services;

■ eligible children attending private schools are not excluded;

■ parents/guardians of participating children are to be involved in the programs; and

■ programs/services are evaluated to determine their impact on children's basic skills achievement.

State Education Agencies (SEAs) conduct the following activities to support the goals of Chapter 1 MEP:

■ identify and recruit eligible migrant children;[4]

■ enroll eligible migrant children in the Migrant Student Record Transfer System;

■ assess the unique needs of migrant children;

■ design programs and services for regular and/or summer school terms;

■ coordinate these programs and services with other states, agencies, and programs that serve migrant families;

■ involve parents in MEP and establish Parent Advisory Councils; and

■ evaluate the effectiveness of programs and services relative to desired outcomes.

SEAs are authorized to administer these activities directly or through subgrants to local operating agencies such as school districts, nonprofit agencies, or other public agencies. In 1992, every state and jurisdiction, except for Hawaii, American Samoa, and the Virgin Islands, received MEP grants.

Migratory workers travel from community to community in order to work. They often settle in a single community for two months or less. Consequently, their children are seldom in school long enough to participate in school activities; some spend only two to six weeks in any one school district during the harvest season. Well over half are not achieving at their grade level." [3]

The primary goals of Chapter 1 MEP are to serve the unique educational needs of children who migrate as a result of their families' work in agriculture, dairy, or fishing, and to help children who have ceased migrating to overcome educational difficulties resulting from a previously mobile lifestyle. On an annual basis, State Education Agencies (SEAs) apply to the Secretary of Education for funding to help them meet the goals of the program.

If educators are to translate statutory requirements into workable programs for migrant children, they must find a way to satisfy both statutory and regulatory requirements without sacrificing program effectiveness. MEP must be adaptable since migrant children live in different states at various times of the year. To make the programs more flexible, staff at each level of the educational hierarchy—local, state, and Federal—must synchronize their efforts to provide a coordinated national program for migrant children.

Federal Role in MEP

At the Federal level, the Office of Migrant Education (OME), within the U.S. Department of Education (ED), administers MEP. OME issues regulations, allocates funds, awards contracts, and routinely performs regulatory oversight responsibilities (such as monitoring).

While these duties are similar in nature and scope to those in other Federal programs, OME has an additional set of responsibilities. Statutorily, OME allocates funds to states according to a formula, develops a standard form to certify the eligibility of migrant children,[5] develops and disseminates a policy manual that describes program requirements for subgrantees,[6] and coordinates activities with the states.[7] MEP made major gains when OME formalized program operations by disseminating both a policy manual and a standard certification form. Each ensured that program requirements were consistent across states. In addition to developing policy, OME also oversees *coordination of interagency, intraagency, and interstate activities.* Such efforts are ongoing and are accomplished in a variety of ways.

In 1991, ED identified 18 programs across the Federal Government that served migrant families.[9] Although most agencies work with each other voluntarily, MEP is one of the few programs that operates under a mandate of *interagency coordination*. In this area, OME's efforts are primarily limited to participating in *interagency* committees and entering into agreements with other Federal programs.

Within ED, most of OME's *intraagency coordination* activities involve the Office of Compensatory Education Programs. Even though OME requires commitment from its grantees to coordinate, the Commission found communications between MEP and other ED programs generally limited to higher levels within the organization, such as between the Office of the Assistant Secretary for Elementary and Secondary Education and the Office of the General Counsel.

Consequently, the Commission recommends that ED consider a more formalized coordination process for encouraging intra-agency coordination within ED. The Commission suggests that ED encourage its program officers to employ monitoring strategies (e.g., joint program monitoring) that present as little disruption to the school staff as possible. This suggestion reflects the Commission's concern about the burden placed on local schools when program officers arrive at different times.

OME has been overseeing contracts that facilitate *interstate coordination* of MEP services among states since 1978. To ensure that states were involved, in 1988 Congress required OME to include them in the consultation and approval of these coordination contracts.[10] In 1992, OME formalized state involvement by creating a process that allows states to provide input without compromising the integrity of the procedure for awarding Federal contracts. The Commission believes that consultation should not be limited to state directors as members of the National Association of State Directors for Migrant Education (NASDME) but should also include local project staff who are responsible for providing services to migrant children.

The Commission found that to achieve this goal of interstate coordination ED has adopted practices to ensure that technical assistance and coordination are at the heart of MEP. The most frequent forms of coordination are the provision of technical assistance through contractors,[11] the participation in NASDME meetings, and the dissemination of joint memoranda with other Federal programs to encourage activities that benefit migrant children.

Overall, the Federal role focuses on administrative activities which facilitate the implementation of MEP in every state. Besides performing the traditional functions of an office in a regulatory agency (issuing regulations, allocating funds, reviewing programs for compliance, etc.), OME provides technical assistance and coordination services. These activities assist the states in meeting the needs of migrant children. OME's leadership has furthered this end by actively encouraging ongoing communication between ED and the states.

State Role in MEP

Congress authorized MEP as a state grant program so that through SEA leadership, programs and services could be targeted to the states and the areas within those states where migrant children are found. Each state operates its MEP based upon the number of migrant children within its jurisdictions, the time periods migrant children are in residence, the state's size, and the need for services.

SEA Administrative Activities.[12] Each SEA has flexibility in the way it administers MEP within its own jurisdiction although standards exist to ensure some uniformity in program implementation. For example, the state must establish a formal complaint procedure which describes the process for resolving program grievances; however, the specifics can vary by state. In addition, if the state establishes its own rules, regulations, and policies for MEP, then the state must convene a state committee of local administrators, teachers, and

"Coordination and cooperation can never be mandated, and the willingness to cooperate does not occur until people understand the uniqueness of the migrant child, the migrant lifestyle, and the Migrant Education Program...Once you capture the heart and soul, the mind and body will follow and usually do for many years; and I believe that this fact alone has helped make migrant educators unusually committed and the Migrant Education Program uniquely successful. The interrelationship between attitude and cooperation and coordination cannot be separated..."
—ROBERT LEVY[8]

parents to act in an advisory capacity.

SEAs are permitted to award subgrants to LEAs, nonprofit agencies, and other public agencies through an application process. The Commission's review of FY 1991 state plans, which are the applications that the states submit to OME for grants, indicated that all use subgrantees to provide services to migrant children, except New Hampshire and the District of Columbia. The most frequent recipients of these subgrants are LEAs.

The primary role of the SEA is administrative, i.e., to ensure that MEP services are offered to meet the needs of migrant children and that funds are spent within the guidelines of the statutory and regulatory requirements. Although each state administers MEP differently, some practices are similar in all states. These similarities and differences can best be seen through the analysis of the specific functions that are required by MEP.

Identification and Recruitment.[13] To ensure that all migrant children have access to MEP services, each state must identify and recruit (I&R) eligible children who reside within its borders. I&R is one of the most critical components of MEP since it determines whether migrant children will have access to MEP services. It also affects MEP funding allocations to the state.[14]

In most states, the SEAs and their subgrantees share I&R responsibilities. The SEA's primary role in this process is administrative: overseeing and training local recruiters, communicating with state-level organizations to locate migratory workers, and monitoring the overall quality of statewide I&R activities. In some

states with areas of high concentrations of migrant families, the local MEP is responsible for its own I&R; however, in other areas where the migrant population may be more scattered, the state usually conducts its own statewide I&R.

In order to ensure that the children being served are eligible under the MEP definition of migrant, ED encourages the states to accurately identify children by allowing no more than 5 percent to be inappropriately classified as eligible.[15] In accordance with statutory and regulatory requirements, each state's recruitment effort must be statewide, thorough, and comprehensive.

Migrant children are identified in a variety of ways. State staff responsible for recruitment usually communicate with associations, other state offices, and organizations that can provide information both on the location of agricultural, dairy, or fishing activities and on periods of peak employment. Statistics from the Migrant Student Record Transfer System (MSRTS) provide additional information. By evaluating profiles of past-year enrollments, state staff can determine where and during what time periods migrant children are likely to be residing in their state.

In essence, I&R is a labor-intensive activity, particularly when children are in the process of migrating. I&R is also costly for states with large rural areas and scattered migrant populations. As a result, SEAs often require their local subgrantees to hire local recruiters. An additional benefit of using these local recruiters is that they are known within their communities and can readily locate migrant children. Other recruitment strategies include using SEA staff or part-time staff to recruit in areas without local MEPs,[16] conducting statewide recruitment through one[17] subgrantee, and/or requiring local school superintendents to notify SEA staff of eligible migrant children.[18]

Use of MSRTS.[19] MSRTS is a national computerized database that stores information on migrant children and transfers it to the MEP in the new area when the child moves. The child's transition into a new school is smoother if these records are complete and accurate. Consequently, SEAs must design ways to ensure the integrity of the child's records.[20]

Although the Commission found that MSRTS has accomplished some of its original goals, problems still exist in the accuracy of the information and the timeliness with which it is exchanged. Recommendations for resolving these problems were included in the Commission's report to Congress.[21] As part of its recommendations, the Commission suggested reducing the amount of information included on MSRTS, involving parents, improving quality control, and transferring information electronically. We are pleased with the response from ED and NASDME to this report. Both groups have adopted the spirit of the report and are in the process of modifying MSRTS. The Commission, however, cautions that its recommendations were offered as a complete package to be considered in its entirety.

Assessment of Needs.[22] SEAs and their local subgrantees are required annually to assess the needs of MEP children and to use this information to design programs and to select eligible children, especially those with the greatest needs.[23] Only those children who now reside or are expected to reside within the district are assessed and then only in those areas or subjects of program concentration. When deciding which needs should be addressed, SEA staff must consider the availability of other programs, personnel, and library resources.[24]

The process of assessment presents challenges to the states because some of their MEP populations are not in school and much of the assessment information is held by other entities (e.g., LEAs and MSRTS). For these reasons, California initiated a system that uses certain MSRTS elements to capture the characteristics of the state's migrant children; the system is known as the Student and Program Needs Assessment (SAPNA)/Migrant Education Needs Assessment and Evaluation System (MENAES).[25] The Commission heard testimony regarding its value. For the first time, both local and state staff had profiles on groups of students.[26] While the Commission commends these efforts to improve the information reported to MSRTS, it is concerned that SAPNA/MENAES, which is mainly a management tool for the states, may interfere with the primary mission of MSRTS—the exchange of student records.

The Commission appreciates how complex a process it can be for a state and its projects to gather accurate data on the progress of migrant students. While states must conduct assessments, comprehensive information on migrant children remains elusive. Unfortunately, the information needs of state administrators (for program management) differ from those of local service providers (for program planning). Consequently,

> "...we see all of these entities as members of one body whose common purpose is to meet the educational needs of the migrant child, and this body we see not as one member but many. And just like the human body uses its members for different functions, this body of migrant entities uses its different members...for different functions...And many times...we use the hands for another activity, use the eyes for another activity; but sometimes we need eye-hand coordination."
>
> —DR. TADEO REYNA[29]

each requires its own set of tools and procedures for assessing migrant children that will provide the information necessary to design effective programs. Mandatory testing may be the most efficient method for states to acquire information on the basic skills knowledge of migrant children but it may also provide unreliable information about them since many migrant children are recent immigrants with limited-English skills.

The Commission believes that Federal policy should be sensitive to these problems and encourage realistic practices; otherwise, SEAs may be in the unenviable position of having to choose between following the spirit or the letter of the law.

Designing Program Services.[27] SEAs are authorized to use MEP funds for supplementary programs and services that meet the special educational needs of migrant children during the regular school term, as well as during the summer term. MEP funds can pay for personnel, equipment, materials, staff training, support services, construction of school facilities (if necessary), and coordination activities with other programs for migrant children. In contrast, MEP funds cannot be used as general aid or to support programs that are the legal responsibility of the LEA, such as a desegregation program.

The SEA generally assumes administrative and leadership roles with respect to the funding, location, term, and general design of its MEP. However, the local projects determine how the basic program objectives will be implemented and include a description of the process as part of their application. SEA staff approve local project applications and then monitor the program to ensure that the services delivered are those described in the application.

State Coordination Activities.[28] In addition to OME's coordination activities, MEP also requires extensive coordination activities by the states. Coordination must occur among the agencies and Federal programs that serve migrant children and families, among the states to ensure the transfer of student information, and among all local MEP projects.

The SEAs generally promote interagency coordination among the agencies that serve the migrant family by forming committees composed of agency representatives. The committees meet regularly to plan and coordinate services. These meetings help MEP state directors to learn when and where migrant families will be working so that they can plan more coordinated services for migrant children and, thereby, help to reduce program costs.

In an ideal situation, coordination among agencies allows each agency and program to share resources to expand the scope of its services. For example, by sharing information about the same migrant farmworkers, the Migrant and Seasonal Farmworker Job Training and Partnership Act (JTPA) Program can assist MEP in identifying and locating families; Migrant Health can conduct health screenings; and Migrant Head Start can provide preschool services to children. This referral process enables a family to access services from several programs without applying separately for each.[30] In some cases, services from various programs are in one location so all the needs of a family can be addressed.[31]

SEAs also make sure that interagency activities occur at the local level and provide assistance if the agencies are not working together. In general, MEP applications include descriptions of the activities local subgrantees plan to use when working with other agencies. SEAs then monitor the programs to ensure that the planned activities occur.

The Commission confirmed that one of the negative effects of migration is the lack of continuity that tends to disrupt the migrant child's education. Effective interstate and intrastate coordination helps to ameliorate this problem by encouraging continuity through curriculum, credits, and services.[32] The Commission recognizes that each state is responsible for designing a curriculum to suit the needs of its students. However, such independence—and the increasing autonomy of some LEAs—makes interstate coordination of educational services for the migrant child exceedingly difficult.

Interstate coordination within MEP is accomplished by the use of MSRTS, by consultation with NASDME, and by the awarding of special grants/contracts administered by OME. A portion of each state's MEP funds is set aside at the Federal level to support the MSRTS contract, since MSRTS facilitates the nationwide exchange of student information. NASDME supports interstate coordination by sponsoring national conferences and regional meetings where SEA and local operating staff can share training and information.

Parental Involvement.[33] *"One of the things that migrant education taught us [is that] as parents, we have the power of changing the minds of our children."—Anastacio Andrada*[34]

SEAs are required to ensure that MEP projects involve parents in meaningful ways in planning and implementing programs for their children and themselves. Projects offered in the regular school term must convene Parent Advisory Councils that include parents of children participating in the program. In particular, MEP projects must find ways to involve parents who lack literacy or have limited-English skills.

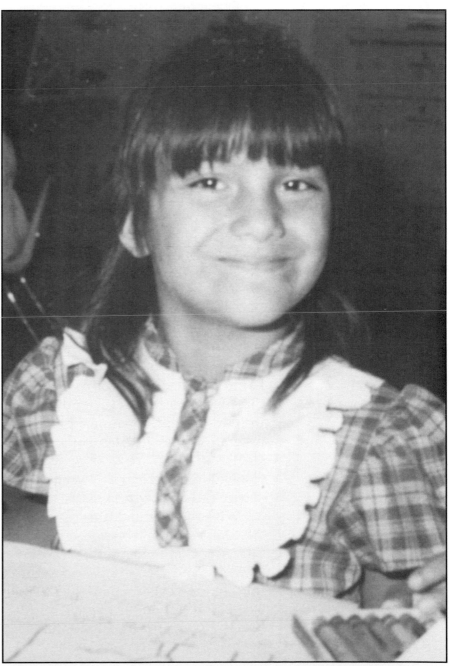

■ *Interstate Migrant
Secondary Service Program*
coordinated services to
junior and senior high
school migrant students
in 11 states.

■ *Interstate Migrant
Secondary Team Project*
addressed the problems
of California's intrastate
migrants and trained a
national group of migrant
education experts.

■ *Migrant Dropout
Reconnection Project* targeted migrants who had
dropped out of school
and helped them gradu-
ate or obtain an equiva-
lency diploma. The pro-
ject newsletter, sent to
identified dropouts, pro-
vided information on
ways for them to "recon-
nect" with school. This
outstanding project was
awarded a grant by ED's
Dropout Prevention
Program.[38]

The SEA's primary role in this area is
to ensure that local projects fulfill
this obligation.

The Commission is pleased to
find that over half of the states out-
lined activities in their MEP plans
that go beyond the legal requirements for parental involvement.[35] In
addition, some agencies not required
by law to have councils, were offering them. By doing so, they were following the spirit of the mandate.

Evaluation.[36] At least once every 3
years, a MEP project must conduct a
formal evaluation to determine the
impact of its program on the migrant
children it serves. SEAs must submit
information annually on the migrant
children who participated in the programs and biennially on how successful the project was in meeting its
goals. In addition, local MEPs must
determine how successful formerly
migrant children have been in main-
taining achievement gains for at least
2 years.

Though SEAs have always been
required to evaluate MEP and report
their results to ED, the states and the
Federal Government have tried over
the years to develop a process that
suits the needs of both the states
(sufficiently accurate for program
planning) and ED (sufficiently uniform to generate a national profile of
program success). Meanwhile, the
states and OME are working to
resolve the difference between what
is required and what is practical.

With this in mind, the
Commission has several suggestions.
First, the Commission encourages
Congress and OME to continue supporting the development of a flexible
evaluation system for migrant education. Second, Congress is also urged
to review the current reporting

schedule to ensure that LEA and
SEA requirements are synchronized.
Third, the Commission suggests that
ED explore vehicles to gather information on the proportion of LEP
migrant children who participate in
other supplementary programs such
as Chapter 1.

Special Projects to Enhance MEP

In 1978, Congress authorized a
discretionary grant program (Section
143) to support interstate coordination activities. These grants were
funded by ED, but administered by
the states. Although more than 100
grants were funded, most were too
narrowly focused to meet the program goal,[37] and they did not clearly
differentiate between the general
educational needs (e.g., language
enrichment) and the specific educational needs (e.g., high school credit
transfer) of migrant students. OME's
role in interstate coordination
includes ensuring that these contracts
and grants meet their stated objectives and that states are consulted in
the process.

In 1985, legislative amendments
gave ED more control over program
design.[39] In response to these
changes, OME asked the states to
identify priority areas for coordination. Given their need for technical
assistance in providing services to
migrant children, the states requested that resource centers be established. Eventually, the Program
Development Centers were created
to provide technical assistance. These
Centers became tools to help the
states facilitate coordination within
states and across regions.

As part of the 1988 legislative
changes, Section 143 became Section

1203 and the coordination projects under this Section became national in scope. Those projects that are currently funded under Section 1203 are listed in Appendix E, Exhibit 2.1. While most appear to focus on valuable national efforts for coordination, the Commission is concerned that some sections of the two projects, the Migrant Stopover Center and the National Secondary Credit Exchange and Accrual Project, may not be meeting their intended goals.

The Migrant Stopover Center, which provides a variety of services to families traveling in the central stream, was neither requested by NASDME nor enthusiastically supported by OME. One of its services is short-term college counseling, which does not appear to be a viable activity for a stopover location.[40] The Commission encourages ED and project administration to work cooperatively to identify more appropriate activities.

The National Secondary Credit Exchange and Accrual Project, which was originally created to assist high school migrant students transfer credits between schools, shifted its focus away from its main goal toward the development of a formula to calculate the national migrant dropout rate. However, the Commission is encouraged by a review of recent contracts which suggest that the project may be refocusing on its original goal of credit exchange and accrual. The Commission further believes that the transfer of credits for currently migrant students is very important and it urges ED and other agencies such as the Chief State School Officers, the National Goals Panel, and the National Governors Association to support and encour-age the project's original goals of secondary credit exchange for migrant children. It would be a tragedy for MEP children if any part of this Section 1203 project failed.

Given that the major obstacle to the transfer of credits for migrant students is the lack of a common policy on credit accrual across states,[41] this project is certainly a high priority and has the potential to ease this problem.

"…there is nothing more disappointing to a student than to have passed a course only to discover that the course was not accepted. It is not hard to imagine how their disappointment can grow into real disillusionment, a reluctance to re-enroll in school or ever to graduate."[42]

While this chapter describes the structure and core of the activities that are the basis for MEP, the ultimate goal of the program is to help migrant farmworkers improve the quality of their lives:

"In our role as advocates for farmworkers' families, we must help other institutions change so that we can ultimately empower migrant families to meet their own needs."[43]

The Commission also believes that MEP should serve as an advocate for migrant children in local communities. The program should be more aggressive in finding and serving migrant children and their families who need services from state, Federal, and other programs. In addition, ED should provide support for state administrators in ensuring that local MEPs meet their stated goals and objectives. Furthermore, the Commission suggests that Congress consider, during the next reauthorization, legislative language which would permit the Section 1203 grant process to be opened to other public and private groups.

CHAPTER THREE

Meeting the Needs of the Migrant Child

"The Day the Crops Failed...When I went to my back yard everything was frozen and I was very frightened, it's because of the cold weather. My family and I couldn't eat any more good vegetables. We only have beans, eggs, and several radishes. We need some money, so we can buy food. We all live in a trailer in a camp. My mom's tomatoes, at work, got frozen...If we put on the gas stove to warm up, we would have to pay lots of money and [we] don't have enough."

—EGOBILIA IBARRA, *Grade 3*[1]

Migrant children are characterized by a diverse set of traits. They possess a wide range of academic strengths and weaknesses. Some migrate during different seasons to different places for varying lengths of time and some do not migrate at all. Such a diverse set of traits provides states and local programs with the unique challenge of designing programs and support services with the flexibility to meet the considerable academic, linguistic, and health service needs of this population.

During the course of conducting research and hearing testimony, the Commission was encouraged to find that many Migrant Education Program (MEP) staff aggressively sought out and served migrant children in need of instructional and social-service assistance. Conversely, the Commission was discouraged to find that based on the changing demographics within the migrant workforce, some children migrating now have even greater needs than those of the past. Identifying these children and providing appropriate services are two of the tasks that state and local agencies are addressing (See Appendix F).

In 1991, more than 600,000 children were certified as eligible for Chapter 1 MEP throughout the United States.[2] This program funds supplementary educational and support services to children ages 3 through 21 whose parents are presently migratory (currently) or whose families have moved in the past 5 years (formerly) (see Appendix C). While national statistics indicate that almost half of these children moved[3] sometime during a 12-month period,[4] statistics describing the status of migrant children show that states have widely different proportions of currently and formerly migratory children. (Appendix E, Exhibit 3.1.)

MEP provides a range of services to about three-fourths of the eligible population.[5] Services are based upon a migrant child's needs, the availability of MEP funding, the existence of other funded services, and the time of year when a large number of children are present. Although MEP is a supplementary program that targets specific services to specific needs, it also provides full services both in the areas of instruction and support to migrant children. As a result, a variety of programs are available for a broad range of age groups from preschool to age 21 which are served during either or both the regular and summer school terms.

MEP Population Compared to Regular School Term Population

In relative size, the MEP population during the regular school term represents slightly less than 1 percent of all children enrolled in public schools across the nation.[6] While the incidence of MEP children varies by state (from about 5 percent in Alaska to less than 0.01 percent in West Virginia),[7] they represent a relatively small proportion of the total public school population in any state during the regular school year. For the hand-ful of districts that operate year-round programs, their students are included as part of the regular term enrollment.

Changes in the location and concentration of the MEP population vary seasonally based on when migrant labor is needed. Consequently, some states (e.g., California and Texas as home base states) serve many more migrant children during the regular school term, while others (e.g., Wyoming as a receiving state) serve the largest number during the summer, and none during the regular school term. Still others because of their vast expanses (e.g., Alaska), serve a sizable population that moves within the state boundary rather than to other states. As a result, the states offer programs and services that are tailored to the size of the migrant population, their length of stay, and their migration pattern.

California, which has a large intrastate migratory population, serves the largest concentration of migrant children during the regular term and offers special projects to targeted populations during the summer months. Nebraska has the largest concentration of children during the summer term, so MEP services are provided in the summer rather than during the regular term. By contrast, in New York where migratory movement is within the state and where a sizeable portion of formerly migrant children reside, relatively comparable numbers of children receive services during both the regular and the summer terms.

Identification & Recruitment Are Critical

Identification & Recruitment (I&R) are the processes through which migrant children are identified and deemed eligible for MEP. Since children who are migrating and those who formerly migrated are eligible, recruitment activities must target both groups. Activities range from basic administrative procedures such as recertification of those previously identified to intense outreach activities. Some common methods of recruiting include posting announcements in public buildings such as churches or stores, visiting migrant labor camps, and even "spreading the word" to other migrant families new to an area.[8] Recruitment occurs primarily through local MEP projects although some states use regional centers or one location for statewide recruiting.[9]

MEP staff (e.g., recruiters, home-school liaisons, teachers, etc.) responsible for recruitment activities play an important role in the program since they are usually the first MEP contact the family has. Once a prospective family is identified, staff explain the services available through MEP and obtain basic information from the parent or guardian to determine whether the child is eligible for the program. Many recruiters also assess family service needs[10] and serve as advocates for migrant children to ensure that they receive appropriate school services and placements[11].

One problem caused by migration is the lack of continuity of services across states. MEP children recruited in one state may not be recruited when they move to another state. A recent analysis of MSRTS records found thousands of students who had left one state and entered another without being recertified as eligible for MEP.[12] This might happen when the child migrates to an area without a migrant program. The Commission views recruitment as one of the most critical components of MEP, particularly since it affects those who are currently migrating and who may be the most difficult to find and serve. The Commission encourages MEP recruiters to develop more aggressive methods for identifying currently migratory children since they may also be the children most in need of academic and support services.

Counted, But Not Served

Not all migrant children deemed eligible for services actually receive them.[13] Although eligible children are counted for the purpose of determining funding, some may not necessarily receive services. There are several possible reasons for this dis-

Leadership Training Programs, designed to teach leadership skills to teenage migrant youth, are held on weekends. Florida offers leadership institutes to middle and senior high school students who are at-risk of dropping out of school. This program helps students develop leadership skills while they earn credits for promotion or graduation.[32] In Oregon, weekend leadership institutes permit students to develop mutual trust, cooperation, and self-esteem. These programs are held on weekends so that migrant children with limited-English skills can train with their peers[33] rather than with the general population. These programs vary in design but their common objective is to raise the self-esteem of migrant youth by exposing them to new experiences.

crepancy. Migrant children are entitled to receive the same basic and supplementary services available to all children within a specific program. Consequently, some or all of their needs may have been met through local, state, and Federal resources rather than through MEP. However, since MEP has limited funds, if a MEP is not available to provide services, some children may not be served, particularly if other programs are not available.

Of the 550,865 children enrolled in MSRTS during the 1989-90 regular school term, states reported that 66 percent (360,839) were MEP participants. The services they receive can range in intensity, for example, from daily language instruction to tutoring several times weekly. Exhibit 3.2 illustrates that over a 6-year period the proportion of eligible children who receive MEP-funded services during the regular school term ranged from a high of 73 percent to a low of 65 percent. However, the actual numbers of children served by MEP have increased continuously since 1987.[14]

Needs of MEP children

As is true with other educationally disadvantaged populations, migrant children generally come from families with low incomes, inadequate housing, and serious health problems.[16] What makes migrant children unique is their mobility which is caused by their parents' employment in agriculture and fishing. Consequently, on an annual basis, some children change schools once, others change several times,[17] and still others attend schools both within and outside the United States.[18]

School Year	MSRTS Enrollments	MEP Participants	Percent Served
1984-85	438,958	311,615	71%
1985-86	440,733	323,601	73%
1986-87	448,914	300,674	67%
1987-88	471,619	308,249	65%
1988-89	513,137	333,042	65%
1989-90	550,865	360,839	66%

Exhibit 3.2
MEP Eligible Versus Participating During the Regular School Term 1984-85 through 1989-90[15]

A recent national study of migrant children documented that approximately 39 percent of the migrant students who attend the regular school term and 45 percent of the migrant students who attend the summer school term move within a 12-month period.[19] During the 1991 calendar year, MSRTS statistics showed that 48 percent of the population moved at least once during that time.[20]

A national profile of migrant students suggests that:

■ a high proportion (84 percent to 94 percent) qualify for free or reduced lunch;[21]

■ over one-third are one or more grades behind their age-appropriate grade level;[22]

■ for approximately 40 percent, fluency in English interferes with classroom work;[23]

■ some have had little or no exposure to formal education;[24]

■ over 40 percent are estimated to be achieving below the 35th percentile in reading;[25] and

■ the proportion who have needs diminishes over time once children cease migrating.[26]

Differences between Currently and Formerly. Some educators view both currently and formerly migratory children as having greater needs than other disadvantaged populations.[27] Further evidence suggests that a greater proportion of currently migratory children have needs that exceed those of their formerly migratory counterparts,[28] and that within the currently migratory population, differences exist between those who recently entered the migrant workforce and those who migrate annually.[29] In part, these differences result from the changing demographics of the migrant farmworker population. As one local MEP director reported to the Commission:

> The change in our migrant population over the last ten years has been significant. The profile has been one of steadily increasing numbers of nationalities, languages, cultures, and needs… It is not uncommon to find a ten-year-old child who has never put one foot through the door of a school in his life.[30]

States also report differences in their currently migratory population that are related to when they move. The FY 1991 MEP Grant Application from Arizona noted that:

> Generally, the needs of mobile migrant students fall into two broad categories—one being those students whose families move in a regular cycle which means late arrivals into the school program and early departures. These students' needs center around flexibility in both timing and content of the delivery of instructional services. The second broad group of mobile students are those whose families move from place to place within a more confined geographic area and their movements have less predictability. These are more often dysfunctional families with more intense support service needs.[31]

Programs Designed to Meet Needs

To address the need for intense support services, MEP, as a full-service program may fund instructional, medical, and social services. However, to receive these services, migrant children must have a need that falls within the boundaries specified by the state or by local projects.

Strategies for providing services vary from project to project because of differences in the needs of the population, the availability of other programs and services, and the fiscal resources of MEP. Some local projects that operate year-round customize their services in response to the seasonal changes in the numbers and types of migrant children who attend. Other projects offer services only during the regular term or the summer term, whenever the greatest numbers of migrant children are present. Some sites offer projects that serve only migrant children within their district. In contrast, other projects provide services across a region that includes several school districts.

Many programs offer full-day instructional services as well as tutoring, home-based services, compensatory instruction, and special projects such as Leadership Training. Differences in instructional strategies are most notable between regular and summer term projects since MEP is usually the only instructional program available during the summer.

Regular Term and Summer Term Projects. Although MEPs are usually classified by school term, the pro-

Exhibit 3.3
Number of Migrant Children
Receiving MEP Services
By School Term 1984-1990[34]

Year	Regular School Term	Summer School Term
1984-85	311,615	100,895
1985-86	323,601	112,350
1986-87	300,674	104,751
1987-88	308,249	105,419
1988-89	333,042	125,427
1989-90	360,839	127,980

One project in Florida has nine components. The preschool supports a Head Start-like program. At the primary and elementary grade levels instructional tutors assist migrant children in the regular classroom. Class size is reduced (using local and MEP funds to support the regular classroom teacher) in Language Arts classes in middle schools and high schools. Also available are after-school tutorial programs with accompanying child-care services for younger siblings. This program also offers after-school recreational programs, a dropout prevention program, and medical and social referral services.[35]

When the regular school term ends, the summer term MEP project in New York begins its home-study program. Later in the summer, a day and evening program begins when larger concentrations of currently migratory children arrive. Day programs are offered to elementary children and evening programs are offered to middle and high school students. For those who cannot attend either program, a home-study program is available.[40]

grams share many features regardless of when or where the service is offered, differing for the most part only in the numbers of children they serve.

Unlike the regular term, all children who are counted for summer term funding must be served.[36] Furthermore, programs during the regular term supplement existing school district programs, while during the summer, MEP is frequently the only available service.

The greatest number of children are served during the regular school term (Exhibit 3.3). The amount of instructional time may range from less than an hour to several hours per week depending on how instruction is provided.[37] Furthermore, a greater proportion of summer term as compared to regular term students receive more than one MEP-funded service.

Exhibit 3.4 shows the number and percent of the population that received different types of instructional services during the 1989-90 Program Year. In both school terms, the largest percentage of children received MEP-funded reading and mathematics services, while the smallest percentage received vocational services.

As one local project director in

California stated to the Commission regarding summer programs:

The major focus of migrant education in summer schools is not only to remediate unlearned skills, but also provide students with a stimulating, rich curriculum that integrates higher-order thinking skills, meaning-centered curriculum, student-centered activities, and perhaps most important of all, learning how to learn. The second focus is not to stop the learning process but to see that it continues.[39]

Services Are Need-Based. Each migrant child is assessed to determine whether he or she needs educational and support services. Should a need exist, project staff might design a program appropriate for the student's needs by selecting a combination of services provided by MEP or other funded programs. Conceivably, some children might not receive MEP services because their needs are met through other funded programs, while other migrant children might receive services through a combination of MEP and another funded program.[41] Among children who did not participate in MEP, less than one-third received Chapter 1 and less than 10 percent participated in programs for students who are limited-English proficient.[42] Those children who do receive MEP services participate in other programs only at a slightly higher rate.[43]

Although these statistics paint a

Exhibit 3.4
Number and Percent of Children Receiving
MEP Funded Instructional Services 1989-90[38]

Service	Regular School Term		Summer School Term	
Instructional Area	Number	Percent	Number	Percent
English As a Second Language (ESL)	72,868	20%	31,874	25%
Reading	141,499	39%	63,035	49%
Other Language Arts	60,898	17%	57,751	45%
Mathematics	100,903	28%	64,893	51%
Vocational	12,184	3%	13,884	11%
Other Instructional Services (e.g. driver education)	53,716	15%	51,301	40%
Unduplicated Count	360,839		127,980	

less-than-clear picture of who is and is not served and why, there are projects particularly in the regular term where multiple sources of funds (e.g., MEP and bilingual programs) finance instructional supplementary services.[44] Consequently, whether a migrant child can participate in MEP as well as other funded supplementary programs differs from school district to school district. Thus, the degree to which migrant children participate in MEP and in other programs is a function of the match between each child's need and the array of existing programs.

Support Services. Migrant children receive a number of services created to offset some of the problems associated with poor nutrition, inadequate medical services, etc. As with instructional services, more children received supporting services during the 1989-90 regular term than during the summer term, except for nutrition and transportation services which serve larger numbers of children during the summer. Exhibit 3.5 shows that similar proportions of the children received medical, dental, and guidance services regardless of school term.

Targeted-Service Groups. Although MEP can provide funded services to eligible children between the ages of 3 and 21, more than 60 percent of the children served by MEP are enrolled in kindergarten through grade 6.[46] In fact, only slightly more than half of the local projects in a 1990 national sample offered services to those aged 18 through 21.[47] At a national level, almost equal proportions of currently and formerly migratory children receive MEP services. On a state-by-state basis, differences in the percentages of the served population that is currently migratory range from 99 percent (i.e., Montana) to less than 20 percent (i.e., Massachusetts).[48]

Priority in MEP services is to be given to currently migratory children if they have a need. While some programs are clearly designed for children moving between school districts—such as the Portable Assisted Study Sequence (PASS) which permits secondary students to continue course completion through independent study—the Commission's research suggests that services generally do not vary relative to migratory status. Rather, it appears that time of year and the availability of resources or other programs are more likely to determine whether MEP serves a higher proportion of currently or formerly migratory children.

Exhibit 3.5
Number and Percent of Children Receiving
MEP Funded Supporting Services 1989-90[45]

Service Area Supporting Service	Regular School Term		Summer School Term	
	Number	Percent	Number	Percent
Guidance/Counseling	178,134	49%	58,777	46%
Social Work/Outreach	64,065	18%	34,657	27%
Health	81,778	23%	30,804	24%
Dental	35,493	10%	18,834	15%
Nutrition	35,940	10%	56,387	44%
Transportation	34,416	10%	60,063	47%
Other Supporting (e.g., translation services, insurance)	153,909	43%	68,894	54%
Unduplicated Number of Participants	360,839		127,980	

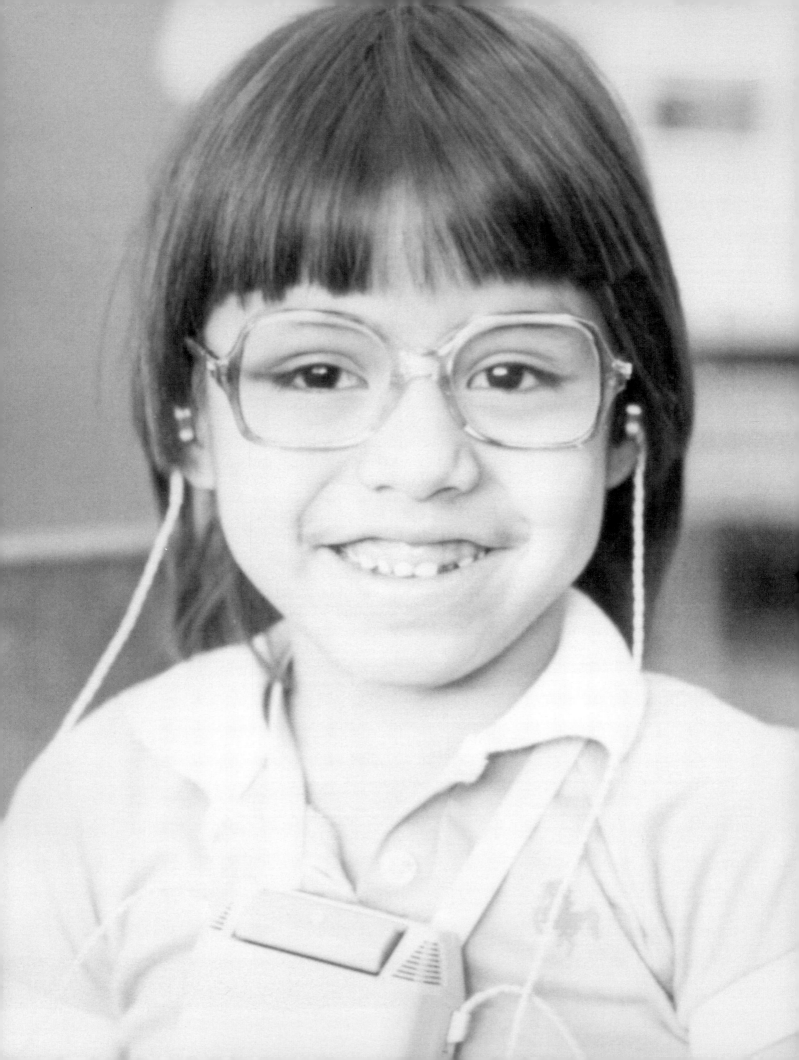

CHAPTER FOUR

Migrant Populations with Unique Needs

Even within such a disadvantaged population as migrant children, there are some whose needs are distinct. The Commission was mandated to review the status and the needs of four such groups—preschool-aged children, migrant children with disabilities, gifted and talented migrant children, and migrant children who are at-risk of dropping out of school or who have dropped out.

Preschool-aged migrant children, a recent legislative priority for the Migrant Education Program (MEP), are of particular concern to the Commission. Because of the developmental nature of the preschool years, what happens during these years is important for all children but especially critical for the migrant child. Consequently, preschool interventions must be comprehensive and provide intensive health, education, nutrition, and parental support services. In addition, programs must be responsive to the needs of migrant families who are not able to afford high-quality early childhood programs.

Another group requiring special interventions is migrant children with disabilities. While they represent only a small portion of the total number of migrant children, their needs are significant. Federal legislation requires that all children with disabilities be identified and served; however, migrant children with disabilities still face difficulties in being properly diagnosed and receiving appropriate services. Much of the difficulty is directly attributable to linguistic, cultural, and lifestyle attributes over which the migrant child has no control. Consequently, there is a need to look carefully at identifying migrant students with disabilities as well as providing interventions and coordinating services for these children.

Migrant children who are gifted and talented may be overlooked initially because of linguistic, cultural, and lifestyle factors which complicate their identification. Unlike migrant children with disabilities, gifted and talented children are not entitled to receive MEP special educational interventions. Consequently, even gifted migrant children who are identified may not receive services.

Migrant children who are at-risk of dropping out or who have dropped out of school may do so to help support the family, or because they have been unable to amass enough credits to graduate from high school because of their mobility. Although several MEP programs show promise in helping migrant students complete high school, they are only available on a limited basis.

While some migrant children do succeed in school, there are others whose needs require special interventions tailored to their age group, disability, or other educational support service needs. Each section of Chapter 4 discusses the special problems and concerns associated with each of these groups—Preschool-Aged Migrant Children, Migrant Children With Disabilities, Gifted and Talented Migrant Children, and Migrant Students At-Risk.

Preschool-Aged Migrant Children

It is widely believed that children who participate in high-quality, early childhood programs will not only perform better in school but will eventually become contributing members of society.[1] In *America 2000*, the National Governors' Association and the President endorsed this belief and made it a national goal—by the year 2000 all children in America will enter school ready to learn (See Appendix F).

Thanks to the efforts of many early childhood providers, more young migrant children today are entering school better prepared. However, there are still many young migrant children and their families who live in poverty and are neither able to find nor afford the high-quality early childhood education and health care services they need. While some of these services are available at no or low cost to migrant children and their families, often the parents' inadequate English skills, mobility, or their reluctance to seek assistance for a variety of reasons interfere with their receiving services.

The Commission believes that young migrant children will best be served by a well-integrated community support system that includes all existing preschool, health, nutrition, and social service programs. Although coordinating such diverse programs is difficult, communities are struggling to develop models to coordinate their early childhood services despite many obstacles.[2] With a coordinated social service delivery system—which we currently lack—migrant parents can provide their young children with the health services, experiences, and skills necessary to succeed in school.

Programs Serving Young Migrant Children

Three programs at the Federal level—Migrant Education Program (MEP), Migrant Head Start, and Migrant Even Start—provide services only for migrant children (Appendix E, Exhibit 4.1). Other programs such as regular Head Start and Chapter 1 Even Start, which are also available to the general population, can provide services to migrant children.

Migrant Education Program. In 1988, Congress demonstrated the importance of serving preschool migrant children by allowing MEPs to receive funding to serve children between the ages of 3 and 5 who were identified as MEP-eligible. Prior to that time, preschool-aged migrant children could receive MEP services under certain conditions; however, the cost of these programs was not reimbursed by the Federal Government. Because of legislative changes, the U.S. Department of Education (ED) now requires states receiving MEP funds to identify those migrant children aged 3 to 5 and serve those whose needs are not being met by any other program.[3] Although costs cannot be reimbursed, programs can serve children ages 2 or younger only if, without such services, an older sibling could not otherwise attend MEP.

Migrant Head Start. Migrant Head Start programs are broad-based and interdisciplinary, family-centered to support the family's principal role in the development of the child,

designed to promote "the child's everyday effectiveness in dealing with both present environment and later responsibilities in school and life,"[4] and coordinated with the services of other community agencies.[5]

Migrant Head Start provides highly comprehensive services and requires high standards of service in the areas of education, health, nutrition, social services, and parental involvement.[6] As the most evaluated early childhood program, research on Head Start has demonstrated that young children who participate in high-quality Head Start programs are at first developmentally, socially and emotionally more successful than their peers.[7]

Migrant Even Start. The Migrant Even Start Program was originally enacted into law in 1988 and is required to collaborate with other community programs to avoid duplication of services. The basis of this program is to help both children and their parents at the same time. Program components include a preschool program for the children and adult education and parenting programs for the parents, which assist them in learning how to help their children succeed in school. Even Start enables parents and children to become true partners in education by providing parents with the literacy skills necessary to help their children with their school work, to read to their children and to obtain better jobs, thereby improving the family situation.

The Commission believes that both Migrant Head Start and Even Start contain model elements that MEP educators should build upon in designing programs for migrant preschool children.

Roadblocks to Coordination

Essentially, migrant children are entitled to every Federal program for which other children of low-income families are eligible.[8] In some areas where one MEP program may not be reaching its total eligible population, these migrant children might be served by other preschool programs. For example, MEP in New Mexico plans to serve only 46 percent of its preschool population because other programs such as regular Head Start and Migrant Head Start already provide services to the children.[9]

Some Migrant Head Start grantees consider their services to be more responsive to the needs of children and working parents because, as private nonprofit organizations, they are free of the constraints usually governing school systems.[10] Although the Commission is not certain that this is true in all cases, we believe MEP providers should identify the most cost-effective and responsive program design.

While in some places an abundance of early childhood programs creates a larger safety net of services, it can also result in fragmentation if many programs provide the same functions and services to the same clients. Duplication of effort is not only inefficient, it may also be contentious.[11] During a time of limited fiscal resources, duplication can lead to competition and animosity among service providers—a situation which inhibits coordination.

Commission research uncovered one example concerning the overlap in services provided by MEP and Migrant Head Start. MEP providers view the 1988 modification to MEP legislation that extended services to children 3 years of age as a positive step for those who wanted to serve preschool-aged children but lacked funds. In contrast, other programs serving this population view this expansion as an encroachment into their service responsibilities and as a change not in the best interests of either migrant children or their families.[12] In particular, some Migrant Head Start providers believe that the public school systems are unable to provide the flexible services that migrant families require and about which they are unwilling to ask the early childhood community for advice. Although the Commission is uncertain how widespread this problem is, one early childhood provider described the situation as follows:

"Unfortunately,...there's virtually no real collaboration going on between the local school systems and the private, nonprofit or other child care providers anywhere in this country...I know...the local Migrant Head Start provider runs a sixteen to twenty-week program, because the agricultural season...has become that long. The local Migrant Education Program, on the other hand, has traditionally run a six-week program because that's when the schools are available to them. So the migrant children come in at the school's convenience for a pre-school program run for the weeks that it's convenient for the schools to run it."[13]

On the other hand, the Commission also heard testimony which highlighted how a long-term and ongoing partnership developed between competing state agencies which served the same migrant farmworkers and their families:

"...in 1964...a social worker...and a home-school visitor...were [each] responsible for the recruitment and enrollment of respective program children. One evening when [we] arrived at the same camp, [we] mutually agreed...to hold a joint meeting with [our] superiors and funding sources...Such a meeting was held with the following results: 1) the county would be divided in half by assignment; 2) one person would enroll all children for both programs; 3) age limits were set for day care and education; 4) [we] would meet jointly with both supervisors...Parents, growers, health and church officials were pleased with the results. They knew who to contact...In 1965...we organized [a] meeting of all local agencies and their responsible state officials...Today, nearly 30 agencies still meet annually to review services, introduce new staff, and refine roles.[14]

The good news is that in some places coordination is occurring daily, despite obstacles.[15] The Commission is aware that several MEP and Migrant Head Start programs are sharing funds, personnel, training, and other resources.[16] As a result of these efforts, migrant early childhood providers hold joint training sessions, utilize the same intake form, share resources, and sometimes operate in the same building.[17] As another example, the Minnesota Migrant Child Development Program Steering Committee has been developing coordination strategies for almost 20 years.[18]

Program Services Vary Widely

The Commission found a rich diversity of models to serve young migrant children. The differences among the models are based upon the variability of participant needs, geographic location, and program philosophy. While such diversity often leads to innovation, the quality of services across programs is generally unknown. The Commission would urge these groups to carefully review their guidelines and performance standards to ensure that they are clearly stated and obtainable.

Continuity across programs is a critical factor in program design for those migrant families who are highly mobile. Several early childhood programs aspire to improve inter-and intrastate coordination by actually moving with families. For instance, the Texas Migrant Council's Pre-

school Program staff relocates with the families as they move upstream during the harvest season and acts as a liaison between the migrant family and local service agencies. The Council operates over 34 projects in Texas, Indiana, Kansas, Ohio, Washington, and Wisconsin.[19] One of its major strengths is that bilingual personnel—a rare commodity in many receiving states—move with the migrant families.

Working migrant families, whose wages generally fall below the poverty level, have significant childcare needs. Since both parents may work in the fields just to provide for their family's necessities, very young children may be left unattended in a car near the field, actually taken into the fields, or left at home in the care of an older sibling who must miss school. For parents fortunate enough to locate quality childcare programs, the program hours may not coincide with the parents' long work day nor be responsive to the unique needs of migrant families. In comparison, the Commission is aware of areas in which services are offered from early morning to late evening and even on weekends.[20] The Commission urges childcare programs to expand their services, wherever possible, and to meet the needs of the families they serve.

Programs may also vary by population density or by geographic location. For example, in an area where a large population of migrants resides, the optimum program is designed to keep the children within the community. The program's location along the migratory stream also affects its operating schedule. For example, Migrant Head Start programs in home base and receiving states run at

"One of the experiences we have the most problems with is in our summer education for our children [up North]. When we arrive, usually the programs have already started, and this is in early June. The programs are held from three to four weeks, and our season is much longer than that. We [work] from July to August and part of September. We have to take our children to the field, which about ninety percent of us do, because there are no babysitting facilities that we can use. There are some babysitters, but they charge them anywhere from two to three dollars, per hour, and that's per child."[21]

—JUANITA CASTILO

alternating times of the year based on fluctuations in the harvest schedule.[22]

Early Interventions Needed

Current health and nutrition profiles of migrant families indicate that many young migrant children begin life precariously and continue to struggle as they enter school and later in life. Consequently, programs for young migrant children should prevent early health, nutritional, and developmental set-backs which tend to put them at a later disadvantage.

Poor Health Profiles. Although there is limited research on the health status of migrant farmworkers and their families, the data consistently portray a population with health needs similar to those in a third-world country.[23] A recent national report underscored the poor health conditions of migrant farmworkers by concluding that "hired farmworkers are not adequately protected by Federal laws, regulations, and programs; therefore, their health and well-being are at risk."[24]

The Commission's review of studies on the health status of young migrant children found this population to be especially vulnerable to malnutrition, dental problems, low-birth weights, high infant mortality, and developmental abnormalities.[25] The tragedy of these findings is that such problems can be prevented, in part, by early intervention. Unfortunately, migrant children's health needs are often ignored until a crisis arises. By that time, the child may have suffered irreparable damage with long-term consequences.

One particularly troubling health problem is the improper immunization of young migrant children. The Commission heard testimony about children who were over-immunized or, because of a lack of access to health care, under-immunized.[26] Despite on-going efforts to maintain immunization records through the Migrant Student Record Transfer System (MSRTS), significant problems relating to the timeliness and accuracy of records on immunization still exist.[27] Given their substandard living conditions and interaction with many people, migrant children are especially susceptible to—and can quickly transmit—infectious diseases. Therefore, national immunization campaigns should provide priority services to migrant children.

Prenatal and Infant Healthcare. Regularly scheduled preventive healthcare is a luxury that many migrants can neither afford nor find. However, the factors which characterize agriculture (i.e., continued exposure to pesticides known to cause birth problems,[28] inadequate field sanitation,[29] and the high incidence of hospitalization and physical disabilities caused by farm-machinery accidents[30]) create an even greater need for services.

Factors related to rural isolation, lack of transportation, and language barriers restrict the availability of healthcare, especially in upstream states.[31] Inconsistent access to prenatal care,[32] incompatible eligibility criteria for Medicaid across states, and limited access to migrant health due to the program's fiscal constraints, may further limit healthcare options for some migrant women and their young children.[33] In some states, families may wait at least a month for a medical appointment.[34] Such a long wait might preclude mobile families from receiving treatment mainly because they may have to migrate before the date of their appointment.

Nutritional Status. Relative to the general student population, children who start school hungry are four times more likely to suffer from fatigue, three times more likely to suffer from irritability and concentration problems, and twice as likely to suffer from frequent colds.[35] This is especially disturbing in light of Commission testimony that described participation rates of migrant families in programs designed to provide nutritional supplements, i.e., the Women, Infants and Children Program (WIC) and the Food Stamp Program are much lower than expected.

The lower-than-expected participation is due, to some extent, to regional differences in eligibility requirements.[36] Although migrants are given a priority status when participating in the Food Stamp and WIC programs, this does not guarantee that services will be provided. Other reasons for nonparticipation include pride in not receiving public assistance, a lack of program information, and an inability to produce proper documentation.[37]

Fortunately, there are other efforts to provide nourishment for young migrant children. About 40 percent of the migrant children enrolled in school-sponsored preschool programs are eligible to receive free or subsidized meals.[38] However, less fortunate children who cannot locate a summer program or who are not otherwise enrolled in school may go hungry.

Programs for Parents of Infants and Toddlers. Many experts believe that the first 3 years of a child's life create the foundation for future learning.[39] Therefore, parents are in the best position to influence their children's early development. Commission testimony indicates that some migrant families, especially those living in poverty, may be unable to provide their children with experiences to help prepare them for school.[40] For these children and their families, high-quality, early childhood and parenting programs can nurture a child's intellectual, linguistic, and social development.[41] Many of these programs rely on an intensive home-visiting component,[42] especially by early childhood education and health specialists, as a method for promoting development and lowering mortality.[43]

Unfortunately, most Federal and state early childhood and parenting programs are neither mandatory nor do they enroll children younger than 3 years. Less than 1 percent of the early childhood programs nationwide provide services for infants and toddlers.[44] In fact, infants and toddlers represent only about one-third of Migrant Head Start's total participant enrollment.[45] These statistics may indicate the need for a stronger emphasis on services for infants and toddlers, especially since the benefits would appear to be substantial.[46] Therefore, the Commission believes that the benefits of parenting and home-visiting programs for migrant infants and toddlers should be explored further.[47]

Limited Access to Preschool Programs

High-quality, affordable, early childcare and education programs are unavailable to many migrant families with young children primarily because of income, service availability, rural isolation, mobility, or language barriers. Middle-class families are more likely to participate in preschool programs than are low-income families such as migrant families. In 1991, according to the National Education Goals Panel, 4 out of 10 children ages 3 to 5 years from families with incomes of less than $30,000 were enrolled in preschool compared to 7 out of 10 children from families with incomes of more than $75,000.[48]

The Commission repeatedly heard that access to early childhood programs is limited. Although the Commission could not obtain exact percentages of children served, waiting lists for these programs are perhaps the best indicator of their short supply. As one early childhood provider in California explained:

"We have a waiting list of approximately 80 children and this waiting list would probably triple. The reason it stays this low is because the parents understand and know that the waiting list really never changes. Once [they] get into the program, they don't leave until the end of the program..."[49]

The Commission recognizes that appropriately serving preschool migrant children is an expensive proposition. High-quality early childcare and education programs that provide comprehensive and intensive services were estimated to cost an average of $4,800 per child in FY 1988.[50] By contrast, in FY 1990 Migrant Head Start received approximately $2,600 per child.[51] Consequently, MEP providers are struggling to fund services for preschool-aged children without diminishing services for other children.

Some service providers claim to have found cost-effective ways of providing high-quality services. One program reduced staff costs by hiring migrant mothers and eventually assisting them in becoming certified as early childhood specialists.[52] Another cost-effective technique is through home-based services where a child-development specialist regularly teaches parents the skills they need to help their children.[53]

The Commission is encouraged by the fact that participation rates within migrant-specific, early childhood programs have steadily increased during the past several years. ...1989-90, MEP served 13,104 preschool migrant children during the regular school term and 12,833 during the summer term.[54] In comparison, Migrant Head Start served less than 6 percent of the total eligible population in 1986.[55] Although the number of children served in FY 1992 increased, a large number of children still remain unserved.[56]

Overall, the participation of migrant children in programs varies nationwide by program. For example, in 1990, eight states did not provide MEP preschool services to migrants. In states that did, the percentage of preschool children receiving services ranged from between 1 and 92 percent of the total migrant population served.[57] However, on a national basis, prekindergarten children represented only 4 percent of the total population served by MEP during the 1989-90 school year.[58] Preschool participation rates for migrant children vary little between regular and summer terms. Rates, however, vary by migrant status, with the currently migratory receiving more services than the formerly migratory preschool children.[59]

To some extent, recruitment and identification procedures may determine accessibility to preschool programs. A 1991 survey of MEP preschool providers suggests that the recruitment of children depends upon whether an older sibling has already been identified through a regular school program.[60]

Program Access is Critical

The Commission believes that most migrant parents—like parents everywhere—provide their young children with love and support; however, in order to compete in school, children need some of the experiences that the migrant lifestyle cannot provide. Without the experiences commonly found in high-quality early childhood programs, many migrant children may enter school less prepared and have difficulty adjusting to the school environment. One early childhood provider explained to the Commission:

"The need for children to get socialization experiences to learn English, to be exposed to the kind of experiences that they can't have in their lives as migrants is critical to their future school success. Going to zoos, going to beaches, going to the fire station, sitting in a policeman's car, these are all important experiences that children need for their language development as well as their knowledge of the world. There's no way the migrant child can compete without having some of these experiences, which most middle-class children have as a matter of course."[61]

Research verified this assumption. A recent study found that participation in preschool programs helps migrant children (74 percent) perform at grade level.[62] By comparison, 51 percent of the children who had not enrolled in preschool performed below grade level. Although the effects on academic achievement were negligible, children who participated in preschool programs were less likely to drop out of school[63] and less likely to be retained in kindergarten or first grade.[64]

While the Commission believes that most migrant children enter school eager to learn, they may not be as prepared as others to do so. Early childhood education and other preschool services provide the health, nutrition, and educational support that is especially important for those young migrant children whose families are highly mobile, poorly educated, and inadequately paid. Although federally sponsored programs have helped many young migrant children, many more remain unserved.

Migrant Children with Disabilities

Migrant children with disabilities continue to be one of the most elusive and challenging populations to serve. In 1984, an Interstate Migrant Education Council (IMEC) conference focused national attention on this issue.[1] Although migrant educators are now more aware of the issue, the Commission finds that two of the problems associated with serving these children nearly a decade ago still exist today.

First, data on migrant students with disabilities are sketchy and not systematically collected by states. The data available on children with disabilities suggest that significant barriers still exist in identifying and serving these children. Second, the lifestyle of migrant children, which is often characterized by mobility, limited-English proficiency (LEP), and poverty, complicates the accuracy of assessing children who have certain types of disabilities. Because some of these children have other needs in addition to a disability, ongoing communication between the Migrant Education Program (MEP) and Special Education programs that serve the same children is vital.[2]

Individuals with Disabilities Education Act

Migrant children with disabilities are protected by the same laws that govern state and local school-district services to all children with disabilities.[3] As a result of the Individuals with Disabilities Education Act, states which receive Federal funds under this act must ensure that all children, regardless of the severity of their disability, receive an appropriate public education at public expense. The states must comply with specific directives concerning testing, developing individualized services, and providing an appropriate classroom placement.[4]

The Act also requires that the school consult the parents during all phases of the screening process and inform them of the procedure for challenging decisions regarding their child.[5] Finally, the law commands the states to conduct systematic searches to identify and serve all children with disabilities.

Other parts of the law are also important to migrant children. Whenever possible, the primary language should be used when assessing the child and communicating with the parents, especially if the child and parents have limited-English skills. In addition, the diagnosis must consider linguistic factors.[6] Unfortunately, a preliminary study conducted by the Commission suggests that some of these provisions may not be adequately enforced and that some migrant children with disabilities may not be receiving the services to which they are entitled.[7] The Commission would urge educators at the local level who are responsible for providing services to children with disabilities to aggressively seek out and serve these students.

Participation in Special Education

Compared to the general population, fewer migrant children are identified as having certain disabilities. Analysis of the data raises the following question: Are migrant children being accurately diagnosed or are these statistics suggesting actual differences in disability problems unique to this population? To some extent, diverse practices across states and schools may explain why fewer children are identified with certain disabilities. In addition, recent increases in the numbers of all children reported with disabilities may reflect an increased awareness in these children's needs, rather than an absolute rise in the number of children with disabilities. Indeed, the number of children with disabilities in the general population who receive services has increased by 26.4 percent since 1976.[8]

Although the Federal Government reports annually to Congress on the status of children who receive services for their disabilities, data on migrant children are not reported separately.[9] However, statistics from the Migrant Student Record Transfer System (MSRTS) and a national study reveal that only 6 percent of the MEP population is identified as disabled while 11 percent of the general population is identified as disabled. Furthermore, differences between migrant children and the general population are also apparent when examining the percentages of each population with respect to each disability category. A greater proportion of migrant children are found in five out of eight disability categories than exists in the general population. (See Exhibit 4.2.) Thus, relative to the general population identified as disabled, migrant children appear to be under-represented as a group but appear to be over-represented in several disability categories.

Differences in Identification and Participation Across Regions

A recent national sample found that migrant children with disabilities also vary by geographic region: in Central States, 8.8 percent of all migrant children received Special Education services; in Eastern States, 5.1 percent were served; and in Western States, 1.9 percent were served.[10]

Similarly, information collected from the 1989-90 State Performance Reports showed dramatic differences by location in the percentage of migrant children with disabilities. For example, Alaska served one-third of its almost 6,000 students who are eligible to receive Special Education services, while four states reported providing no services.[11] Overall, both national-level data (ranging from 6.7 to 14.2 percent)[12] and local-level data[13] reveal differences in partipation rates.

Although comparisons to the national Special Education population by region are not available, the data appear to indicate that a relationship exists between circumstance and location that, in large part, determines whether children with disabilities are identified. As a result, migrant children because of their mobility are more likely to encounter

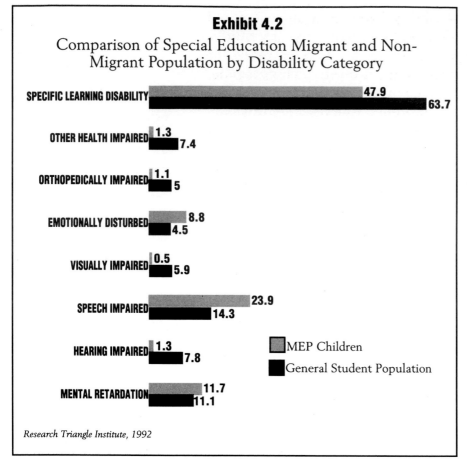

Exhibit 4.2

Comparison of Special Education Migrant and Non-Migrant Population by Disability Category

SPECIFIC LEARNING DISABILITY — 47.9 / 63.7

OTHER HEALTH IMPAIRED — 1.3 / 7.4

ORTHOPEDICALLY IMPAIRED — 1.1 / 5

EMOTIONALLY DISTURBED — 8.8 / 4.5

VISUALLY IMPAIRED — 0.5 / 5.9

SPEECH IMPAIRED — 23.9 / 14.3

HEARING IMPAIRED — 1.3 / 7.8

MENTAL RETARDATION — 11.7 / 11.1

■ MEP Children
■ General Student Population

Research Triangle Institute, 1992

differences in how their disabilities are identified and the types of services they might receive.

Disproportionate Representation By Disability

The Commission found some curious national trends when examining percentages of children identified by type of disability. As Exhibit 4.2 indicates, in only one category (Mental Retardation) are migrant children identified at about the same rate as the general population.[14]

Other sources, in addition to a recent national survey, have also found higher rates of easily identifiable physical disabilities such as hearing, visual, orthopedic, and other health-related impairments than those found in the general population.[15] The fact that migrant children

are found to have physical or medically related disabilities at a rate higher than the general population highlights the need to investigate better health interventions and more comprehensive strategies for serving migrant children.

Better Health Interventions Needed. In addition, such evidence highlights the need for further information about the relationship between young migrant children's nutrition and healthcare and their susceptibility to developing certain disabilities.[16] In addition to poor health and malnutrition, disabilities may also result from farmwork injuries (e.g, loss of limbs).[17] Migrant children are also more susceptible to pesticide contamination than adults since children can absorb more pesticide per pound of body weight.[18]

Numerous health clinicians testified that the prenatal and follow-up care of migrant children for potentially disabling childhood illnesses is sporadic at best.[19] In addition, medical treatment may be delayed because MEP funds can only be expended as a last alternative in treating disabling health conditions.[20] This is especially serious in light of corresponding research that found migrant children to be susceptible to some diseases—such as ear infections, which if untreated may cause permanent hearing loss.[21] Unfortunately, many of these debilitating illnesses may have an impact on the child's future success in school.[22]

Better Assessments of Language Minority Children Needed. While migrant children are more likely to be over-represented in the physical disability categories, they are more likely to be under-represented in milder disability categories (e.g., speech impairments and emotional disabilities), which can be masked by limited-English skills.[23] Assessing language minority children with disabilities can be a complicated process and is difficult to perform effectively.

Numerous assessment approaches exist for children who are not proficient in English, yet none appear to be completely satisfactory.[24] The demand is now great for assessment instruments and procedures to ensure that LEP children with disabilities are neither overlooked nor misdiagnosed.[25] However, until these materials become readily available, the Commission urges school districts to contact professional organizations to locate individuals who can conduct assessments in other languages. This is especially important in order to ensure that all children, including migrant children, receive the services to which they are entitled by law.

Other problems, especially in rural school districts where resources are scarce, were uncovered during testimony before the Commission. As one state specialist explained to the Commission:

"...districts were extremely uncomfortable in attempting identification of migrant children for Special Education. A few districts identified all language minority children as speech and language delayed in order to access Special Education resources to serve them. Most districts avoided identifying migrant or language minority children altogether, even when there were significant indications of a focus of concern that would ordinarily have triggered a Special Education referral. Their reasoning was that the process of sorting through language, culture, and [disability] factors is far more time-consuming and complex for LEP children, and Special Education staff lacked language, cultural, and knowledge competencies to perform such evaluations."[26]

In response to these problems, the state established a special committee to foster communication and coordination across the state MEPs and Special Education Programs. This committee provided statewide training in assessing language minority children.[27] As a result of this initiative, MEP identification rates for the state improved. Strategies such as these could serve as models to other states struggling with this problem.

Interrupted and Delayed Services

It is unclear how differences in referral procedures,[28] assessment, and delivery of services across the nation effect the rate at which migrant children with disabilities are identified and served. The availability of services may be directly effected by funding and resource limitations within certain areas.[29]

For currently migrant children who move frequently, especially between schools in the United States and Mexico, services will differ depending on the state and school district in which they reside. The children may experience interrupted services, delays in assessment, and conflicting teaching methods. Presumably, such children face greater obstacles to being identified and served than do formerly migratory children. In fact, testimony and other data show that currently migratory children do indeed face greater obstacles to receiving services.[30] A recent national study, however, indicates that such differences are negligible.[31]

Barriers to Assessing and Serving Migrant Children

The Commission identified several barriers that need to be addressed when assessing and serving migrant children with disabilities. These include barriers to time and resources, training and language, cultural issues, summer services, and communications.

Time and Resource Barriers. Evaluations for determining a disability can be extensive and often complex for children who are LEP.[32] Some districts forego the evaluation when they know the child will move in the near future; the school year is ending; or insufficient resources exist to evaluate a large number of children. For currently migrant children who move frequently, an evaluation might not be completed before the child transfers to another school district. In this situation, the need for or status of the evaluation must be entered in MSRTS or the parent must be properly informed to ensure the next school district is notified. For these reasons, the Commission encourages all MEP staff to keep migrant parents informed of the educational progress and screenings (complete or incomplete) of their child. As informed parents, they are better able to act as advocates for their disabled child.

Training and Language Barriers. The possibility of underclassifying or misclassifying migrant children, especially in mild disability categories, is further complicated by issues surrounding the testing of LEP children.[33] A major barrier to providing appropriate services for LEP children is the shortage of trained personnel qualified to work with these students,[34] especially in rural school districts and during summer programs. Because of the language and cultural issues involved in evaluating and serving these students, special techniques and training are required.

The Commission is aware of higher-education programs[35] that offer courses for Special Educators interested in teaching migrant or language-minority children with disabilities.

Cultural Barriers. Especially when dealing with an increasingly immigrant population, cultural barriers often contribute to a family's misunderstanding about how their child will be treated in school. The family's perceptions may interfere with the child's access to needed Special Education services. For example, some children are actually hidden at home.[36] Other families believe a child born with a disability is a punishment from God and, therefore, a source of shame.[37] Some fear that their child will be taken away.[38]

Another issue to consider is that the migrant child may have received different services in other countries, states, or school districts. For example, the incongruities in the Special Education systems between Mexico and the United States may be confusing. In Mexico, children with disabilities are placed in separate schools. Upon coming to United States, if these same children are placed in regular classrooms they may have difficulty coping largely because of the differences in language, teaching methods, and peer groups.[40]

Summer Service Barriers. Testimony revealed that access to services is limited for migrant children with disabilities who move during the summer.[41] A recent national study found that fewer migrant children are eligible for Special Education services during the summer term than during the regular term.[42] According to law, only those children whose Individualized Education Programs specify the need for summer services are entitled to them. However, if the child moves during the summer another school district may not honor such a request.[43] In some cases, services are denied because the district is unaware of the existing Individualized Education Program or lacks the necessary staff or resources to provide the services. Such situations raise questions about compliance to the law. Because of reduced staffing, schools may not be able to provide summer services for blind and deaf migrant children. It may be even more difficult to serve those who come from Mexico, which uses a different sign language system.[44]

Communication Barriers. To a large extent, MSRTS has tried to improve communication among school districts within the United States by including a Special Education code in its database. However, MSRTS information on student participation in Special Education Programs is incomplete for reasons relating to the voluntary nature of data entry across states, privacy concerns, as well as the burden associated with providing such information.[45] Better communication across school districts, states, and perhaps even between the U.S. and Mexican governments is required.

Integration and Coordination Required

The Commission's testimony and research found that coordination was not always evident at the local level, across schools, states, and countries, nor is it evident between providers in MEP and Special Education programs.[46] While educators in both

fields have historically viewed their missions as fundamentally different,[47] these differences have resulted in migrant children receiving somewhat disjointed services across both programs and within the regular school program.[48] This is largely a result of the way schools structure services for students in with disabilities.

The amount of time some students leave the classroom to receive Special Education instruction varies. A recent national study found that Hispanic high school students in Special Education were more likely to be placed in a separate resource room rather than in the regular classroom. Overall, the study found that Hispanics spent only 38 percent of their time in regular classrooms as compared to other groups who spent, on the average, about 50 percent of their time in regular classrooms.[49] Although these findings relate to the general population, they raise the related issue of the desirability of interventions which segregate Special Education students[50] and the need for integration between the Special Education and the regular education systems.[51] The Commission urges local staff to work towards providing integrated services for migrant children with disabilities so that the children can benefit from both supplemental and regular classroom instruction.

Parental Involvement in Special Education Programs

Commission testimony and research found that some parents may not be well-informed about the status of their children within the Special Education program, in most cases because of inadequate English or reading skills. Furthermore, the information presented may contain technical jargon which is unfamiliar to many parents.[52] Finally, disabilities may be treated differently in their home countries,[53] causing even greater frustration to parents accustomed to other ways of dealing with such conditions.[54]

The Commission believes that schools should keep parents informed of their children's evaluation, involved in planning services, and advised of their children's progress as required by existing Special Education laws. Since MEP providers are familiar with the cultural and linguistic issues surrounding migrant children, they should work closely with Special Education providers to ensure that parents fully understand their rights so that they can become their child's best advocate.

Research and testimony indicate that identifying and providing appropriate services for migrant children with disabilities remains difficult largely because of barriers to service (trained personnel, adequate assessment procedures) as well as factors within the child's background (language, culture, poverty). Regardless, the Commission supports the statutory and regulatory requirements that specify each school district is to conduct a systematic search to identify and serve all migrant children with disabilities regardless of how long the child resides within the district. The Commission also encourages states and local school districts which receive migrant children who have already been identified as eligible to receive Special Education services, to initially accept such identification and place them in appropriate classrooms so that they do not fall farther behind.

Gifted and Talented[1] Migrant Children

The Migrant Education Program (MEP), created as a compensatory educational program, appropriately concentrates on serving those migrant children who are on the verge of academic failure. Although many migrant children are in need of compensatory instruction, there are others whose exceptional academic potential may require different and more challenging programs.

While there are difficulties in identifying and providing appropriate services for gifted students in the general population, the problems are magnified for gifted migrant students. Because they are culturally, socially, and economically different from the gifted mainstream, gifted migrant students are often overlooked for special programs. When these students are identified, little attention is given to the background cultural and socioeconomic factors that may interfere with their performance and ability to achieve.[2]

Participation in Programs for the Gifted

It is not surprising that the national status of gifted children, especially gifted migrant children, is largely undocumented. Research is sparse and data collection on this population is sporadic, mainly because the Federal Government does not require states to collect or to report information on gifted children. Furthermore, programs for these children are funded and administered separately by state agencies and local schools, and any information reported by the states is done voluntarily.[3]

In 1990, a survey of 47 states found that the percentage of children served by gifted and talented programs ranged from 1.8 to 12.1 percent of their total state population.[4] In contrast, less than 1 percent of the migrant children participating in MEP were involved in a special program for the gifted and talented.[5] This low participation rate appears to be consistent with other research which points to the historical under-representation of at-risk (i.e. culturally diverse and low-income) children in gifted and talented programs.[6]

Identifying Gifted Migrant Children

Unfortunately, the needs of gifted migrant children are seldom addressed or officially recognized because, in general, they do not exhibit the same outward signs of exceptional abilities as does the national student population. As one researcher of gifted migrant children explained:

"The gifted and talented [mainstream] student is commonly characterized as reading two or more grade levels above that of chronologically aged peers. The migrant gifted and talented child, with interrupted schooling and lack of access to reading materials within the home environment, may be doing well to read at grade level."[7]

It is often difficult to discern the "giftedness" of children who have changed schools several times, have limited-English skills, and live in poverty. Since traditional means of identifying gifted students may not be useful with migrant students, alternate means of assessment are in order. This is especially pressing since children from economically disadvantaged backgrounds, i.e. migrant, are under-represented in programs for gifted students.

Using Multiple Measures to Assess "Giftedness"

There is little consistency in the identification practices and criteria used to determine "giftedness" in any population, a fact that further complicates the process of identifying gifted migrant children.[8] The lack of consistency poses a problem for any student (especially the migrant student) who attends more than one school during the term: A student considered gifted in one school, might not be in another.

Migrant children may be bypassed for gifted programs because screening procedures commonly used to identify and assess "giftedness" may overlook those who are at-risk.[9] Nearly 90 percent of all states reported using traditional assessment methods such as standardized tests to identify participants for gifted programs.[10] Historically, the traditional measures have been more effective in identifying children from the mainstream culture. Even teacher nomination, the single most-commonly

> "Although there were a greater number of Hispanic students when I was in high school, teachers still strongly clung to their preconceived notions about minorities. There was one particular teacher who affected me greatly...Like most minorities, I was automatically placed in the non-college bound biology class. The first day of class we were assigned to the mini lab. In the process of completing the lab, my partner, also a migrant student, broke the slide. The teacher stopped the class and proceeded to inform us of how stupid we were. I have never felt so humiliated in my life. The slide had not been broken intentionally. It was not the fact that I had been embarrassed that angered me. Rather, it was being condemned as a stupid child that bothered me. Her expectations of me were obviously very low. Two weeks later I was moved to a college preparatory biology. Her response was, 'I thought you were just another one of those Mexicans.'"
>
> —LIDIA ESPINOZA[13]

used measure of identification, is unsuccessful in identifying migrant gifted students at the same rate as the national population.[11] While this identification technique should be less rigid than standardized tests, the Commission heard instances where teachers unconsciously discounted the capabilities of migrant children.[12]

The most devastating use—or lack of use—of tests may come from the inadvertent practices of some MEP providers. A study conducted for the Commission found that some MEP providers were reluctant to refer their students to be tested for gifted programs for fear that the students would lose self-esteem if they failed to meet rigid cut-off scores for eligibility.[14] The Commission understands such concerns but would encourage teachers not to deny children the opportunity to try, especially those who want to take the test. Rather, these teachers should help their students develop self-esteem through other avenues, such as academic achievement.

Because some traditional assessments are limited in their power to identify a broad range of "giftedness," educators are appropriately investigating new approaches to assessment. In recent years, nontraditional assessments have become a respected way to evaluate competence in a variety of disciplines. The concept is simple—determine the student's competence by observing the student at work. By combining traditional measures, as just one aspect of the assessment, with nontraditional assessments such as student portfolios and performance assessment, assessors would have a more balanced and culture-free approach to identifying migrant students who are gifted.

The Commission believes that state and local educators should work towards identifying and adopting multiple-eligibility criteria for programs and nonbiased assessments for identifying gifted migrant children. In particular, special assessments are needed for MEP students with limited-English skills, who may be hindered temporarily by their language abilities.[15] The Commission urges MEP providers to contact professional organizations to locate individuals who can conduct assessments in other languages.

Mobility Issues

Gifted MEP children who move frequently may also fail to be included in a program for gifted students. While there have been attempts to ameliorate such problems through the use of the Migrant Student Record Transfer System (MSRTS), these efforts appear to have had limited success.[16] Students who arrive after the start of school may miss the annual program screening,[17] find that existing programs are already oversubscribed,[18] or leave before the screening is completed and the results are available.[19]

Interruption of services is further complicated by the fact that curricula for gifted children differ across states and schools. This can be especially troublesome for secondary school-aged migrant students who participate in advanced course work required for college admittance.[20] The Commission believes that the Portable Assisted Study Sequence and the National Secondary Credit Exchange and Accrual Project should be flexible enough to address the needs of this population.

Gifted Programs Limited

Funding for the gifted continues to be precarious[21] in light of the understandable need to fund remedial instruction. Indeed, at the Federal level, the Jacob K. Javitz Program for the Gifted and Talented is the only program that targets gifted children. Funding for gifted programs, albeit limited, comes from the states and almost half of the states provide gifted programs to less than 5 percent of their total student population.[22]

Limited funding has curtailed the number and quality of programs available for gifted migrant children. Not only are services extended to few children but—as one expert fears—the scope of interventions offered is minimal and many gifted children still spend most of their time languishing in the regular classroom with an unchallenging curriculum.[23] The Commission believes that local and state MEP providers should advocate access to available programs for gifted migrant children.

Since it is not clear how many programs for the gifted exist, the Commission believes other avenues for providing services to gifted migrant children should be explored. One witness suggested that MEP and Chapter 1 services be extended to migrant gifted children.[24] However, such an approach may require a fundamental change in perception, as well a change in authorizing legislation, as to what constitutes "a need" for services under current program (e.g., MEP and Chapter 1) criteria.

Alternative Approaches

A study conducted for the Commission suggests that some gifted MEP students are under-challenged and have set their academic goals too low.[25] There are several ways to help gifted migrant children realize their potential.

Traditional methods of separating gifted children through "pull-out" programs or homogeneous groupings by ability are currently being called into question by those who promote a more integrated approach to teaching children. Rather than be exposed to a high-ability curriculum for only a few hours a week, gifted migrant children should also be exposed to a high-ability curriculum during their hours in the regular classroom.

The integrated approach is gaining support through the development of individualized learning plans for at-risk gifted children such as migrant children.[26] With these learning plans, children could remain under the supervision of the teacher within a regular classroom but work at their own pace. This strategy is useful in assuring that students also master the regular classroom curriculum. An added advantage to the individualized approach is that program adjustments are quickly and easily made by the teacher in response to ongoing informal assessments of student progress.[27] As such, the instructional plan takes into account the unique abilities, learning styles, motivation, and background characteristics of the child.

While the individualized learning plan has promise, one issue requires further consideration. This approach can be too labor-intensive for regular classroom teachers who may have limited experience in designing differentiated learning plans for their high-ability migrant children.[28] Nevertheless, given the range of educational readiness of migrant children, local educators may want to consider the merits of individualized programming for this group of gifted children.

Other ways to challenge gifted migrant students can easily be pursued by local administrators. These include encouraging children to participate in academic competitions; establishing mentor programs with successful lawyers, doctors, or other professionals who were former migrant students; and using community resources—such as universities—to establish programs which rein-force and nurture the aspirations of migrant students.[29]

While these alternative approaches hold promise for inspiring gifted migrant students to excel, recent research indicates that these children are largely unchallenged during most of the school day.[30] The Commission believes that migrant children who have the potential to excel in school should have the opportunity and the assistance they need to succeed.

Migrant Students
At-Risk

The children of migrant farmworkers are often described as at-risk. Although the term has many connotations, for this report, children who are at-risk are those most in danger of dropping out of school. Two predictors which commonly identify children who are at-risk are poor academic performance and grade retention. Both are associated with migratory children who change schools frequently and who might also be recent immigrants to this country.

The National Educational Goals Panel has also identified a list of characteristics which increases the likelihood of a student dropping out of school. Of these, the two most often linked with migrant children are limited-English proficiency and poverty.[1] The consequences of poverty can be long-range, often affecting future generations. For example, a recent study found that 64 percent of the children in households headed by young high school dropouts are impoverished, which means those children are likely to become dropouts, thereby continuing the cycle.[2]

Identifying At-Risk Migrant Students

In addition to family income which is considerably below the poverty line, other factors in the migrant lifestyle which can contribute to children leaving school before graduating include, but are not limited to the inability to accumulate sufficient credits to graduate because of interrupted school attendance, inconsistent record keeping among and between schools, and adolescent pregnancy and its associated lack of adequate child care services.[3] Since many of these at-risk predictors are associated with migrant students, it is not surprising that these students have the lowest graduation rate of any student population and that their rate of completing postsecondary education is equally dismal.[4]

One obstacle to determining the number of migrant students who are at-risk of dropping out is that no standard definition of *dropout* exists.[5] Although the Department of Education (ED) is in the process of developing such a definition,[6] until the task is complete it will be difficult to describe the population of dropouts in general, and migrant dropouts in particular. The Commission applauds ED's efforts on behalf of developing a standard dropout definition and recommends that ED work with the National Education Goals Panel and the National Association of State Directors of Migrant Education (NASDME) to establish and implement a nationally accepted definition of the migrant dropout. We also recommend that national migrant dropout rates distinguish between migrants born in the United States

and those who are foreign-born.

Dropout data are further obscured by the increasing numbers of immigrant students entering the schools. In many cases, it is virtually impossible to determine if those migrants who are counted as dropouts ever attended school in the United States. If we are to have educational outcome data that truly reflect the impact of our educational system, we must know whether the immigrant child was ever enrolled in U.S. schools, the age at which first enrolled, and the length of time in attendance. At the very least, this information would help MEP evaluators distinguish the program impact from the exposure students actually had to the program.

Yet another obstacle in determining dropout rates for migrant students is that comparable data describing the general student population are incomplete, at best. According to a 1989 report of the National Center for Education Statistics, the number of ways used to calculate dropout rates might be part of the reason.[7] Although a number of studies have calculated dropout rates, their estimates vary depending on the method used to collect and report the data. Furthermore, dropout statistics are not gathered in a format that allows ED to determine the effect that migration has on whether a migrant student will drop out. Even the available databases—including the Migrant Student Record Transfer System (MSRTS)—do not contain information researchers can use to compute the total potential or the actual migrant dropout rates.

Since migrant students are difficult to track, dropout statistics describing them can only suggest current trends. For example, we know that more migrant students appear to exhibit at-risk characteristics than do students of other at-risk groups. We also know that approximately 75 percent of the MEP-eligible population is Hispanic[8] and that dropout rates for Hispanics between the ages of 16 and 24, nationwide, are higher than the rates for other ethnic groups.[9] More significantly, while the rates for all groups have declined steadily over time, dropout rates for Hispanics have increased over the last 5 years to 32 percent,[10] which may reflect growth in the numbers of immigrants among the Hispanic population.[11] Yet a commonly cited study of migrant dropout rates, the Migrant Attrition Project, concluded that the dropout rate among migrants had declined to 45 percent,[12] a substantial improvement over the 89 percent dropout rate reported in a 1975 study.[13] The findings of the two studies are not comparable and their causes can neither be attributed to a specific remedy nor an educational intervention without further research.

Perhaps the best evidence that migrant dropout rates might be reversing is that more migrant students are reaching twelfth grade. Many educators consider this reversal to be a hopeful trend since migrant students who stay in school so long are highly motivated to graduate. The supporting statistics are dramatic. Between 1984 and 1990, the numbers of migrant students enrolled in twelfth grade jumped 43 percent to 30,745, while the overall migrant student school enrollment increased just under 13 percent.[14]

Migrating into Rural Areas Intensifies At-Risk Factors

Since many migrant farmworkers and their children live and travel into rural areas, we must also consider additional factors which put them even more at-risk. As reported in a 1990 study, rural schools estimate that they have higher percentages of at-risk children than do urban areas. The study also reported that the social and economic pressures facing rural students are at least as difficult as those facing the inner-city youth—an important consideration since two-thirds of the school districts in the United States and one-third of the school children live in rural areas.[15]

Another major problem in many rural areas is the lack of social, psychological, and family services. This is especially true in the more remote and impoverished areas where migrant families tend to live.[16] Many rural communities lack adequate medical personnel, Special Education programs, and drug-abuse programs.[17] Ironically, these services are essential for at-risk populations such as migrants. For this reason, the Commission recommends that the Program Coordination Centers target rural, isolated areas for additional technical assistance and work closely with the Rural Technical Assistance Centers. The Commission further recommends that the Office of Migrant Education (OME) increase its monitoring of secondary school programs in the more isolated areas with an emphasis on coordinating services and outreach efforts.

The Effect of Retention on Migrant Students[18]

The Commission often heard testimony that migrant students who move fre-

quently are under pressure to keep up academically with their nonmigrating peers. Compounding this pressure is the fear that they will not be promoted at their next school—a fear substantiated by the Grade Retention and Placement Evaluation Project (GRAPE), a MEP-funded study. The study found three major at-risk factors leading to high dropout rates for MEP students. These students are older than their grade peers, they exhibit poor academic achievement and they come from families of low socioeconomic status.

GRAPE also determined that 35 percent of MEP kindergarten students in 1988 were one or more years older than their classmates as compared with only 5 percent of the general population. By second grade, 49 percent of the MEP students were in a grade below their age peers as compared with 21 percent of the general population. After second grade, the percentage of MEP students who are in grades below their age peers remained 25 percent higher than for the general population until ninth grade when MEP students began to drop out in larger numbers. This study also found that 65 percent of the MEP students in grades below their age level had been retained while in kindergarten or first grade. Such figures, when juxtaposed with the MEP dropout rates, present a chilling relationship between grade promotion, grade retention, and future academic success and highlight the need for quality early childhood programs.

These factors strongly suggest that schools need to provide alternative programs that improve academic achievement, thus eliminating the need for grade-level retention. While retaining migrant students in the early grades is done with the best of

"In the wintertime, we have 47 centers in Texas. We get up to about 5,000 children. In the summertime, we close our operations (in Texas) and we relocate staff...we go to the states of Ohio, Indiana, Wisconsin, Kansas, Panhandle (Florida), and Washington. So we serve the migrants while they are there...my staff goes in March—that's when our migrants leave, late March, and they shuttle for 3 days; get up there and they open up a center. The first day that work starts, they open up the center and we operate the center from 4:00 in the morning. The bus starts picking up kids at 2:45, 3:00 in the morning."[22]
—R. GUERRA

intentions, especially if the student has limited-English skills, research continues to suggest that it may not be helpful. One option being considered in some areas is grade promotion combined with intensive individual remediation. The Commission suggests that ED (through OME and NASDME) and the National Education Goals Panel identify alternatives to retention being used successfully by schools—such as programs that combine promotion with supplemental remediation as well as any other innovative approaches being developed—and broadly disseminate this information.

The Role of the Family

The Commission heard repeatedly that the family plays a significant role in a child's decision to stay in school.[19] If a program is to be successful in deterring a migrant student from dropping out or in encouraging a dropout to return to school, it should stress to parents the importance of their role in inspiring their children to obtain an education. This is especially important for older youth who often leave high school in response to the economic needs of the family. The parents of these youth must agree that, over the long term, the value of the student to the overall well-being of the family will be greater with continued education:

"While many of these Hispanic workers will earn good wages during the years of young adulthood, most will be unable to withstand the physically grueling pace indefinitely and will face either mid-life career changes or severely reduced earnings within 5 to 15 years after entering the harvest workforce."[20]

Earn-to-learn programs or those offering education in conjunction with a part-time job often provide just enough money to keep students in school. Such programs work best when the school, the employer, and the parents can cooperate to serve the interests of the students.[21]

Programs to Help Students Who Lose Credits While Migrating

All high school students must accrue credits in required courses in order to graduate on time. Unfortunately, mainstream course-credit programs frequently cannot accommodate the travel patterns of the migrant family.[23] Students, unaware that graduation requirements vary by school district, usually learn this fact after they are denied a high school diploma for insufficient credits. Understandably, these students often become discouraged and are more likely to be tempted to earn money by working in the fields.

"I have attended 13 different schools in cities and towns in Texas and Oregon. I started out as a freshman...in Salem, Oregon, hoping I wouldn't have to move anymore. Well, my family and I made several more trips to Texas and moved to different towns in Oregon. As I continued school, I started to realize that I was getting further and further behind because of course failures and frequent moves. By the middle of my junior year, my parents decided to move to Woodburn, Oregon. That's where I met Mr. Maldonado, a migrant counselor, who introduced me to [Portable Assisted Study Sequence] PASS. I have made up a number of required classes and I hope to graduate this year with my class. I am grateful for the PASS Program and Migrant Education because it has helped me so much. The sad part about all this is that I am moving again and will have to be graduating from [another] high school."[24]

This is why credit accrual programs, established through MEP, are considered critical to keeping migrant students in school. The two major programs in the United States are both based on the premise that the MEP student can complete course work towards high school graduation even when the family is migrating. PASS[25] and the National Secondary Credit Exchange and Accrual Project (SCEAP) are especially important because they provide counseling to help students graduate from high school and continue their education.

PASS originated in California in 1978 as a component of a Secondary High School Dropout Project. PASS provides 40 courses for middle and high school students within a semi-independent study program. Course credits can be issued either by the school district where the migrant student finished the course or by the home-base school.[26]

In states with local migrant projects, MEP supports the availability and distribution of PASS courses at no charge to migrant students. To date, this procedure has been successful. Since 1987, the number of PASS units completed nationally has almost doubled; the number of semester credits granted has tripled; and, 25 percent more migrant students have been helped to graduate.

In addition to PASS, a Mini-PASS is available to sixth, seventh, and eighth grade students (ages 13 to 15) in Colorado, Idaho, Illinois, Michigan, New York, and Wisconsin. Developed in Wisconsin in 1985, Mini-PASS offers 26 courses and each semester course contains all the materials the student needs to complete the course.

Although both programs are much needed, PASS has been criticized because of the quality and skill level of the course materials. In response, NASDME, ED, and migrant educators are currently revising all courses to ensure that they meet the states' minimum curriculum requirements and reflect the skills and competencies taught in most public schools.

The other program, SCEAP, was established by ED in October 1990 and funded through a 3-year cooperative agreement. The project was designed to create a national system of credit exchange and accrual to increase the high school graduation rates for all migrants.[28] The Texas Education Agency office in Edinburgh, Texas, an area that has a high concentration of migrant students (60,000, of which 30,000 are currently migratory), won the award. Three satellite offices are located in Washington, Illinois, and New York.

The major problem migrant students encounter with credit transfer is the lack of a common credit unit policy across school districts and even within the same state.[29] To address this problem, the project will develop a model for secondary credit and exchange, which will incorporate the best features from PASS and any other correspondence courses; a national graduation rate formula; a database of generic correspondence courses; and interstate credit agreements.

The project is also trying to establish a national consensus on ways to accept summer credits and to record all earned credits on MSRTS. The first year's report, issued in September 1991, only focused on the graduation rate formula and did not discuss progress of a national credit accrual program. Years two and three will be devoted to reviewing curricula in major sending and receiving states; formulating agreements among states leading to a voluntary system of credit exchange and accrual; providing technical assis-

Maria Banuelos, a 17-year old migrant student from Washington, is the oldest of five children. Her family cuts asparagus in the spring, picks berries in the summer, and apples in the fall. She has helped cut asparagus for the past 5 years. During the asparagus season, the family works in the fields from 2 a.m. to 8 a.m., when Maria goes home, eats breakfast, showers, and goes to school. It is hard work, but she does it to help earn money for her family. An eleventh grade student, she is completing her sixth PASS course with a PASS grade point average of 3.6. PASS has helped her complete the credits she lost. Her goals are to graduate from high school, attend business college, and then go to a 4-year university to become an electrical engineer.[30]

tance; and providing in-service training to help states establish, improve, and/or expand secondary programs. As stated in Chapter Two of this report, the Commission believes that this is one of the most important initiatives currently underway at ED and urges that its efforts be encouraged and that a common credit unit policy be adopted.

Few Programs Target Migrant Students Who Drop Out

Although approximately 18 Federal programs currently provide assistance to dropouts or at-risk students,[31] only two, the HEP and the Migrant and Seasonal Farmworkers Job Training Partnership Act (JTPA) program, specifically target migrant or seasonal farmworker dropouts. Ten of these 18 programs are administered by ED; the Departments of Labor and Health and Human Services administer the other programs.

Several are explicitly designed to help the dropout or the at-risk student. However, little information is available about how successful these Federal programs are in helping students complete their schooling.[32]

The Commission found that the resources of MEP are further stretched by the needs of the changing demographics of the migrant labor force. Increasingly, the migrant streams are comprised of less educated immigrants who may not be aware of the importance of an education for themselves and their children. These migrant families require different interventions from those used in the past.

MEP also funds many successful migrant state and local dropout programs. Some of these are funded under Section 1203 as interstate

coordination programs and others are funded under the basic state grants, as part of a district's dropout prevention activities. One such 1203 project, which issued the *Dropout Retrieval Report*, concluded that efforts to bring migrant students back to a regular or alternative school must first consider why the students choose to drop out.[33] More specifically, the report found that there are certain core qualities that a successful migrant dropout prevention project must contain:

■ *A work-study program.* This is important since helping the family is often one factor in the student's decision to leave school.

■ *A flexible schedule and a convenient location.* Classes must be provided at the camps and during the early morning and late evening hours to accommodate the migrant student's travel and work schedule. Summer schools which are close to or at the camps provide one of the best methods for accruing credits, for tutoring students in skills required to pass competency tests, or making up lost courses. To be useful, however, such courses must be accepted for graduation credit at other schools.[34]

■ *A pre-general education diploma (GED) program to prepare students who are illiterate or are reading at a low level.* Such assistance reduces the frustration of those not yet reading at the GED-required level of sixth grade. Programs can be adapted to involve the parents who might not have the skills necessary to help their children.[35]

■ *A "migrant-only" dropout prevention advisor.* Each school district should employ a person familiar with the characteristics of at-risk students to offer early intervention.

■ *Role models.* To see a successful former migrant in a professional setting can help the student better understand the importance of a high school diploma.

■ *Community involvement.* Establish work-study programs to dispel stereotypes and fears in the minds of community members and the migrants.[36]

In addition to such projects, the Commission has heard testimony that highlights MEP's successful interventions for at-risk students. One example is the Migrant Dropout Reconnection Project which has encouraged many out-of-school youth and potential dropouts to get a high school diploma. The project also offers a toll-free phone number and a newsletter to help students locate the closest projects and services.[37] The Commission recommends that successful dropout prevention strategies developed by MEPs be made available to all schools attended by migrant children.

MEP's High School Equivalency Program (HEP)

HEP, the only ED program designed to accommodate out-of-school migrant youth, originated in the Office of Economic Opportunity as a discretionary grant program in 1967. It was designed as an employment/training program for high school dropouts and has always had training overtones. In 1973, HEP became part of the Comprehensive Employment Training Act Program administered by the Department of Labor and in 1980 it was transferred to ED. In 1987, HEP grants were extended from 1 to 3 years and awarded on a competitive basis. The major services or assistance offered through HEPs are counseling, placement services, healthcare, financial aid, stipends, housing for residential students, and exposure to cultural and academic programs.

Today, HEP is funded by Section 418A of the Higher Education Act and administered by OME and serves an average of 3,000 students annually.[39] Grants are given to institutions of higher education and non-profit organizations. Currently, neither geographical location nor the size and proximity of the migrant population is considered when awarding the grants, so some areas of high migrant concentrations do not have HEP services.

The Commission addressed the issue of geographic distribution, among others, during the 1991 hearings concerning the reauthorization of HEPs and the Collage Assistance Migrant Programs (CAMPs).[40] At that time, the Commission asked the Subcommittee on Education, Arts, and Humanities to consider the following recommendations: expand the program cycle from 3 to 5 years; include geographic distribution as a criterion in funding future HEPs/CAMPs; include eligibility for Section 1201 of the Education Amendments of 1988 and/or Section 402 of JTPA as a criterion of HEPs/CAMPs' eligibility; appropriate adequate funding for HEPs/CAMPs; and reject the concept of capacity building for a service delivery program as an inappropriate constraint on these programs.

Uninterrupted funding of HEPs is vital if they are to continue preparing migrant workers or their dependents to attain the same level of preparedness of regular high school graduates so that, as much as possible, they can choose among the full range of high school outcomes. To be eligible for HEP, a person must be a migrant

> "That day I was alone at home and thinking. 'What was going to happen with my future?' I went to the mailbox. The first letter that I saw was a bill, bill, and another bill. I saw another letter that was for me. REAL TALK [The Migrant Dropout Reconnection Project Newsletter]...that's when I started looking for the possibilities that would help me."
>
> —EMILIA[38]

On March 15, 1988, Anna Elizabeth Robles received her GED certificate from the University of Tennessee HEP. The path from eighth grade dropout, mother, and migrant worker to self-sufficiency has not been easy. The daughter of migrant farmworkers, Liz still remembers the pain and rejection she felt from teachers and students when attending school in her native Texas. Today, Liz is a successful store owner whose shop carriers Mexican staples and ingredients not available in nearby stores for migrant farmworkers who work in the area. Not content to be just a shopkeeper, Liz has become a spokesperson and advocate on issues affecting the local migrant workers. Liz illustrates the reason why the University of Tennessee HEP established satellite programs. Although Liz was motivated to finish the requirements for high school graduation, she would not have been able to do it without the satellite program since her income and her presence were required by her family and children. The University of Tennessee HEP satellites have helped over 500 students like Liz become assets to their communities.[47]

worker or seasonal farmworker, or a dependent of one for least 75 days during the past 24 months; lack a high school diploma (or a GED); not currently enrolled in school and be at least 17 years of age; and be in need of the academic assistance, support services, and financial aid that the program provides. HEP students generally come from low-income families. The HEP/CAMP National Evaluation Project Study found that more than 75 percent of recent program participants reported total annual family (with an average of seven members) incomes of under $10,000.

A 1989 ED study of HEPs collected data describing individual HEPs, student characteristics, and outcomes. The major findings of this study were that HEP has had a stable base of projects since its inception[41] and 85 percent of the programs are operated by institutions of higher education; most participants are Hispanic; more than half of the average total hours of program services were devoted to instruction, and during the remaining hours participants received counseling, health, and support services; and many have strong training components. The average rate of GED completion for 1986-87 was 70 percent, ranging between 24 percent at the Milwaukee Area Technical College and 100 percent at the University of Colorado. Of the 1987 HEP graduates, 40 percent enrolled in technical vocational schools, 37 percent at 2-year colleges, and 23 percent at 4-year schools.[42]

Over the past 23 years, HEPs and CAMPs have served about 65,000 people.[43] During this time, HEP has evolved mainly into more of a commuter program that serves a small area. Today, students are more likely

to be older (mid-twenties), more recent immigrants, have lower skill levels, and have limited-English proficiency—factors that contribute to a more difficult transition into postsecondary education or into society.[44]

Some HEPs are housed on college campuses, thus enabling migrant students to be part of a world that is different from their own. Other campus-based HEPs let students choose housing to suit their needs; they can choose either residential, in which a student lives on campus away from the distractions of family life, or commuter, which allows the students to live at home to help their families. Other HEPs are not on a college campus, but are satellites of a campus-based HEP. These programs offer the student the prestige of being associated with a college program.

Effectiveness of HEPs

A 1984 study of HEPs funded by the HEP/CAMP Association found that 80 percent of the HEP students obtained their GED at the end of the course and most continued their education in either vocational or postsecondary schools or found new jobs as a result of their upgraded skills.[45] This success becomes even more significant considering that HEPs usually operate between 8 and 12 weeks. In addition, the students graduated from the programs with greater self-esteem and confidence in their abilities to lead productive lives.[46]

The story of Jesus Estrada, currently working on his doctorate, is one example of the many HEP successes heard by the Commission. Mr. Estrada graduated from the first Oregon HEP class in 1967 and is now director of a successful University of Tennessee HEP with satellite programs in three other states.[48] The Commission believes Mr. Estrada to be just one example of how HEP has positively influenced the lives of its participants.

Through testimony and research, the Commission learned of several recurring concerns about HEP. The first deals with relative costs. Compared to other programs that offer a high school diploma as its outcome, the annual per student cost of HEP ($2,335) is relatively high. State-administered adult basic education programs offer students ($40 per pupil of Federal, excluding institutional and state support) the opportunity of earning a high school diploma at a lower cost.[49] However, most migrant students who drop out do not take advantage of these programs for several reasons. These programs are usually in operation when the family is migrating; they do not offer transportation so that students can attend class regularly;[50] and they do not provide vital assistance (financial, academic, or other support services) which are major components of HEP.

The second area of concern is the level of student disadvantage of HEP participants. The data are unclear about the educational level of the students when they begin these programs. Yet based on information compiled by the HEP/CAMP National Evaluation Project and other research, program participants appeared to be representative of the children of migrant workers.[51] They came from families involved in migrant agricultural labor either away from or close to their permanent residence. Few had parents with high school diplomas. Most families spoke a language other than English at home, one-half were the first gen-

eration born in the United States and the others were equally divided between foreign born or those whose parents or grandparents were born in the United States. Twenty percent of the participants were married. On the average, the participants appear to be as disadvantaged as the migrant population in general.

Because of limited funds, it is possible that HEPs selected only those students most likely to benefit from and complete the program; however, it is also possible that only those with the capability and/or motivation to succeed signed up for the program. Without additional resources, all those who are eligible to participate in HEP (i.e., meet the minimum criteria) will not be able to do so, and this segment of the migrant population will remain under-served.

The last factor is the difficulty in measuring the impact of HEP. The ability of HEP graduates to secure nonmigrant employment is a desired outcome of HEP. However, data describing the employment history of HEP graduates are generally unavailable. Regardless of this concern, a high proportion of HEP participants meet the educational goals of the program by obtaining a GED. Of those, all continued their education either at a vocational school or a college. Such actions are the first step toward a successful future outside of migrant employment. Once these students meet the HEP goal of obtaining a high school diploma, their employability or their prospects for employment should be similar to those of the general population, at best, or comparable to those with similar disadvantages, at the very least.

CHAPTER FIVE

Postsecondary-Age Migrant Students

Thirty years ago there was no record of a son or daughter of migrant farmworkers ever having graduated from college.[1] While the situation has improved somewhat, there are still few opportunities available to prepare the highly able migrant child to participate in the academically demanding situations of higher education.[2] This is especially true for postsecondary migrant students who, in spite of the hardships imposed by migrancy, have successfully completed high school.

As the only national-level support program directed solely at migrant college students, the College Assistance Migrant Program (CAMP) is a rare and extremely vital program that affords access and equity for migrant students who seek postsecondary education[4]. The support services offered, such as professionally trained migrant student counselors, are especially important to the student who, in many instances, is the

first person in the family to complete high school— much less go to college.

The Transition to College

CAMP assists qualified first-time college students to make the transition between high school and college. These students tend to be at higher risk of failure than other first-time college students[5] by virtue of their inadequate academic preparation and their disadvantaged background, which frequently requires them to work while attending school. To help the students develop the motivation and skills necessary to complete higher education, CAMP was conceived as a full-service program. The services designed to meet these needs can range from financial aid (tuition, fees, a stipend, and room and board) to career counseling, tutoring, cultural and social activities, and college-orientation programs.

To be eligible for CAMP, a person must be a migrant worker, a seasonal farmworker, or a dependent of either for at least 75 days during the last 2 years. Each participant must be qualified to enroll as a full-time freshman and must require academic assistance and financial aid.

CAMP helps students master the skills essential for college and academic success, such as study and test taking skills, learning strategies, note taking, and time management. CAMP also helps students with course work by providing tutoring and other instructional support for those who need it.

History of CAMP

CAMP originated as a U.S. Office of Economic Opportunity discretionary grant program in 1972. The following year, CAMP was transferred to the Department of Labor and became part of the Comprehensive Employment Training Act program. In 1980, CAMP moved to the U.S. Department of Education. CAMP grants were extended from 1 to 3 years in 1987 and then to 5 years in 1992.

Both CAMP and the High School Equivalency Program (HEP)[6] are authorized by Section 418A of the Higher Education Act and are administered by the Office of Migrant Education. CAMP and HEP are funded through discretionary grants awarded on a competitive basis to institutions of higher education (IHE) and nonprofit organizations, without regard to their geographical location or proximity to sizeable migrant populations. The longest operating program, St. Edward's University (Austin, Texas), has operated for many years. The newest grantee is the University of

Tennessee (Knoxville).

Over the years, funding for CAMP has been in jeopardy. For 6 years, beginning in 1980, as part of overall budget cuts the Administration annually requested the termination of HEPs and CAMPs since financial aid was available through other programs, although none focused on migrant students. The 1987 budget proposed that CAMP be combined with the Special Services for Disadvantaged Students Program into a new Special College Services Program. In contrast to the $7.1 million appropriated for HEP and CAMP in 1986, the appropriation requested for the newly consolidated program was $3.9 million. Had the termination or consolidation of CAMP taken place, the subsequent reduction of financial and supporting services would not have enabled students from such disadvantaged backgrounds and fragmented educational histories to meet the educational goals of CAMP.

Although funding for CAMPs has remained relatively constant over the years, the average undergraduate tuition charges (adjusted for inflation) have increased for public and private universities, other 4-year, and 2-year institutions from 1977 to 1987.[7] Consequently, the number of students served through CAMP funding has decreased by one-half (Exhibit 5.1).

It remains unclear, yet important to consider, how increased tuition costs combined with limited CAMP opportunities will affect the future aspirations of able migrant students to seek higher education.

How Programs Vary

All CAMPs are characterized by

an intense commitment to recruitment. As with other programs for migrant farmworkers and their children, one of the difficulties in serving this population is that they must first be identified and recruited.[9] CAMP counselors rely on a network of resources, which are not part of the traditional college recruitment and application process, to help them identify eligible migrant youth. The network includes the migrant home-school coordinators, the high school guidance counselors, local agricultural community contacts, and people within the migrant labor community.[10]

In addition to recruitment, CAMPs are permitted to provide services such as testing and special academic, career, and personal counseling; tutoring and supplementary instructional services; and other essential supporting services to assure the success of CAMP participants. While CAMPs have experimented over the years with ways to provide services that best meet the needs of their students, research has identified several factors found to be effective. These factors include providing clear, measurable student outcome goals; matriculating participants who meet or exceed the program's entry-level requirements; and providing program interventions designed to support identified student needs.[11] The Commission encourages CAMPs to work towards incorporating into their programs factors that research has identified as being effective in meeting program objectives.

CAMPs are designed to be either commuter or residential, or to let students decide which best meets their housing needs. Unlike commuter programs, costs for CAMPs that offer residential options are greater since funds must be allocated for housing. CAMPs which provide housing offer participants the experience of a supervised campus environment which they otherwise might not have. CAMPs which allow students to commute are especially appealing to students who want to continue their education but must also fulfill family and home responsibilities.

CAMPs sponsor a variety of summer enrichment and community involvement programs. For example, St. Edward's sponsors a 10-day program and the University of Colorado has a 5-week program. St. Edward's also sponsors a three-tier community-campus mentor program through which it establishes a series of relationships between CAMP participants and members of the community. The program is based on the concept that appropriate role models provide migrant students with the motivation to build a successful life outside of migrancy. Each CAMP participant is mentored by a successful member of the Austin business community who was once a migrant worker. In turn, the CAMP participant becomes the mentor of a third grade migrant student. At California State University, Sacramento, CAMP students have "adopted" 2 miles of busy highway through the Adopt-a-

Exhibit 5.1
Appropriations for CAMP, 1984-1991[8]

FY	Appropriation	No. of CAMPS	No. of Students
1984	1,950,000	10	710
1985	1,200,000	5	440
1986	1,148,400	6	435
1987	1,200,000	4	274
1988	1,300,000	5	290
1989	1,500,000	5	287
1990	1,720,000	6	280
1991	1,952,000	7	347

CAMPs maximize the efforts of other service providers. John Jensen, Director of HEP and CAMP at Boise State University, described the following example:

"The Idaho Nuclear Energy Laboratory (INEL) approached CAMP about interesting more migrant students in science and mathematics. INEL provided us $10,000 for instructors. Several were former CAMP students. The State (Idaho) Migrant Office worked to secure funding for transportation. Boise State University provided facilities, computer labs, and scientific equipment. We were able to provide a great math and science workshop for 40 seventh and eighth grade migrant students through this networking and sharing of resources."[16]

Highway program. The CAMP students are encouraged to learn that volunteering in their community should be part of their personal and professional lives.[12]

The Economics of CAMP

The costs for funding CAMPs vary depending on the types of services provided and the amount of fiscal support the hosting institution can offer. For example, students also receive a stipend, which varies from $128 per month at Boise State University (Boise, Idaho) to $243 at St. Edward's University.[13] Without support services such as stipends, these migrant students are less likely to complete the first year of college.

CAMPs have traditionally operated through IHEs, although they may be administered by either IHEs or private, nonprofit organizations. The level to which the IHE can subsidize its CAMP with institutional funding varies considerably. Over the years, St. Edward's University, for example, continues to increase the fiscal support it extends to its CAMP. St. Edward's contribution to CAMP amounted to $250 per student in 1972 and grew to $7,000 by 1992.[14] In addition, Boise State University subsidizes its CAMP by arranging for and sharing resources with other local institutions.[15] As IHEs address the competing demands on each of their dollars, it may not be possible for them to continue to subsidize CAMPs at the current level.

On the surface it would appear that CAMPs are more expensive per participant than other ED higher education programs. For example, the average cost per CAMP participant in 1987 ranged from $4,154 at Boise State to $3,214 at St. Edward's

University. By contrast, the average cost for students participating in the Special Services for Disadvantaged Students Program was only about $455 (in program year 1984-85).

Comparisons to other programs are misleading. CAMP, as a full-service program, helps the migrant student deal with all aspects of the college experience by funding all the vital support services participants need to succeed in college.[17] Unlike CAMP, a program such as Special Services for Disadvantaged Students, which has similar goals, does not provide the same level of support services. In addition, information is unavailable on the access of migrant youth to these nonmigrant specific postsecondary programs.[18]

From another perspective, the success of CAMP students and their positive impact on the community more than justifies the costs.[19] Based on the percentages of students who earn a college degree, are fully employed, and enjoy an income well-above the poverty level, CAMP has been successful.[20]

"In the simplest of terms, students who are successful in completing the objectives of CAMP will repay the total amount invested in them by the United States Government within two years of completing their...college degree. The repayment comes in the form of personal income taxes, estimated on the basis of average size of family and the net difference in income between those who completed the programs and those who did not. The higher the overall success rate, the more cost-effective the programs become."[21]

Why CAMP is so Important

For CAMP participants, the program has helped to reverse some of the devastating effects of the migratory lifestyle that make it difficult for migrant children to complete high school, much less college. "*One way of viewing the task faced by migrant children is to compare their participation in education with a runner required to enter a race twenty yards behind the starting line."*[22]

As individuals who come from backgrounds of poverty and low levels of parental educational attainment, the children of migrant workers seem doomed to disadvantage. Educational researchers whose findings hold little hope for this group continue to report on the strong relationship between family background, personal characteristics, and academic success. All things being equal, the children of migrant workers continue to be among the least likely to complete high school and postsecondary education.[23]

In many instances, culturally diverse students of low socioeconomic status, such as the children of migrant farmworkers, reside outside the mainstream networks and are ill-equipped to take advantage of educational opportunities.[24] Few of these students have out-of-school experiences which relate to the school culture; or counseling to help them identify what they might be able to accomplish; or knowledge about

career or vocational choices, especially those which are outside their realm of experience.[25] Such knowledge is critical for migrant students who wish to transform their aspirations into achievement. Consequently, the service aspect of CAMP continues to be a vital and integral element in its successful operation.

The services provided by CAMP are especially important to the almost 15 percent of the participants surveyed for the HEP/CAMP Evaluation Study felt academically unprepared for college. They required the additional support services provided by CAMP to enable them to compete at the college level, yet they lacked the preparation to benefit from the services.[26] By their own admission, some students entered CAMP without the knowledge of what was expected of them, what entry-level skills were essential, and what the programs had to offer.[27] Almost without exception, students with these deficits failed to reach program objectives and were unsuccessful in doing so at a later time.[28] These students rarely achieved the levels of education and career advancement attained by those who completed the first year of college.[29] Although some do eventually complete the first year of college, they almost never catch up to those who did so while enrolled in CAMP.[30] While some students were not able to meet CAMP objectives, their participation in postsecondary education, even for a short time, is a noteworthy accomplishment.

Accomplishments of CAMP

In spite of the educational odds against migrant students who enter CAMP, an overwhelming majority of participants complete the basic educational objectives of the program.[31] For example, a recent study of CAMPs[32] found that in 1987, 81 percent of the 180 CAMP participants completed their freshman year. The completion rate varies from 100 percent at California State University, Sacramento, to 50 percent at Boise State University.[33] Additional current data, such as the college graduation rate and the nonmigrant employment rates of CAMP students, are sketchy and only available through limited longitudinal studies.

A 1985 longitudinal study found that a total of 92.4 percent of CAMP participants successfully completed their first year of college[34] (much higher than the national norm of about 50 percent among all first-time entering freshmen)[35] and about 56 percent remained in school and graduated from college. Considering that the results of the HEP/CAMP Evaluation Study were presented in 1985 and that only those students who entered CAMP in 1980 or 1981 could reasonably have been expected to finish a 4-year degree by 1985, the overall results were strong.[36] At the California State University, Fresno, 94 percent of its CAMP participants completed their freshman year and 67 percent went on to earn a bachelor's degree.[37]

Students who attended both HEP and CAMP were more likely to have completed a degree program, and have higher employment and income profiles upon college graduation than did those who attended only one of the programs.[38] The statistics are even more impressive for women. Women who attended CAMP substantially outperform women in the national sample with regard to occupational status and income.[39]

Employment and income data on CAMP participants suggest a progressive pattern of moving from lower levels of employment and income to higher levels as students progress through the educational system, graduate from college, and enter the mainstream workforce.[40] A number of graduates have gone on to become migrant educators,[41] lawyers, doctors, and other professionals.[42] Furthermore, the CAMP participants were proud of their achievements. When asked their opinion, they indicated that they were doing considerably better than their friends.[43]

In a manner of speaking, the CAMP participant is the ultimate formerly migratory student, who will never have the need to return to the fields. CAMP participants are living testimonials, especially to other migrant students, that motivated and able migrant students can succeed academically when given the opportunity and the support.

Such conclusions would have been more difficult to formulate without the extensive longitudinal data collected through the 1985 HEP/CAMP National Evaluation Project. The Commission supports the longitudinal study efforts of the HEP/CAMP Association and encourages continuation of this study through foundation funding or voluntary institutional support.

Gaps in Providing Services

More eligible migrant students apply to participate in CAMP Programs than there are spaces available. On the average, each program receives approximately 200 applications for every 40 slots.[44] The Commission heard testimony that the lack of programs to meet the demands of the eligible migrant students is one of the concerns continually expressed by the educators who serve them.[45]

This is especially troublesome when taken in perspective of how successful HEPs have been in meeting their program objectives. During 1986-87, 70 percent of the HEP participants completed the GED. Of the 1987 HEP graduates, 60 percent enrolled either in a 2- or 4-year college,[46] or a total of 1,087 individuals.[47] Since only 274 CAMP slots were available that year, the remaining 813 students could not have attended CAMP had they wanted to go.

What further compounds the demand for services is the absence of CAMPs in the eastern stream.[48] The current geographic distribution of existing CAMPs was established as a result of the competitive grant application process. There has never been a requirement to consider geographic distribution in funding CAMPs. In the future if more money becomes available for CAMP, the Commission encourages greater distribution of these projects to ensure that they operate in each stream and in proximity to migrant populations.

Considering the level at which CAMPs meet their objectives and the demand for CAMP slots which far exceeds the supply, why haven't CAMPs (and HEPs) become a programmatic priority? One explanation may be that other large educational programs for disadvantaged students (i.e., TRIO, Chapter 1 Basic) are located in almost every Congressional district in the United States. TRIO has a strong constituency base; all states are represented, and students all over the country benefit from

"Migrant Education was designed so that the migrant students wouldn't abandon school before graduating from high school. The result for the last 8 years has not only been that we have had higher percentage...who have graduated from twelfth grade but that also we have gone on to community college in larger numbers, state universities of the State of California, private colleges, vocational careers and, above, the effective participation of parents.
—J. Cabedo[50]

those programs. The situation is different with respect to CAMPs. Unfortunately, with so few programs (7 CAMPs and 23 HEPs) in only 15 states, many people are unaware of the purpose for and the success of the programs and, therefore, do not consider the programs a priority.

Another explanation might be that, in general, there is little widespread support on behalf of increasing higher education opportunities for migrant students. Except for a handful of committed legislators and a few college presidents, HEP and CAMP have no other champions. The HEP/CAMP Association membership of 29 directors meets annually and attendance is modest. Since most directors are newly appointed to their positions and knowledgeable only about their respective programs, they may not be aware of the importance of informing the general public about CAMP. The Commission urges this group to inform the public of the successes of their students.

Another group is beginning to focus its attention on the educational needs of disadvantaged students. The State Higher Education Executive Officers, based on the results of a survey[49] on state priorities for higher education, found that the need to improve minority student achievement was listed second only to the need to improve undergraduate education. According to the survey, many states are focusing attention on identifying, recruiting, and supporting minority students, and including migrant students.

Related Initiatives

A new Federal program was authorized this year as part of the Higher Education Act, which is designed to specifically help migrant students achieve their higher education goals. The program, called Mini-Corps,[51] provides college students with the option of working while training to become a teacher or related professional. The program grants a small stipend to help students offset the expenses of the degree program and begins after the student successfully completes the first year of postsecondary education. Mini-Corps students training to become teachers can work as aides to teachers of younger migrant children while also providing a positive role model for them. In this capacity, the program helps trainees to strengthen their self-esteem, affords an opportunity for them to help others, and provides an enormous resource for at-risk students in various programs.

As proposed, the Mini-Corps Program addresses many of the recommendations advocated by the Interstate Migrant Education Council, the State Higher Education Executive Officers, the Education Commission of the States, and other groups who encourage students as they move from kindergarten through college.

During the past 3 years, the Commission has heard testimony describing the efforts of high school counselors and CAMP staffs through whose efforts, migrant farmworkers and their children are at long last gaining access to the educational opportunities that so many mainstream individuals take for granted. These students who have overcome the disadvantages associated with their migratory lifestyles clearly demonstrate the importance of and need to expand successful programs like CAMP.

CHAPTER SIX

Coordinating Programs and Services

The educational outcomes of children are affected by many inter-related factors. In addition to a child's predisposition for learning, other needs exist which if left unmet may adversely affect academic success. Consequently, interventions must be preventive, continuous, comprehensive, and coordinated—a fact which the Migrant Education Program (MEP) has embraced since its inception.[1]

Coordination is an important function within MEP. From an administrative standpoint, coordination is the vehicle by which service providers can avoid duplication of effort, increase efficiency, and eliminate gaps across programs to more efficiently serve the children of migrant families. From the perspective of migrant children with multiple learning needs, coordination is the mechanism which facilitates continual access to services and ensures that their needs are addressed.

Although coordination models vary, three types of coordination are relevant for MEP. The first type, *the coordination of instructional programs*, affects the child within the school district. In some instances, a migrant child is eligible for several local, state, and Federal education programs. Ideally, these programs should be coordinated to provide migrant children with the additional academic support they need. Commission research suggests that more school administrators appear to be exploring ways to fully integrate programs for children with multiple needs. In reality, however, some migrant children may not benefit from the additional support partly because the schools they attend may not have developed strategies to coordinate instruction within and across their regular and supplemental programs.

The second is *the coordination of instructional services among several states and schools*. Curricula, tests, graduation requirements, etc. should be coordinated, if not standardized, to provide much needed continuity for migrant children who move frequently.

The third type of coordination is *the coordination of educational and social service programs*. As members of families who struggle along the margin of poverty, migrant children often have needs which require more than remedial instruction. Indeed, many migrant children are found to have health, nutrition, and other social service needs which may adversely affect their ability to learn.

Coordinating Federal and State Policies

The Commission is aware of the many accomplishments of local educators and social service providers in coordinating services for migrant families, often despite the lack of coordination at higher governmental or institutional levels. In an effort to further support local providers, state and Federal officials should strive to better align their policies to facilitate, instead of inhibit, coordination.

As local, state, and Federal governments have grown over the years, so has the fragmentation of their programs and services. The end result is an increasingly inefficient social service delivery system which is highly compartmentalized, crisis driven, and unwieldy to manage.[2] At the Federal level, this situation is partly the result of a Congressional structure that extends policy-making authority for the same social service programs across several Congressional committees and Federal agencies.

The Commission's review of Federal migrant assistance programs also revealed fragmentation of ser-

vices within the Executive Branch where more than six Federal agencies provide programs to migrant and seasonal farmworkers and their families. Because many of the programs have evolved independently, duplication of effort frequently occurs among these programs.

Although programs may develop policies and operate independently, some have conflicting or incompatible policies which may penalize the migrant families they were designed to serve. One policy issue which is commonly cited by migrant service providers is the varying definitions of migrant farmworker used across programs to determine eligibility for services. This causes problems for administrators who try to collect data or integrate services.

To date, there are as many as 12 different statutory and regulatory definitions for migrant farmworker in the Federal Government.[3] For administrators, these diverse definitions not only make it difficult to consolidate outreach and intake procedures; but they also create a situation where data across programs serving migrant farmworkers cannot be compared.[4]

For migrant families, the existence of inconsistent eligibility criteria means that programs will find it more difficult to coordinate the delivery of services simultaneously in one location, further penalizing the families they were designed to serve. When this happens, family members must contact a number of agencies to find the services they need and must complete a number of intake forms that may request the same information. The Commission heard repeatedly that program standardization would encourage the delivery of services in a more consistent and com-prehensive manner.[5]

Overcoming Barriers to Coordinating Federal and State Policies

Efforts to coordinate policies across migrant programs may be hampered by the independent nature of the legislative authorities which create each program and those agencies involved in administering them. Regardless, interagency committees are frequently formed to coordinate services for migrant families at both the Federal and state levels.

Two interagency committees exist at the national level. The first committee, the Interagency Committee on Migrants, was formed in 1985 and consists of program-level officials from the Federal Government. It meets about four times a year primarily to exchange program information. Because it lacks any formal recognition or policy-making authority, the Committee is unable to coordinate policy, e.g., eligibility criteria.[6] A second committee, formed in 1990, is the Migrant Inter-Association Coordinating Committee and Coalition. Last year in Buffalo, New York, the Committee sponsored the first national conference that brought together representatives of the following programs: MEP, Migrant Head Start, Migrant Health, and Migrant and Seasonal Farmworker Job Training and Partnership Act (JPTA).

The Commission is also aware of other task forces at the state level.[7] Some of these task forces are created by state governors and draw their members from state agencies, non-profit organizations and, in some cases, the farming industry. The Commission encourages these groups to expand their initiatives to include other agencies and associations in other areas of education, welfare, and health.

Beyond participating in interagency meetings, several agencies have drafted "Memoranda of Understanding" to formalize the coordination of policies across their programs. These Memoranda outline the ways in which agencies agree to collaborate and share their resources.[8] Although the implementation of these agreements relies upon the willingness and commitment of the signing parties, they represent a starting point for improving program coordination for migrant families.

Coordinating Instructional Programs

Coordination occurs at the school level across various educational programs which serve MEP children. Under ideal circumstances, all programs which provide instructional services would be well-coordinated and integrated within the regular school program to ensure that children receive a sequential and continuous curriculum. Unfortunately, this does not always happen. Once all policies associated with special programs converge at the local level, school administrators face the enormous challenge of trying to comply with the sometimes conflicting restrictions and accountability requirements associated with operating programs from multiple funding sources.

The Commission is aware that some program administrators often perceive accountability measures associated with these various programs as unnecessary, if not arbitrary:

"There's a tremendous, and understandable, frustration felt by the local school people when they see money...earmarked for one area when they know they have greater needs in other areas...I have often heard the criticism that [non-MEP] children can't sit in chairs designated as "migrant" chairs, especially when auditors come. We must show that we're not using any of our "migrant" dollars on anyone else. Such actions cause bad feelings and resentments."[9]

As a result, administrators design interventions that, when implemented, may provide only fragmented services to the children.

For a variety of reasons, some schools operate pull-out programs where children leave the regular classroom to receive specialized instruction. While the Commission heard testimony explaining that schools are abandoning this method, research indicates otherwise, especially for basic skills instruction in mathematics, reading, or language arts.[10] One concern about pull-out programs is that students may suffer from the stigma associated with participating in such programs. To compound the situation, teachers may expect lower levels of achievement from children who are in special remedial programs. Unfortunately, children have been known to achieve to the level expected of them and seldom higher.

Another concern about pull-out models is that they allow school administrators to separate staff and resources across different programs, so children who leave the classroom for specialized instruction may lose valuable exposure to the core curriculum and to classroom enrichment activities. As one MEP administrator testified:

"I feel that the pull-out program, while effective in some instances, is at best a band-aid approach. It disrupts the child's education. When the child leaves his regular classroom teacher, he is missing something—even if it's only the interaction in the classroom... We're trying to compensate for things he's already missed. When we pull him out, again, we're causing him to miss something else."[11]

Since the Commissioners are concerned about the adverse effects that pull-out programs may have on MEP children, they are encouraged by other more integrated methods of intervention which are becoming more commonplace.[12]

Coordination and Participation in Other Programs. The Commission found that sometimes children with multiple needs may also be denied access to other supplementary services for which they are eligible. Research suggests that children are served more on the basis of where slots for services are available and not on the basis of which programs best meet their needs.[13] In fact, some children may not participate in programs which lack sufficient funds to serve all needy children.[14] Access to programs may also be limited by restrictions imposed by the state or school on the number of supplementary programs in which children can participate.[15]

Children must participate first in all other programs to which they are entitled before they can participate in MEP. On the one hand, Federal regulations stipulate that local communities and states must meet their financial responsibilities to educate disadvantaged students. On the other hand, these laws may inadvertently encourage schools to structure programs so that children can only benefit from one service at a time.

Participation of MEP children in Chapter 1 may not be as common as it is for other disadvantaged groups. Historically, educators assumed that

Participation of MEP children in Chapter 1 programs may be limited because:

■ state rules may prohibit participation in more than one supplementary program;[20]

■ the way programs are designed may exclude children with limited-English skills;[21]

■ MEP children are not enrolled in a school or in a grade where Chapter 1 services are provided;[22] and

■ MEP children do not meet the eligibility cut-offs for services.[23]

MEP children received Chapter 1 services.[16] Concerned that this may not be occurring, ED directed school districts to include MEP children when conducting needs assessments to select children to participate in Chapter 1. The Commission is pleased by ED's response to this pressing problem, especially in light of the following findings: in Pennsylvania only 26 percent of the migrant children receive Chapter 1;[17] in Massachusetts only 9 percent;[18] and in Florida only 14 percent of the currently and 26 percent of the formerly MEP children were served by other supplementary programs.[19]

The participation rates for migrant children in other Federal supplemental programs are also relatively small.[24] For example, of those students receiving MEP instructional services, only 8.5 percent participated in Title VII (bilingual education), only 5 percent participated in Special Education, and .4 percent participated in gifted and talented programs.[25]

By law, states are required to plan and implement their MEP projects partly by coordinating with other programs.[26] According to one study, the degree of instructional coordination was contingent upon several factors: the mobility of the MEP population, the proportion of MEP students within the district, and the structure of different services MEP provides to the students.[27]

While the Commission acknowledges that the restrictions imposed on school districts may sometimes be perceived as burdensome, it recognizes that these restrictions are necessary to maintain equity in educational opportunity as well as maintain the integrity of Federal programs. However, at the same time,

the states and the Federal Government may need to consider more flexible policies, especially in those instances where coordination may be hampered by competing mandates.

Despite the difficulties some schools face in integrating educational programs for children, the Commission found evidence that many MEP educators at the local level are exploring creative ways to provide better-integrated instructional programs. More schools appear to be working within a program's regulatory restraints while at the same time improving the quality of instruction to children with special needs.

As one superintendent explained to the Commission:

"We believe that all programs need to be part and parcel of the whole, and that we need to look at it from a holistic point of view in that migrant education should not be an independent program isolated from other programs."[28]

Schools adopt certain strategies to accomplish this type of coordination. They fund staff positions through a combination of programs;[29] employ in-class teachers or aides within the regular classroom to tutor children with special needs; and implement interdisciplinary teaching methods which are responsive to the needs of all children.[30] In support of such efforts, Congress and the Federal Government are now adopting more flexible policies for those schools wishing to integrate programs.

Balancing Educational Program Integration and Integrity. Despite the growing popularity of educational program integration and the many positive outcomes of this policy for the migrant child, some MEP policymakers are concerned about how it will affect the "advocacy" or supplemental nature of MEP. Based on the belief that MEP services should be supplemental to other instructional services, program providers have assumed more of an advocate role in helping MEP children secure other services for which they are eligible. In this situation, MEP advocates identify services that will augment the regular school program or actually dispense such services themselves. For example, after-school homework labs, weekend tutoring, and counseling. One local MEP administrator explained the role of their After-School Tutorial Advocates:

"An advocate, working in the middle and/or high schools, analyzes Migrant Student Record Transfer System (MSRTS) data, checks cumulative folders, becomes acquainted with classroom teachers; chases counselors to get information on students, cajoles students to stay after school to be tutored so they won't fail, or sometimes so they can even raise an already credible grade; visits parents to enlist cooperation or simply get acquainted, provides transportation if none is available; convinces principals to issue a grade of incomplete in order to give a late-entering student an opportunity to make up missed work through intensive tutoring; becomes the person at the school who always welcomes, encourages and continually prods the disadvantaged migrant child to do better, to be the best."[31]

However, the Commission believes that MEP should never be considered a substitute for services which the local school program or the state must offer and fund. For MEP providers, this means advocating for MEP children's participation in other Federal and state programs for which they are eligible as well as advocating for a well-integrated regular school program responsive to the needs of MEP children. In particular, MEP staff should work closely with mainstream teachers to ensure that instructional interventions are consistent. For example, MEP teachers of

after school programs should work closely with mainstream classroom teachers. Ultimately, the key to integrating different instructional programs is finding the proper balance between coordination and accountability so that the unique needs of migrant children are met equitably.

Coordinating MEPs Across Schools and States

Another form of coordination important for MEP children is the coordination of MEP services across schools and states. As migrant children move and change schools, they may encounter incompatible educational curricula and may be judged by different standards of achievement. Through interstate coordination initiatives, some MEP providers are reducing the adverse effects migrant children suffer because of mobility. Initiatives to develop uniform curricula and course credits are ongoing. However, many of these efforts are thwarted by the highly variable nature of our educational system—a system which has become increasingly difficult to standardize due to state control and local autonomy.

Commission testimony clearly illustrates the many hardships that migrant students experience as they move in and out of new schools. For children who move, changing schools is a difficult transition—a situation which, even for the brightest migrant children, may result in grade retention or a decision to drop out of school. Some of the problems migrant children encounter as they move include:

■ *Classes that are filled.* Some migrant parents testified that elementary school-aged children from the same family were sent to different schools.[32] At the secondary school level, students find that courses for which they have received partial credit are not available in their next school.

■ *Differences in curricula, teaching methods, and graduation requirements.* As children move, they inevitably struggle to catch up, and they grapple with differences in curricula and teaching methods among schools.[33]

■ *The level of tutorial and counseling services varies.* Some students complained that the level of dedication and concern varied among MEP counselors across schools they attended.[34]

■ *Inconsistent grade placements.* Some students were placed in differ-ent grade levels when they changed schools—a situation which can be disheartening to students and their parents.[35]

■ *Students enrolling late experience discrimination.* Some students are advised not to enroll if they will be in school for a short period of time.[36] One school board policy prohibited students who enrolled in school later than 20 days after school began, to earn credits for the remainder of the semester.[37]

Clearly, students who move frequently need extra assistance to ensure a smooth transition to a new school. Whether or not they can continue their education in spite of minimal interruption depends upon the

types of support available from the school.

To reduce some of the problems children encounter when they move, many MEP educators exchange information with other providers across the country on the educational status of their students. Sometimes such communication is informal and conducted on a case-by-case basis. In other instances, especially where families customarily travel between the same locations, formal processes for conducting interstate coordination have been established.

Other interstate coordination initiatives are facilitated by ED through several mechanisms—Program Coordination Centers (PCCs), MSRTS, and interagency meetings. These PCCs are funded through discretionary grants to the states to provide technical assistance, training, and sharing of practices across several states and local projects within each stream. PCCs also work with other Technical Assistance Centers funded by ED. The second mechanism, MSRTS, collects and stores data on migrant children who are eligible for MEP. It was designed to smooth the transition for migrant children who change schools. Ideally, MSRTS records are shared between the sending school and the receiving school. The third mechanism, interagency meetings, are held annually by each stream to provide the opportunity for local staff to coordinate their programs through sharing practices and attending training sessions.

For secondary school-aged children, interstate coordination can make the difference between dropping out of school or graduating from high school. Although many schools try to communicate with each other

to transfer high school credits, the process is imperfect and depends on how comparable the courses are. Currently, a national-level project is examining this problem and developing strategies to facilitate credit transfer and accrual. Unless educators who work with migrant children are committed to and support this project, its success in standardizing credits will be minimal.

Coordinating and Integrating Social Service Programs

Coordination and integration are also important in addressing those needs which extend beyond the school. The basis for such coordination is straightforward. Migrant children cannot enter class prepared to learn if they are hungry after a morning of picking tomatoes, unable to read the chalkboard because they have never had an eye exam, or tired because of a restless night spent sleeping in the back seat of a car. Indeed, many migrant children have serious needs which may adversely affect their ability to learn.

Recognizing the impact of these needs, MEP providers have linked children to vitally-needed social services outside the school, an initiative which the education community at large is just beginning to explore.[38] In the wake of declining fiscal resources and increasing numbers of families with children who enter school at a disadvantage, agencies can no longer operate in isolation.

Although the magnitude of migrant farmworkers' social service needs is largely undocumented, existing data consistently portray a needy and indigent population. Despite their efforts to remain self-sufficient, three in four migrant fami-

"We have to drive 45 minutes to make appointments for our children's WIC [Women, Infants and Children Supplementary Food Program], and most places do not honor our certification. When we leave here we have to go through another certification. When we leave there we go through still another certification to see if we qualify...when we get over there, they do not honor [the prior certification] so we have to go through the same thing again, finding transportation, having to miss a day's work. Some of our bosses are getting upset."[41]

—JUANITA CASTILLO

lies continue to struggle below the margin of poverty.[39] The symptoms associated with poverty—substandard housing, inadequate diet, and untreated health conditions—are further compounded by the lifestyle and cultural isolation faced by many migrant families.[40] The cumulative effect of such factors places an enormous strain on some families. Even under the best of circumstances, the strain of the migrant lifestyle may interfere with a child's ability to do well in school. Hence, the need for accessible and well-coordinated social services is critical.

In some communities, the coordinated efforts of outreach workers make services well integrated and available to migrant families. In other communities, families are left on their own to identify the programs that offer the services they need. If they are fortunate enough to find services, they once again may become frustrated by conflicting eligibility criteria and other bureaucratic barriers. In addition, this whole process takes time, something many migrants do not have due to long working hours.

Commission testimony and research revealed numerous barriers to social services:

■ rural isolation and the associated geographic distances between services (as much as 70 miles);[42]

■ limited hours of operation which are incompatible with harvest season work schedules (i.e., program offices are not open in the early evenings);[43]

■ few social service providers with bilingual skills;[44]

■ residing in an area of the community where there are limited resources across programs as evidenced by waiting lists;[45]

■ inconsistent program eligibility criteria across states, interrupting services;[46] and

■ lack of knowledge about the existence of services for which they qualify.[47]

Despite their eligibility and need for social services, many migrant families may choose not to seek assistance for various reasons. For example, a recent survey indicated that only one in four migrant farmworker families received public services (usually food stamps) even though three in four of these families fell below the poverty line.[48]

Perceived Barriers to Coordination. Although there may be administrative obstacles to coordinating different social service programs, these barriers can sometimes be more illusory than real.[49] As one MEP administrator stated:

"There are only those [barriers] which might be self-imposed, such as not taking the time. If the will is there, I would see no barriers."[50]

A study conducted for the Commission found attitude, not regulatory barriers, to be a primary obstacle to coordination.[51] According to the study, many program providers will coordinate to the point of sharing financial resources and no further. Thus, "turfism"—bureaucratic territorialism over resources and power—may be a significant, but silent, barrier to coordination.[52] An example was uncovered in a report written for the Commission:

"One Migrant Head Start director interviewed, who operates a program that must turn away substantial numbers of eligible preschoolers for lack of resources, expressed some bitterness at the indifference of the local Migrant Education office. Despite its wider mandate, he said, Migrant Education would not think of transferring its funds to enable Migrant Head Start to serve a larger population. The two were like 'separate empires.'"[53]

In other cases, territorialism is not an issue. Many MEP administrators claim they do not coordinate with other migrant services because they do not exist.[54] Some MEP administrators also claim that limited funding precludes them from finding the time needed to coordinate and to follow up on such efforts.[55]

Effective Strategies for Interagency Coordination. Despite the tendency to become territorial, Commission research and testimony revealed many instances of coordination at the local level that went far beyond simple information sharing and client referrals across programs.[56]

Examples of effective strategies in interagency agency coordination include:[57]

■ organizing a local interagency council on migrants;

■ defining common missions, objectives, and outcome indicators for successful coordination;

■ creating "one-stop" centers where health, education, early childhood programs, nutrition, and other services are located in one facility;

■ developing a common public relations strategy for eliciting community and private sector support;

■ consolidating outreach procedures and forms;

■ designating one case manager to present information about different programs to client families;

■ holding joint staff development training sessions; and

■ split-funding staff across all programs.

The Commission believes that migrant children with needs benefit the most from services which are

well-coordinated whether within schools or within the larger social service delivery system. To this end, the Commission recommends that an interagency council be established with the priority of coordinating services to migrant farmworkers and their families among Federal agencies.

"Most persons interviewed agreed that coordination at the national level is improving, but they also frequently voiced dissatisfaction with current arrangements. Existing bodies do provide for a fair amount of information sharing, but other objectives are not as well served. For example, coordination should provide a mechanism to improve the geographic targeting of services, so that assistance can keep up with changes in agriculture."[58]

If migrant children are to gain access to all the supplemental instructional services to which they are entitled, schools and MEPs must begin to work more closely. Understanding that children's learning potential is not just determined by the quality of classroom instruction, the Commission believes the family and the community to which the child belongs should also be considered.

Successful strategies to provide integrated services to families must be explored further and broadly disseminated to other communities. MEP educators and other social service providers share a common mission. They must provide migrant children and their families with the continuous and comprehensive services they need to remain self-sufficient, as well as the services they need to be participating members of society. Only when migrant families' basic subsistence needs are met can parents focus more attention on supporting the educational growth of their children.

Costs

Congress recognized the importance of Federal assistance to migrant farmworkers when it authorized the Migrant Education Program (MEP) in 1966. The program was designed to ensure that the children of farmworkers who migrated between states in search of work would not be overlooked and that fiscal resources would be available to support supplementary programs and services to help them succeed in school.

While Federal resources for MEP have increased from approximately $9 million in 1966 to $294 million in 1992, the Commission heard testimony that the dollars have not kept pace with the number of eligible children, the spiraling cost of services, and the expanding requirements of program operation. In other words, "they have to do more with less."[1]

In basic terms, the proportion of all Federal dollars spent in support of elementary and secondary education increased during the 1970s and then decreased in the 1980s,[2] even though most programs such as MEP received continual increases in their funding. Over this same period, MEP eligibility was extended to include other categories of agriculture, and MEP's activities for recruiting eligible students were very successful. As a result, more children were identified as eligible to participate in MEP and greater numbers were actually served.

The Basic and Fluctuation of MEP Funding

The method used by Congress to determine how much funding MEP would receive has changed over the years. Originally, funding for MEP was based on external estimates of the number of eligible migrant children in each state. This method was abandoned in favor of using a fixed percent of the total appropriation for Chapter 1 Local Education Agency

(LEA) grants. Today, Congress authorizes total MEP funding which is then allocated to states based on a formula. The net result is that there is no longer a relationship between the number of children eligible to be served and the total amount of MEP funding. Consequently, many programs today are struggling with limited Federal resources to serve a growing and increasingly needy population.

More specifically, finding a reliable basis for funding MEP has always presented a challenge to Federal decision-makers. When MEP was first authorized, Congress did not know how many migrant children were living within each state, where in the state they lived, nor how long they stayed. To deal with this dilemma, Congress used external farm labor statistics to estimate the total number of migrant children and then distributed funds to the states based on estimates for each state.[3]

Since the estimates did not consider the amount of time MEP-eligible children actually lived in a state, the states wanted the funding to reflect more closely a true count of the children and where they lived. In 1974, the hypothetically estimated formula was replaced by data reported through the Migrant Student Record Transfer System (MSRTS) as the basis for funding.

Information from MSRTS is used to compute the amount of time each child spent in a state during a calendar year (FTE).[4] The FTE counts continued to be used as the basis for funding MEP until 1981 when Congress agreed to limit funds for the Chapter 1 state grant programs to no more than 14.6 percent of the total amount appropriated for the entire Chapter 1 program. The limit restricted increases in MEP funding for 3 years until the law was changed.[5]

While overall funding for MEP has increased since it was first authorized, annual changes have been inconsistent. Funding has increased (e.g., 1968 to 1982), decreased (e.g., 1982 to 1983), and remained the same (e.g., 1983 and 1984). With the exception of the second year when funding increased by more than 300 percent, changes from year to year ranged from a high of almost 35 percent in 1977 to a decrease of slightly over 4 percent in 1987.[6] As a result, funding for MEP has spiraled and plummeted as the basis for appropriations has changed.

To understand the impact of the changes in funding over time, it is important to consider how inflation has affected the value of the available funds. By converting MEP funding from the actual dollar amount awarded (current dollars) to one adjusted for inflation (constant dollars), a different picture of the funding situation emerges. For example, dollars adjusted for inflation (estimated constant dollars) show a gradual decline annually between 1982 to the present.[7] In other words, MEP lost "buying power" from the early 1980s to the present even when actual funding increased (Appendix E, Exhibit 7.1).

For MEP educators, the loss in buying power that resulted from changing the base of funding from using MSRTS statistics (actual children) to a non-child basis (Congressional appropriations) has been even more dramatic. By comparing the actual funding against that which would have been appropriated if MSRTS statistics were used, the gap between the two widens and funding can be shown to have decreased relative to the number of children being identified. In fact, in 1991 MEP received only 33 percent of the amount of funding which would have been received if MSRTS statistics were still being used. (See Appendix E, Exhibit 7.2.) From the perspective of both state and local educators, the gap between what is being funded for MEP and what should be funded widens yearly.

The Changing Basis for State Allocations

Each time the MEP funding formula changed, the consequences were felt both at the state and local levels. The Legislative History of MEP (see Appendix C) indicates that formula changes were made to offset the differences in educational costs between states, to stabilize the year-to-year funding states receive, and to encourage states to operate summer term projects by providing additional funds and resources.

MEP funding is currently determined in a different manner and is neither related to the number of children identified as eligible for services nor to the total funding given to Chapter 1 programs. Today, a fixed appropriation is authorized by Congress.

Although Congress no longer uses MSRTS data for determining the total amount of Federal funds for MEP, the U.S. Department of Education (ED) still uses MSRTS to calculate FTE information as the basis for funding grants to states. Since MEP funds are based on the number of migrant children identified in each state, the funding each

state receives varies widely. For example, the 1992 state allocations ranged from over $105 million for California to only $21,183 for the state of West Virginia. In fact, the three states with the largest number of children eligible for MEP— California, Texas, and Florida— receive over one-half of all the funds earmarked for MEP.

While changes in state funding occur annually, no consistent increases or decreases are experienced nationwide. Exhibit 7.3 (Appendix E) highlights the year-to-year fluctuations that occur in some states (e.g., Tennessee and Wyoming), while other states have experienced consistent decreases (e.g., Missouri and Texas). These changes reflect demographic shifts in the general migrant population, the success of recruitment efforts within a state, and whether the state is a home base or a receiving state.

In areas where migrant children reside for long periods of time, there are generally large numbers of migrant families who stay for most of the calendar year (i.e., home-based states) or have settled out. Consequently, these states accumulate larger amounts of FTE credits in contrast to other states through which families migrate for the duration of the harvest season. Since FTE is the basis by which a state receives its MEP funds, those states with larger FTEs receive correspondingly larger amounts of MEP funding.

This process sometimes results in an inequitable distribution of funds. States which accommodate their largest number of migrant children during the summer months earn fewer FTE credits and consequently receive the smallest amount of MEP funds even though they may operate full-day summer programs. This is referred to as the "small-state phenomena." Even if they aggressively recruit eligible children, these states are unable to significantly increase their overall state FTE credits because the children's residency is for such a brief period of time.

While many are concerned about this disparity, the current funding allocations to states remain unchanged. The National Association of State Directors of Migrant Education Programs (NASDME) recognizes the diminishing capacity of small states to provide services. In an effort to distribute MEP funds more equitably, NASDME has formulated suggestions to help ED correct this problem.

The Commission is pleased to learn that ED recently proposed increasing the funds available for recruiting currently migratory students through a competitive grant process. ED is also supporting research to explore the actual costs involved in operating summer programs with respect to the services they offer. The Commission is aware that shifts in funding make the small states appear to be "winners" (e.g., states that now have small FTEs) at the expense of the large states (e.g., states that now have large FTEs).

Because funding for MEP is limited, the Commission encourages ED to seek alternatives so that the real "winners" are the children who can profit from receiving adequate services when they migrate to other states during the summer. These summer programs offer a richness in educational experiences that cannot always be provided during the regular school term and that many migrant children would not have without adequate MEP funding. Therefore, the Commission recommends that ED explore options for distributing funds to states which provide economic incentives to identify and serve currently migratory children.

How States Use MEP Funds

Although states receive MEP funding, it was not until 1974 that they were able to distribute the funds to local school districts, nonprofit organizations, and public agencies. In its review of the states' plans for FY 1990, the Commission found that about 80 percent of the funds that states receive from MEP are awarded to other agencies that provide services directly to migrant children.[8] The remaining funds are used by the states to support other activities such as program administration, identification and recruitment, MSRTS, and contracts.

The costs associated with administering MEP at the state level are supported partly by Chapter 1 funds[9] but mostly by MEP funds.[10] The states reported spending slightly less than half of their state administrative funds for administration and slightly more than one-third for instructional and support services.[11] Given that funding for the program has eroded dramatically over the years, the Commission encourages states to give highest priority to funding direct services for the children.

While each state receives MEP funds annually, Federal regulations permit states to carry the funds over a 2-year period. In contrast, regulations require local projects to return annually to the state any funds that the project did not spend. While the

Commission is aware that sometimes unanticipated situations can create a budget surplus, variations exist in the amount of money that some states can and cannot carry over (see Appendix E, Exhibit 7.4). Relative to a state's total allocation, these amounts may seem small; however, in total dollars, some states finish the year with sizeable surpluses of unspent funds.

Although there were insufficient data to determine whether the amounts carried over were only for a year or were part of yearly patterns of budgeted funds, the Commission is concerned about carryover and encourages the Congress to address this issue in its next reauthorization of MEP.

In conducting research to determine the extent of the carryover, the Commission learned that no formal expenditure reports are submitted by SEAs to ED. While ED maintains accounting records of the dollars paid each state and OME requests that estimates of carryover be sub-

mitted with each year's State Grant Application, the Federal Government does not require states to submit annual expenditure reports. Since ED has the authority both to redistribute funds and to ensure the effective use of MEP dollars, the Commission is requesting that ED institute a uniform reporting system of MEP expenditures.

States have more flexibility in the ways they can distribute MEP funds to local operating agencies even though MEP grants to states follow prescribed rules based upon the FTE counts of children and per-pupil expenditures. A recent national study of MEP suggests that approximately half of the states use a formula to determine the amount of funds to award local MEP projects. Others use a formula that considers student need and FTE. Several include migrant status in the formula.[12] These states can then give a higher priority to providing services for currently migratory children, whose needs are often greater than those of formerly migratory children.[13] The Commission suggests that states use a weighting process in determining local subgrantee funds to provide an incentive for identifying, recruiting, and serving currently migratory children.

Allocation of Limited Resources

"When dollars are tight, ...the first things to go are monies for travel and staff development. Next goes the money for support staff, and finally, materials and instructional staff."[14]

Over the past 3 years, the Commissioners heard a number of individuals representing local projects and state programs emphasize the need for more funding. Meanwhile, as the number of children who are eligible for MEP has grown and administrative requirements have increased, the competition for limited-Federal resources has become keen.

When resources become scarce, educators try to maintain the integrity and intensity of their instructional programs by eliminating nonessential activities.[15] There is, however, very little evidence that the number of children receiving services has changed, even though the value of the funding received by the programs has decreased. This finding may be, in part, a reflection of how information is reported to ED rather than an indication of actual practice. Since the current reporting system does not provide information on staffing and the nature of services that are funded by local, state, or other Federal sources, it is impossible to determine whether funds from other sources are supporting MEP at the local level.

Yet, according to state-reported data, the number of children receiving MEP services has continued to increase during both the regular and the summer school terms since 1984-85, which was the first year for reporting participant information.[16] However, changes are evident. In regular school term projects, the number of teachers is decreasing and the student-teacher ratio is increasing.[17] It remains unclear how these changes reflect the ability of local educators to use other funding sources to serve MEP children.

A recent national study suggested that the annual cost for migrant programs per child on average is slightly under $500. However, the cost for regular term programs ranged between $400 to as much as $7,000 per student, while summer term programs ranged between $300 to $4,000 per student.[18] Although these observations are based on a less-than-representative sample of programs and cannot be generalized to all migrant programs, the data reflect the diversity of services and geographic locations in which MEP projects operate.

While costs vary across states and projects, several issues must be considered. Is the cost reasonable based on the services provided? Is the impact of the service worth the cost? Are all migrant children receiving adequate services? The Commission would encourage migrant programs to be designed in such a way that children receive the services they need.

As a result of numerous discussions about funding, the Commission recommends that state and local project allocations be based upon the number of children served rather than the number identified. As part of this funding formula, currently migratory children should be assigned a greater weight. To ensure that this process does not lead to children receiving less than adequate services, we encourage all educators to adopt cost-effective strategies which ensure that migrant children receive services to meet their needs. Given the limited funds available for migrant education, the Commission would urge educators to exercise restraint in incurring administrative expenses. The Commission is also urging a future inter-agency council to review current requirements to ensure that programs are not duplicated, that needy populations are not missed, and that needed services are provided.

Parental Involvement

"It is common knowledge that education, like charity, begins at home, and that the family is the primary institution for socialization."[1]

The Commission believes that migrant parents play the most important role in the development and education of their children. As their first teachers, migrant parents are in the unique position to support and guide the progress of their children. The very nature of migrancy makes the interdependent relationship between children and their parents particularly important since parents must often act as both teacher and advocate. When migrant parents understand and assume the role of teacher/advocate, migrant children are more likely to succeed despite the obstacles provided by their lifestyles.

Parental involvement is vital for the educational achievement of migrant children. A review of 29 studies on parental involvement pro- grams found that when parents participated in the programs, their children improved in reading, mathematics, and other school subjects.[2] Other studies show that migrant children who have successfully completed their education were encouraged by at least one family member.[3] The Director of the Delaware Migrant Education Program (MEP) described how a former migrant was inspired by his family:

"His father and brother taught him something about patience and perseverance. His mother...showed him how to be proud of who he was as well as telling him how important education was."[4]

Another former migrant, also now working as a migrant education specialist, claimed:

"[My] family saw things in me I never saw myself. My family never gave up on me, even when I made mistakes. They encouraged me to go to adult night school so I could get my diploma.[5]

The power of parental influence is illustrated by a study of high-achieving migrants. The study found that high-achieving migrant students have parents with positive attitudes towards school. These parents of high-achievers could give examples of ways in which school helped their children. They also spent considerable time communicating with their children and providing them with successful, educational experiences.[6]

Migrant parents who adapt their lifestyles to the requirements of school attendance positively affected the academic achievement of their children. These migrant parents want their children to have better lives than they themselves lead, and see education as the best avenue to that goal. In addition, the parents frequently persuade their children that studying will guarantee a wider range of choices and provide greater opportunities in life.[7]

What common sense dictates and research confirms is that the involvement of migrant parents encourages educational achievement in their children. It is also clear, however, that parental involvement is neither absolute nor universal.

A Lack of Parental Involvement

In the general population, not all parents are involved in their children's education. One survey found that 71 percent of the parents had not seen their child's classroom, while 67 percent said they had never talked to school officials about academic programs.[8]

Some parents might offer by way of explanation that their childcare demands and work schedules preclude school visits during the day, and others are unable to contact the school or the teacher in the evening.[9] These difficulties would be magni-fied for migrant parents who frequently work 10- to 12-hour days and who frequently lack the verbal skills to communicate with school personnel. A number of other factors contribute to low parental involvement. These include lack of transportation to the school, lack of confidence in speaking at meetings, or the reluctance to challenge the school because of the belief that educators know what is best for the children.[10]

Commission testimony revealed that low parental involvement can also be attributed to a school environment which is not accustomed to working with migrant students. For instance, some parents protested that schools contacted them only when their children were not performing well academically or when they were disruptive. When parents were contacted for disciplinary reasons, communication was with migrant recruiters or other administrative personnel as opposed to teachers.

Although some migrant parents understand the value of an education, their experiences with schools are sometimes negative.[11] The Commission heard descriptions of some unpleasant school situations. For example, one boy was suspended from high school and eventually lost all credits for the school year for reacting angrily after his teacher announced that he would be a failure "just like his parents."[12]

Poor families, particularly the 80 percent who are the working poor (which includes migrants), feel alienated from the national mainstream in general, and the schools, in particular. Most of these parents and grandparents believe that the schools do not really want their children. Unfortunately, many schools do little to persuade them otherwise.[13]

The Role of the Parent

Many migrant parents are often unaware of how they can help their children succeed academically. Commission research and testimony identified several parental involvement strategies beneficial to children's educations, such as creating home libraries, limiting the hours of television that children are allowed to watch each day, talking with children about current school experiences and future education plans, reading with or to their children, and creating an environment in which homework can be done.[14]

Homework can be an especially strong link between home and school. Homework assignments that require parental participation give children the opportunity to show their parents how materials are taught and encourages the parents to discuss the assignment.[15] Discussions between parents and their teen-age children concerning the importance of school, discipline, or other areas of mutual interest are also particularly meaningful since the effect of parental influence continues well into the high school years.[16] Schools are in a pivotal position to help families in forging these links.

Even mealtime conversations about the news of the day, TV programs, or movies can stimulate children's curiosity and sharpen verbal skills. Furthermore, tales of the family's history can help children develop a sense of heritage, personal identity, and cultural pride.[17]

The family's most important responsibility is to teach values and create the ethical foundation that is fundamental to society and democracy. Children learn to love others by being loved, to respect and value the rights of others by being respected and valued themselves, and to trust when they have unconditional support from their parents.

The Role of the School

Research attests to the strength of the relationship between the school and the family for the benefit of the child.[18] The Commission believes that it is the school's responsibility to proactively develop meaningful parental involvement strategies which will draw parents into the school. To make them responsive to the needs of migrant parents, the programs should provide transportation for migrant students and their parents and offer services during the evening. To be sensitive to linguistic needs of migrant parents—particularly immigrant migrants—the program should consider their predominant language and culture, particularly in training, outreach, and self-improvement activities.[19]

Testimony heard by the Commission revealed that many migrant parents are pleased with the effort that schools make to welcome them and their children. One migrant parent described his relationship with the school as warm and supportive:

"The school is always welcoming [my] children and that they always have a place to stay. The school is very happy to have [my] children here...[I] feel happy that the school is teaching [my] children things that [I] cannot teach them."[20]

Schools use a variety of activities to promote parental involvement. Some possibilities include asking them to volunteer (or be paid) to share a talent such as playing an

In one Migrant Even Start program, Tri-State Even Start, program facilitators actually travel from Texas to Washington and Michigan with the migrant families they serve. These facilitators take along instructional packets and bring them into migrant homes and labor camps.[29] Some packets provide information about work, community, school, citizenship, and government. Other packets help parents understand child development and parenting skills through the use of inexpensive hands-on supplies found in the home. By mastering and internalizing these skills, parents will become more confident in their abilities to take an active part in their child's education.[30]

instrument or preparing traditional food with the school children. Some schools invite parents to eat lunch with their children during school visits. Schools also encourage migrant children to participate in school activities since parents are more likely to attend events in which their children take part.[21]

Schools can encourage migrant parents not only to become involved in the school for their own education, but also to advocate on their children's behalf. The advocacy role of the parents increases communication between schools and parents. By notifying parents of courses, programs, and school requirements, the school helps parents gain control over their children's education and keeps them informed of academic opportunities for parents. As an additional benefit, when parents advocate for the academic interests of their children, they will be improving their general knowledge as well as their language skills.[22]

How Preschool Programs Enhance Parental Support

Research shows that children who lack love and support during infancy cannot fulfill the most ordinary human obligations in work, friendship, marriage, and child-rearing. Infants who are neither touched nor talked to may experience depression, weight loss, and even death.[23] The Commission believes that programs which serve migrant children should support activities encouraging parent-child bonding during a child's formative years.

MEP, Migrant Even Start, and Migrant Head Start are migrant-specific programs which strengthen the bond between parents and their chil-

dren by making parental involvement an integral part of their programs. Although these programs are required by legislation to involve parents, the Commission is pleased to find that over half of the states have extended parental involvement beyond the legal requirements of MEP.[24]

Although the programs share common goals of parental involvement and a respect for parents' cultural beliefs particularly in the areas of discipline and child-rearing, each implements the goals differently. Migrant Even Start works to develop positive parent-child relationships and parent education by combining an adult education component for the parents with early childhood services for their children. Migrant Head Start operates when a critical number of families need services, usually for at least a month before and after those of MEP are available. Strategies implemented by these programs enable parents to make frequent visits to the classroom where they are an integral part of their children's learning experience.[25]

Educators should always keep in mind that parents are almost always the child's first and most influential teachers. Parents pass on to their children their culture, language, basic values, and expectations which, for the most part, will shape the course of their children's lives.[26] As such, unless the health and safety of the child is in jeopardy, migrant educators should neither usurp the family's authority, assert undue influence on the child's development, nor attempt to replace the parents in any aspect of the child's life.[27] One former migrant, who received little parental support himself yet still achieved educational success, stated that educating parents was one of MEP's most pressing concerns:

"I personally believe that educating the parents is the biggest problem, and it could be the biggest asset if we can do that successfully."[28]

Migrant educators can help migrant families establish a sense of empowerment, responsibility, and an understanding of the value of an education and, in doing so, can help them function more fully as citizens of the United States.

Involving Parents in School Programs

The very nature of the relationship between migrant parents and their children makes it logical that schools should work closely with the parents of their students.

"The thing which sets migrant children apart from other children is their mobility. This factor demands that the parent provide the continuity, the connecting link. That classroom teacher will not 'pick up' overnight and move along to the next harvesting field to provide instruction. The one constant is the parent. The migrant parent must be taught to teach the child."[33]

A relationship between the school and the home does not exist in all cases. Many migrant parents believe it is the school's responsibility to educate their children and that parental involvement might be misconstrued by the school as interference.[34] In some respects, the schools may be responsible for making parents feel unwanted. Instead, schools might do better to establish strategies for communicating with parents so that the academic needs of their children may be met.

One means of establishing productive communication is to sponsor active outreach to the parents'

homes. The Commission received information describing the effect of an active outreach program:

"For parents of a poor family to have someone from the schools knocking at the door to express interest, kindness, and concern for their child is an electrifying experience in itself. In a program of this type in which we are successfully participating jointly with Collier County Schools, we encounter this amazement at every new home on our list. Almost from the first, there are positive results: better school attendance, better school behavior, and almost inevitably better school grades."[35]

Another method of encouraging parental participation is to make migrant parents feel welcome by conducting meetings with bilingual personnel. By employing bilingual personnel, some of whom may also be migrants, schools can convey their sensitivity to the language and cultural differences of migrant parents. This is a vital step in establishing mutual respect and trust between the school and the home.

Basic variations exist in the ways groups communicate. For example, differences in the communication styles of Hispanic and non-Hispanic White cultures[36] contribute, in part, to the need for conscious efforts to improve communications between the groups. Redlands Christian Migrant Association in Florida credits its success in involving large numbers of parents to the fact that their programs are culturally sensitive and include bilingual services for parents. To involve fathers, in particular, the program includes home visits by male recruiters or husband/wife teams prior to special events, such as holiday parties, picnics, children's awards ceremonies, sports events, etc., and offers programs to address problems related to job hunting or immigration.[37]

To help migrant parents ease their child's transition between Migrant Head Start and kindergarten, the East Coast Migrant Head Start Project publishes a parent-friendly manual. The manual contains a script to help parents learn how to talk to teachers, a set of rules which apply to the public school setting, guidelines to help parents instruct their children about how to catch the bus safely, explanations about free and reduced-price lunches, and suggestions as to what parents can do to help children feel comfortable in school.[31]

Improving Literacy and Parenting Skills

The Commission heard testimony that stressed the importance of creativity and flexibility in developing programs responsive to the migrant parents' educational needs as well as the demands of their work schedules. Among the most successful strategies are those where schools offer evening operating hours so parents can bring their children to be tutored or to work on computers, and where the parents can attend classes. Other strategies include asking parents to sign a pledge that they will attend school conferences and discuss the importance of school and discipline with their children.[38]

One educator suggested "parent rooms" or "clubs" in school buildings where parents can share and discuss ideas, obtain information and resources, and learn from each other about family problems and solutions.[39] The Redlands Christian Migrant Association established De Hombre a Hombre, a men's support group, to help develop family communication skills.[40]

The Family Math Program, developed by the University of California at Berkeley, stresses to migrant parents the importance of mathematics in their children's lives and helps parents make instructional materials to take home. Using common household items, parents create hands-on materials to help their children learn measurement, estimation, and other mathematical concepts.[41]

The Commission also heard testimony about programs and activities offered by some schools. Social services assistance was offered through programs on understanding the elderly, employment services, and information on social security. Educational programs such as budgeting money, sewing classes, buying clothes for children, and making educational toys for preschool children were included. Health activities ranged from screening for diabetes and high-blood pressure to programs on nutrition, dealing with tension, and pesticides.[42] Through programs such as these, migrant parents are learning important skills, as well as proper healthcare for themselves and their children.

Health Needs of Migrant Families[43]

A child's health influences his or her ability to learn.[44] Through the course of Commission hearings and research, it became clear that health issues often go hand-in-hand with educational concerns. As one health provider told the Commission:

"I don't feel that it is possible for migrant children to obtain an adequate education if they cannot obtain adequate healthcare, because so many issues that prevent a child from attending school, long absences, parents who are unable to bring them because they themselves are ill, the stress of having another child in the family who is seriously ill and cannot obtain care; all interfere with the children's ability to sit in the classroom, attend to what is being addressed to them and function as a learning individual."[45]

A particularly important aspect of parental involvement should be to emphasize the role of parents in obtaining proper healthcare for themselves and their children, especially concerning preventable health problems and adequate nutrition.[46] Likewise, migrant parents should also understand the risk that ignoring such healthcare poses for their child. Because poor diets have been linked to five of the ten leading causes of death in the United States, the family must teach children to be personally responsible for their health and to develop healthy attitudes towards their own well-being. Where appropriate, MEP advocates can help parents in this effort by providing them with information about available training in nutrition and about Federal food programs to which they are entitled.

By keeping themselves healthy, parents can serve as positive role models to encourage their children to adopt healthy behavior. In doing so, parents are helping their children live a healthy lifestyle[47] that eliminates major obstacles that can interfere with their ability to succeed in school and beyond.

The Commission recognizes the importance of migrant parents in equipping their children with the tools they will need for a personally and academically successful future. Likewise, the Commission is also aware of the obstacles—which sometimes appear insurmountable—that migrant parents must overcome in order to support and nurture their children. However, research has substantiated the importance of parental support and attention for the academic success of their children. Although many of the programs and projects which provide services to migrant children have taken major strides in involving migrant parents, the Commission would urge those programs that have not yet done so to seek out and involve migrant parents as partners in the education of their children.

Glossary of Acronyms

CAMP—College Assistance Migrant Program

CPS—Current Population Survey

ED—United States Department of Education

EOP—Equal Opportunity Program

ESEA—Elementary & Secondary Education Act

FTE—Full-Time Equivalency

FVH—Fruits, Vegetables, and Horticultural

GED—General Education Diploma

GRAPE—Grade Retention and Promotion Evaluation

HEP—High School Equivalency Project

I&R—Identification and Recruitment

IEP—Individualized Education Program

IHE—Institutions of Higher Education

IMEC—Interstate Migrant Education Council

INEL—Idaho Nuclear Energy Laboratory

JTPA—Job Training Partnership Act

LEA—Local Education Agency

LEP—Limited English Proficiency

MENAES—Migrant Education Needs Assessment & Evaluation System

MEP—Migrant Education Program

MSFW—Migrant Seasonal Farmworker

MSRTS—Migrant Student Record Transfer System

NAFTA—Migrant Seasonal Farmworker

NASDME—National Association of State Directors of Migrant Education

NAWS—National Agricultural Worker Survey

NAFTA—North American Free Trade Agreement

OME—Office of Migrant Education

PASS—Portable Assisted Study Sequence

PCC—Program Coordination Center

PDC—Program Development Center

PPE—Per-pupil Expenditure

PSA—Policy Study Associates

RTAC—Rural Technical Assistance Center

SAPNA—Student and Program Needs Assessment

SAS—Seasonal Agricultural Services

SCEAP—Secondary Credit Exchange & Accrual Project

SEA—State Education Agency

TAC—Technical Assistance Center

WIC—Women, Infants, & Children

Endnotes

Chapter 1

1 Unless other noted, material in this chapter comes from the work of Dr. Philip Martin as presented in testimony before the National Commission on Migrant Education, Washington, D.C., June 22, 1992, and in a paper commissioned by the National Commission on Migrant Education, Washington, D.C., July 15, 1992.

2 Material for this section comes from written testimony by Dr. William O'Hare, Farmworker Demographics: Report to the national Commission on Migrant Education, September 22, 1991.

3 D. Martin and P. Martin, Coordination of Migrant and Seasonal Farmworkers Service Programs (Draft), Paper Commissioned by National Commission on Migrant Education, December 2, 1991 (pp. 1, ii).

4 P. L. Martin and J. S. Holt. "Final Report: Migrant Farmworkers: Numbers and Distribution." Legal Services Corporation, Washington, D.C., April 1987. (A thorough analysis of the migrant demographic literature to 1987)

"Synthesis of Available Research and Data Bases on the Migrant Education Program." Applied Systems Institution, Inc., Washington, D.C., August 1988. (An exhaustive listing of studies, surveys, and data bases on migrant farmworkers)

R. Mines, et. al. "Findings from the National Agricultural Workers Survey: A Demographic and Employment Profile of Perishable Crop Farmworkers." Office of Program Economics

Research Report No. 1. U.S. Department of Labor, Office of the Assistant Secretary for Policy. Washington, D.C., July 1991.

5 William O'Hare, op. cit., p. 4.

6 N. Pindus, F. O'Reilly, M. Schulte, and L. Webb. Services for Migrant Children in the Health, Social Services, and Education Systems: Background Paper. Department of Health and Human Services. July 22, 1992. (p. 4)

7 William O'Hare, op. cit., p. 5.

8 Nancy Pindus, Fran O'Reilly, Margaret Schulte, and Lenore Webb. Services for Migrant Children in the Health, Social Services, and Education Systems: Background Paper. Department of Health and Human Services. July 22, 1992. (p. 4)

9 P. Martin, Paper Commissioned, (p. 32).

10 For a more complete discussion of the Immigration Reform and Control Act (IRCA) of 1986, Seasonal Agricultural Workers (SAW), and Resident Agricultural Workers (RAW), see P. Martin. Paper Commission by the National Commission on Migrant Education, Washington, D.C., July 15, 1992. p. 55-66.

11 William O'Hare. Farmworker Demographics: Report to the National Commission on Migrant Education. September 22, 1991. (p. 14).

12 R. Mines, S. Gabbard, and B. Boccalandro, Findings from the National Agricultural Workers Survey (NAWS), 1990: A Demographic and Employment Profile of Perishable Crop Farmworkers. Office of Program Economics. Research Report No. 1, U.S. Department of Labor, Office of the Assistant Secretary for

Policy, Washington, D.C., July 1991.

R. Mines, S. Gabbard, J. Torres, *Findings from the National Agricultural Workers Survey (NAWS), 1989: A Demographic and Employment Profile of Perishable Crop Farmworkers*. Office of Program and Economics. Research Report No. 2, U.S. Department of Labor, Assistant Secretary for Policy, Washington, D.C., November 1991.

13 As part of the NAWS data collection procedures, over 7,200 farmworkers in 72 counties in 25 states were selected and interviewed since 1989. These farmworkers are representative of about 80 percent of the nation's farm workers who are employed in Seasonal Agricultural Services (SAS).

14 For example, does year-round begin after 6 or 9 months, what is the appropriate boundary to be crossed or distance to be traveled to qualify as migrant, etc.

15 Seasonal Agricultural Services is the type of agriculture in the Immigration Reform and Control Act of 1986 that establishes who can become a legalized Seasonal Agricultural Worker.

16 Based on NAWS criteria, migrants travel at least 75 miles to do farmwork.

17 Mines, et. al. Findings from the NAWS 1990. Washington: USDOL, Office of Program Economics, Research Report No. 1. 1991, and additional data analysis.

18 Seasonal Agricultural Workers are special agricultural workers who did less than 90 days of Seasonal Agricultural Services work in 1985-86.

19 P. Martin. Testimony. (p. 5).

20 P. Martin. Paper. (p. 4).

Seasonal Agricultural Services (SAS) is a subsector of U.S. crop agriculture that employs about 80 percent of the nation's farmworkers who are seasonal agricultural workers (SAWs). It is not possible to determine exactly how much of the nation's farm labor is involved in the SAS agriculture included in the NAWS because SAS was defined by statute, regulation, and court decision. The best estimates are that SAS agriculture includes about 80 percent of the workers employed in agriculture sometime during the year, about 70 percent of the average jobs offered, and 60 percent of the wages paid.

21 P. Martin. Paper. (p. 6).

22 P. Martin. Paper. (p. 47).

23 P. Martin. Paper. (p. 48).

24 P. Martin. Paper. (p. 48).

25 P. Martin. Paper. (p. 52).

26 P. Martin. Paper. (p. 54).

27 P. Martin. Paper. (pp. 54-55).

28 P. Martin. Paper. (p. 47).

29 P. Martin. Paper. (pp. 49-500.

30 P. Martin. Testimony. (p. 21).

31 Although some demographic data are gathered by the following categories— White/Anglo, Black, Asian, Hispanic, etc.—

Hispanics are not a race but rather an ethnic determination. For the purposes of this report, the Commission will use the term "non-Hispanic White" to designate individuals who would otherwise be referred to as White.

32 P. Martin. Paper. (p. 10).

33 P. Martin. Paper. (p. 69).

34 P. Martin. Paper. (p. 5).

35 P. Martin. Paper. (p. 16).

36 The following discussion appeared in P. Martin. Paper Commissioned by the National Commission on Migrant Education, Washington, D.C., July 15, 1992. p. 12.

There is some confusion about the eligibility for MEPs of unaccompanied youth who migrate without their parents. The MEP serves children 3 to 21 who have not completed high school or college regardless of their legal status in the U.S., while JTPA, for example, serves only persons legally authorized to work in the U.S., and if 18, are registered with the Selective Service.

MEP regulations state clearly that a migratory child is one whose parent is a migratory agricultural or fishery worker. Children are considered eligible if they move from one school district to another to join a parent or guardian who moved to work on a farm or fishery. Children who qualify for MEP by moving with or to join their families, remain eligible even they move alone each year thereafter in order to obtain a farm or fishery job.

Although eligibility decisions are made on a case by case basis, it appears that teens who move alone from Mexico to the U.S. to do farmwork when the parents had never migrated to the U.S. are ineligible for MEP.

37 P. Martin. Paper. (p. 11).

38 P. Martin. Paper. (p. 11).

39 P. Martin. Paper. (p. 11).

40 P. Martin. Paper. (p. 11).

41 P. Martin. Paper. (p. 8).

42 R. Mines. communication to National Commission on Migrant Education, October 15, 1991. (pp. 2, 4).

43 For a more complete discussion of the MSRTS, see *Keeping Up With Our nation's Migrant Students: A Report on the Migrant Student Record Transfer System*. National Commission on Migrant Education, September 1991.

44 Keeping Up With Our Nation's Migrant Students: A Report on the Migrant Student Record Transfer System (MSRTS), National Commission on Migrant Education. September 1991. (p. 7)

45 This was the unique count for 1990-1991, according to a March 31, 1992 MSRTS printout.

46 A more complete discussion of eligibility criteria appears in Appendix C.

47 MSRTS statistics for 1990-1991 as

reported on the National Summary profile of the unique count of all migrant children reported as resident or enrolled during the school year on March 31, 1992.

48 The unique count of all migrant children for 1990-1991 as reported by MSRTS on March 31, 1992 was 628,150 of which 329,679 were identified as formerly migratory children and 298,471 were currently migratory children either during the regular or summer school terms.

49 RTI Tables A.3.a and A.3.b indicate 67 percent in the regular and summer school terms were born in the U.S. with 29 percent in the regular and 30 percent in the summer terms were born in Mexico. In both school terms, a higher proportion of the currently migratory population are Hispanic as compared to the formerly migratory population.

50 MSRTS unique count enrollment statistics for 1990-1991 (computer run 3/31/92) for the state of California were 207,561; for Texas, 116,384; and for Florida, 56,890. The sum of these state enrollment statistics represents 61 percent of the unique count of MEP-eligible children enrolled across the nation or 57 percent of the unique count of children enrolled in each state in 1990-1991. Since a migrant child could be enrolled in more than one state during the year, the unique count by state includes children who may have been counted more than once.

51 RTI Tables A.3.b and A.4.b report 384,804 out of 454,813 identified MEP-eligible children in the regular school term and 135,638 out of 160,215 in the summer school term as being between the ages of 6 and 16.

52 P. Martin. Paper Commissioned by the National Commission on Migrant Education, Washington, D.C., July 15, 1992. p. 4.

53 A more detailed description of "currently" and "formerly" appears in Chapter 3 of this report.

54 MSRTS 3/31/92.

55 The patterns of migration described in this section were based on a review of the FY 1991 State Migrant Education Program applications.

56 MSRTS Report: Unique Count Agricultural Workers Migrant Children Reported as Resident or Enrolled During the School Year by migrant Status. July 30, 1991.

57 MSRTS statistics indicate that during the regular school term 78.6 percent of the eligible MEP population is Hispanic and during the summer term 85.3 percent is Hispanic. A representative sample of the national MEP eligible population selected by the RTI study identified 73.5 percent of the regular term and 85.7 percent of the summer term population as Hispanic. However, if the child attended both the regular term and summer term the child is counted twice

since neither MSRTS nor RTI provided racial/ethnic descriptions of the unique count of MEP-eligible children over the entire year.

58 MSRTS statistics include all identified MEP-eligible children enrolled in the MSRTS.

59 RTI statistics are based upon a nationally representative sample of MEP-eligible children.

60 G.E., A. Dever, *Migrant Health Status: Profile of a Population With Complex Health Problems*. Migrant Clinicians Network Monograph Series. 1991 (p. 2, Figs 3, 4, 5).

R. Tidwell (M.D.), letter of April 2, 1979, with accompanying tabulation of a 2-year run of migrant student deaths reports obtain from MSRTS.

61 P. Martin. Paper Commissioned by the National Commission on Migrant Education, Washington, D.C., July 15, 1992. p. 35.

62 B. Cameron, 1981, ibid (p. 37). *Descriptive Study of the Chapter 1 Migrant Education Program, Vol. I*, ibid (p. 25) and Exhibit II.2).

63 P. Martin, Testimony. (p. 19).

64 Information for this section comes from: P. Martin, written testimony for the National Commission on Migrant Education, Washington, D.C., July 15, 1992. (p. 70-74).

65 P. Martin. Testimony before the National Commission on Migrant Education, Washington, D.C., June 22, 1992. p. 19-20.

66 L. Chavez. Testimony before the National Commission on Migrant Education, Washington, D.C., June 22, 1992. p. 38.

67 National Maritime Fisheries of the National Oceanographic and Atmospheric Agency; National Maritime Fisheries Offices in Alaska, Louisiana, and Massachusetts; and the National Fisheries Institute at Arlington, VA, a private industry-supported agency.

68 Marjorie Berry. Testimony before the National Commission on Migrant Education. Fort Myers, Florida. December 15, 1991. p. 84.

69 L. Espinoza. "Report to the Commission: A Personal Perspective." National Commission on Migrant Education. (p. 1-2).

Chapter 2

1 T. Reyna, oral testimony before the National Commission on Migrant Education, Buffalo, New York, April 29, 1991 (p. 298).

2 The four distinct programs authorized by ESEA Title 1 were (1) Chapter 1 Basic Grant Program, (2) Migrant Education, (3) Neglected or Delinquent, and (4) Handicapped. While each authorized program has distinct features, the basic grant and MEP are the only two where the state is not the legal guardian of the child and/or the child is not a resident of an institution.

3 Conference report accompanying P.L. 89-

750, *U.S. Code Congressional and Administrative News*, 89th Congress (p. 3852).

4 The regulations define eligible migrant children if they satisfy criteria in three areas: age, occupation of the child or family member, and recency of migration. These criteria areas are as follows:

Age: 3 to 21 generate funding, but children from birth to age 3 who meet the criteria can be served from birth to age 3 under special circumstances, although they do not generate funding.

Occupation: agriculture or fishing activity for commercial sale or as a principal means of personal subsistence.

Migration Status: "currently" if the child has moved within the past 12 months across district boundaries or administrative areas in a single district, or 20 miles in a district that is 18,000 square miles to enable the child, the parent/guardian, or member of the family to obtain temporary or seasonal work in agriculture or fishing; and "formerly" if the child is not migrating but was eligible as a "currently" migratory child within the past 5 years.

5 P.L. 100-297, Section 1201(b)(2).

6 P.L. 100-297, Section 1436(a).

7 P.L. 100-297, Sections 1203 and 1436.

8 R. Levy, oral testimony before the National Commission on Migrant Education, Buffalo, New York, April 29, 1991 (pp. 285-286).

9 Office of Migrant Education, U.S. Department of Education, *Directory of Services: Federal Agencies and Non-Federal Organizations Providing Services to Migrant and Seasonal Farmworkers and Their Families*, March 1991.

10 Section 1203 of the Hawkins-Stafford Act reauthorized the old Section 143 projects.

11 The Chapter 1 Technical Assistance Centers (TACs) and the Rural Chapter 1 Technical Assistance Centers (RTACs), which are funded by the general Chapter 1 allocation to ED for evaluation, are both required by contract to assist migrant programs. TAC and RTAC areas of specialty include program improvement and evaluation. These services are to complement those provided by the Program Coordinating Centers (PCCs) and, to the degree possible, provide services in a coordinated fashion such as a joint meeting.

12 Statutory Requirements: Sections 1011, 1012, 1202, 1436, and 1451 of Chapter 1 of Title 1, ESEA and Section 437 (a) of GEPA; Regulatory Requirements: Sections 201.10, 201.16, 201.17, 201.18., 201.23, 201.25, 201.46, and 201.47. Sections 76.560, 76.561, 76.563, 76.730, 76,731. 76.734, and Part 80 of EDGAR.

13 Statutory Requirements: Chapter 1 of Title 1, ESEA, Section 1202(b)(1) and (2); Regulatory Requirements: Sections 201.3 and 201.30.

14 Identification and recruitment affects funding since state allocations are based upon the full-time equivalents of eligible migrant children.

15 Statutory requirements specify that a state is allowed a 5 percent error rate in their eligibility determinations. Regulations require states to exercise quality control on their eligibility determinations to ensure that decisions are correct for 95 percent of the children deemed eligible.

16 The FY 1991 SEA MEP State Applications indicate that, where there are no local MEP projects, the following occurs: Kansas uses temporary recruiters (p. 16); Louisiana uses part-time (p. 25); Maine supplements local recruiters with state recruiters (p. 44); Mississippi supplements with part-time recruiters (p. 14); Missouri supplements with a state recruiter (p. 23).

17 Massachusetts uses one subgrantee to operate the entire state program including recruitment. Massachusetts MEP State Application FY 1991 (p. 34).

18 Florida has enacted laws which require all local superintendents to notify the state of migrant children. Florida MEP State Application FY 1991 (p. 31).

19 Statutory Requirement: Chapter 1 of Title 1, ESEA, Section 1203(a)(2); Regulatory Requirements: Sections 201.1(b), 201.20(a), and 201.20(a)(2).

20 Office of Migrant Education, U.S. Department of Education, *Migrant Education Program Policy Manual: Migrant Education Programs Operated by State Education Agencies*, November 1991 (pp. 27-29).

21 National Commission on Migrant Education, *Keeping Up with Our Nation's Migrant Students: A Report on the Migrant Student Record Transfer System (MSRTS)*, September 1991.

22 Statutory Requirements: Chapter 1 of Title 1, ESEA, Sections 1014(b) and 1202(a)(3) and (b); Regulatory Requirements: Sections 201.31, 201.32 and 201.36(a)(1).

23 U.S. Department of Education Policy Manual, 1991 (p. 13).

24 Ibid (pp. 16-17).

25 SAPNA and MENAES use student information for MSRTS to provide assessment and evaluation information for program planning and evaluation. The major difference is that MENAES attempts to provide summary data including pre- and post-test scores for reporting state-level information to ED.

26 C. Lawrence, oral testimony before the National Commission on Migrant Education, Watsonville, California, July 16, 1991 (p. 145);

R. Welty, oral testimony before the National Commission on Migrant Education, Watsonville, California, July 16, 1991 (pp. 148-149).

27 Statutory Requirements: Chapter 1 of Title 1, ESEA, Sections 1201(b) and 1202(a), the basic objectives of Sections 1001, 1011(a), 1012, 1014 and 1018, Section 1471, and subpart 2 of Part F; Regulatory Requirements: EDGAR, Sections 201.3, 201.31, 201.32, 201.34, 201.36, 201.40, 201.43, 201.48, 201.49, and sections 75.600 to 75.615, 76.600, and 80.42.

28 Statutory Requirements: Sections 1202 (a)(1) and (2) and 1203 of Chapter 1 of Title, 1, ESEA; Regulatory Requirements: Sections 201.11(b)(4), 201.30, 201.34, 201.36(e) and (f) and Part 205.

29 T. Reyna, 1991 (p. 299).

30 D. Slaby, written testimony before the National Commission on Migrant Education, Buffalo, New York, April 29, 1991 (p. 5).

31 D. Whittington, oral testimony before the National Commission on Migrant Education, Buffalo, New York, April 29, 1991 (pp. 197, 224).

32 Migrant Dropout Reconnection Project, 1987; Migrant Education Assistance Program, 1986.

33 Statutory Requirements: Sections 1016 and 1202 (a)(4) of Chapter 1 of Title 1, ESEA; Regulatory Requirements: Sections 201.35 and 200.34 of the Chapter 1 LEA Program Regulations.

34 A. Andrada, oral testimony before the National Commission on Migrant Education, Watsonville, California, July 16, 1991 (pp. 102-103).

35 M. Colon and M. Portuondo, *Secondary Analysis of Selected Data on Migrant Education Programs, Fiscal Year 1990*, Department of Curriculum and Instruction, College of Education, Pennsylvania State University, March 1992 (pp. 29-30).

The 1990 state plans revealed the following: School Visitations (36 states) which include visits to classrooms, parent teacher conferences, volunteering, clothing banks, information meetings; Parent Education Programs (32 states) which include literacy training, as well as specialized training ranging from immigration and amnesty classes to developing instructional materials for home use; Home/School Communication (29 states) which include distributing handbooks, surveys, and program reports; Home Visitations (24 states) to deliver information, provide training, identify or follow-up on migratory children; and Extracurricular Activities (16 states) which range from social gatherings to field trips.

36 Statutory Requirements: Sections 1019(b)(1), 1202(a)(6), and 1435 of Chapter 1 of Title 1, ESEA; Regulatory Requirements:

Sections 201.36 (c) and 201.51 through 201.56.

37 C. Stockburger, *The Impact of Interstate Programs on Continuity of Migrant Education*, ERIC/CRESS, New Mexico State University, February 1980 (p. 57); N. Adelman, *Descriptive Study of the Migrant Education Section 143 Interstate and Intrastate Coordination Grants*, Policy Studies Associates, Inc., Washington, D.C., March 1987 (p. i).

38 N. Adelman, 1987 (p. 3).

39 Memorandum from F. Corrigan to C. Whitten, March 12, 1992.

40 Oral testimony of Commissioners Garner and Mata-Woodruff, Washington, D.C., July 31, 1991 (pp. 88-106).

41 E. Ogletree, "Status of Credit Transfer for Migrant Students in the U.S.," Chicago State University, 1984 (p. 14).

42 B. Pessin, oral testimony before the National Commission on Migrant Education, September 23, 1991 (p. 223).

43 B. Reig, oral testimony before the National Commission on Migrant Education, Buffalo, New York, April 29, 1991 (p. 129).

Chapter 3

1 E. Ibarra, *The Day The Crops Failed*, Dade County Migrant Project, Homestead, Florida, February 7, 1990.

2 MSRTS statistics, March 31, 1992.

3 Moved is defined as making a qualifying move based upon MEP regulations.

4 MSRTS Statistics, March 31, 1992.

5 MSRTS unique counts for the year were 571,920, while states participation counts were reported as 411,595. Therefore, 72 percent of the eligible population received a MEP-funded service either during the regular- or summer-school term.

6 A Henderson, et. al. A Summary of the State Chapter 1 Migrant Education Program Participant and Achievement Information, 1992. (p. 24)

7 Ibid.

8 This synthesis of identification and recruitment strategies is based upon descriptions provided in: *Descriptive Study of the Chapter 1 Migrant Education Program, Volume II: Summary Reports of Intensive Case Studies*, prepared for the U.S. Department of Education by Research Triangle Institute, Research Triangle Park, North Carolina, January 1992; Also see: E. Marks, *Case Studies of the Migrant Education Program*, Policy Studies Associates, Inc., July 1987 (pp. 30-32).

9 These I&R strategies are based upon the Commission's staff review of FY 1991 state MEP grant applications.

10 D. Slaby, oral testimony before the National Commission on Migrant Education,

Buffalo, New York, April 29, 1991 (p. 186).

11 A. Goniprow, oral testimony before the National Commission on Migrant Education, Bethesda, Maryland, February 14, 1991 (pp. 157-163).

12 Migrant Education Messages and Outlook (MEMO), "Eastern Coordination Improves," Vol.9 No.5, November-December 1991 (p. 9).

13 The number served versus the number eligible is based only upon statistics for the regular school term. During the summer term, only children who receive MEP funded services can be enrolled on MSRTS.

14 MSRTS enrollment statistics are based upon July 30, 1991, computer runs. MEP participants statistics were extracted from A. Henderson, et. al., *A Summary of State Chapter 1 Migrant Education Program Participant and Achievement Information*, 1990 (Table 9, p. 25), 1992 (Table 2.1, p. 22).

15 Ibid.

16. N. Pindus, et al., *Background Paper: Services For Migrant Children In The Health, Social Services, and Education Systems*, July 1992 (p. 10).

17 R. Levy, oral testimony before the National Commission on Migrant Education, Buffalo, New York, April 29, 1991 (p. 294). Mr. Levy reported that some students traveled to as many as seven states in one year.

18 V. Marani, oral testimony before the National Commission on Migrant Education, Watsonville, California, July 16, 1991 (p. 10).

19 Research Triangle Institute, *Volume I*, 1992 (p. A-13, Exhibit A.8.a).

20 MSRTS, March 31, 1992.

21 Research Triangle Institute, *Volume I*, 1992 (p. 20, Exhibit II.3.a; p. 21, Exhibit II.3.b). Statistics are for both regular and summer term programs.

22 Ibid.

23 Ibid (p. 16, Exhibit II.2). Statistics are for both regular and summer term participants.

24 E. Marks, 1987 (p. 68). The Commission also heard testimony in Florida that, given the rise in immigrants and refugees in migrant farm labor, it is not unusual to find a ten year old child who had never attended school. N. Pullum, oral testimony before the National Commission on Migrant Education, McAllen, Texas, December 15, 1991 (p. 133).

25 Research Triangle Institute, *Volume I*, 1992 (p. A-21, Exhibit A.12). Regular term only.

26 Ibid (p. 27, Exhibit II.4.a; p. 28, Exhibit II.4.b).

27 Ibid (p. A-23, Exhibit A.14.a; p. A-24, Exhibit A.14.b).

28 Research Triangle Institute, *Volume I*, 1992 (p. 20, Exhibit II.3.a; p. 21, Exhibit II.3.b).

29 J. Henderson, oral testimony before the National Commission on Migrant Education, McAllen, Texas, December 4, 1990 (p. 96).

30 N. Pullum, 1991 (pp. 132-133).

31 Arizona MEP State Application FY 1991 (p. 2).

32 MEMO, "Florida's Summer Institutes: A Program That Works," Vol.9, No.5, November-December 1991 (pp. 16-17).

33 MEMO, "Oregon Project Provides Leadership Training," Vol.9, No.5, March-April 1992 (pp. 16-17).

34 MEP participant statistics were extracted from A. Henderson, et. al., *A Summary of State Chapter 1 Migrant Education Program Participant and Information*, Regular-Term Statistics 1990 (Table 9, p. 25), 1992 (Table 2.1, p. 22); Summer-Term Statistics 1990 (Table 20, p. 43); 1992 (Table 2.12, p. 44).

35 B. Rudes, et al., *Handbook of Effective Migrant Education Practices, Volume II: Case Studies*, prepared for the Office of Planning, Budget and Evaluation, U.S. Department of Education by Development Associates, Inc., February 1990 (pp. II-70, II-77).

36 Summer term funding is only based upon children who participate in MEP while in the regular school term MEP funding is based on MEP students' residency regardless of whether or not services are received.

37 Based upon case study information. Research Triangle Institute, *Volume I*, 1992 (p. 10).

38 A. Henderson, et al., 1992, Tables 2.4 and 2.14 pp. 29 and 49.

39 Z. Costa, oral testimony before the National Commission on Migrant Education, Watsonville, California, July 16, 1991 (p. 130).

40 B. Rudes, et al., 1990 (pp. II-178, II-179).

41 Research Triangle Institute, *Volume I*, 1992 (p. 37, Exhibit II.6).

42 Ibid (p. 57, Exhibit III.2).

43 Ibid (p. 60, Exhibit III.3).

44 Volume II of the Research Triangle Institute study suggests that use of multiple funds is occurring. The problem is that the extent of this practice can not be documented by the quantitative statistics reported in this study.

45 A. Henderson, et al., 1992 Tables 2.4 and 2.14 pp. 29 and 49.

46 State reports for 1989-90 indicate that 91 percent of the regular term and 66 percent of the summer term participants were enrolled in kindergarten through grade 6. A. Henderson, et al., 1992 (p. iii).

47 Research Triangle Institute, Volume I, 1992 (p. A-52, Exhibit A.27).

48 Statistics based upon state reports for 1989-90. A. Henderson, et al., 1992 (p. 12, Table 1.4)

Chapter 4
Preschool-Aged
Migrant Education

1 National Commission on Children, *Beyond Rhetoric: A New American Agenda for Children and Families*, 1991; National Education Goals Panel, *The National Education Goals Panel Report: Building a Nation of Learners*, 1991.

2 See Chapter 6 of this report.

3 Office of Migrant Education, U.S. Department of Education, *Migrant Education Program Policy Manual: Migrant Education Programs Operated by State Education Agencies*, November 1991 (p. 76).

4 34 CFR 1304; B. White, *Educating the Infant and Toddler*, D.C. Heath and Company, Lexington, Massachusetts, 1988 (pp. 27-28, 34-38).

5 Head Start Act, Section 642(c).

6 Office of Human Development, U.S. Department of Health and Human Services, *Head Start Program Performance Standards (45 CFR 1304)*, November 1984.

7 H. McKey, et al., *The Impact of Head Start on Children, Families and Communities: Final Report of the Head Start Evaluation, Synthesis and Utilization Project*, CSR, Inc., Washington, D.C., 1985 (p. 20).

8 For a description of these programs, see: S. House, "CRS Report for Congress, Federal Programs for Children and Their Families," Congressional Research Service, Washington, D.C., January 2, 1990; U.S. General Accounting Office, *Child Care: Government Funding Sources, Coordination and Service Availability*, October 1989 (Appendix I).

9 New Mexico MEP State Application FY 1991.

10 B. Mainster, oral testimony before the National Commission on Migrant Education, Fort Myers, Florida, December 15, 1991 (p. 70).

11 D. Martin and P. Martin, *Coordination of Migrant and Seasonal Farmworker Service Programs*, Administrative Conference of the United States, April 1992 (pp. 32-36).

12 S. Kagan, *Excellence in Early Childhood Education: Defining Characteristics and Next-Decade Strategies*, prepared for the Office of Educational Research and Improvement, U.S. Department of Education, July 1990.

13 B. Mainster, 1991 (p. 75-76).

14 P. Coble, written testimony before the National Commission on Migrant Education, Gettysburg, Pennsylvania, August 7, 1990 (pp. 1-4).

15 Migrant Education Messages and Outlook (MEMO), "Migrant Head Start Ties Grow,"

Vol.10, No.1, March-April 1992 (p. 6); F. Fuentes, written testimony before the National Commission on Migrant Education, Buffalo, New York, April 29, 1991 (pp. 12-15).

16 F. Fuentes, 1991 (pp. 12-15).

17 Ibid.

18 Ibid (p. 14).

19 U.S. Department of Health and Human Services, *National Head Start Bulletin*, November 1988 (p. 5).

20 R. Guerra, oral testimony before the National Commission on Migrant Education, McAllen, Texas, December 3, 1990 (p. 48).

21 J. Castillo, oral testimony before the National Commission on Migrant Education, McAllen, Texas, December 3, 1990 (p. 24).

22 F. Fuentes, 1991 (pp. 9-10).

23 B. Walsh, written testimony before the National Commission on Migrant Education, McAllen, Texas, December 3, 1990 (p. 10); E. Zuroweste, written testimony before the National Commission on Migrant Education, Gettysburg, Pennsylvania, August 7, 1990 (p. 1).

24 U.S. General Accounting Office, *Hired Farmworkers: Health and Well-Being At Risk*, February 1992 (p. 3).

25 A. Dever, "Migrant Health Status: Profile of a Population with Complex Health Problems," *Migrant Clinicians Network Monograph Series*, Austin, Texas 1991 (p. 12); A. Dever, oral and written testimony before the National Commission on Migrant Education, Buffalo, New York, April 29, 1991.

M. Good, *A Needs Assessment: The Healthy Status of Migrant Children as They Enter Kindergarten*, Department of Nursing, San Jose State University, 1990 (pp. 47, 57).

D. Runyan and P. Morgan, *Nutrition and Migrant Health: Trends in Nutritional Services at Migrant Health Centers*, Georgetown University Child Development Center, 1987 (p. 15).

E. Watkins, et al., *Improving the Health of Migrant Mothers and Children: Final Report*, Department of Maternal and Child Health, School of Public Health, University of North Carolina, February 1990 (pp. 32, A-9).

26 T. Decker, written testimony before the National Commission on Migrant Education, Gettysburg, Pennsylvania, August 7, 1990 (p. 2); D. Mason, oral testimony before the National Commission on Migrant Education, Buffalo, New York, April 29, 1991 (pp. 3-4);

V. Lee, S. McDermott, and C. Elliot, "The Delayed Immunization of Children of Migrant Farm Workers in South Carolina," *Public Health Reports*, Vol.105, No.3, May-June 1990 (pp. 317-320).

27 In a prior report, the Commission found that data on these records was incomplete, inaccurate, and sometimes obsolete. Furthermore, it

is not certain to what extent MSRTS immunization records are universally accepted by physicians and schools nationwide. See: National Commission on Migrant Education, *Keeping Up With Our Nation's Migrant Students: A Report On The Migrant Student Record Transfer System (MSRTS)*, September 1991.

28 V. Wilk, *The Occupational Health of Migrant and Seasonal Farmworkers in The United States*, Farmworker Justice Fund, Inc., Washington, D.C., 1987 (pp. 95-96).

29 U.S. General Accounting Office, 1992 (p. 18).

30 S. Pollack, "Health Hazards of Agricultural Child Labor," *Migrant Health Clinical Supplement*, National Migrant Resource Program, Inc., 1990 (p. 2).

31 D. Runyan and P. Morgan, 1987 (p. 16).

32 Ibid (pp. 13, 60).

33 National Association of Community Health Centers, *Medicaid and Migrant Farmworker Families: Analysis of Barriers and Recommendations for Change*, 1991 (pp. 4-5); U.S. General Accounting Office, 1992 (pp. 5, 25).

34 A. Dever, "Migrant Health Status," 1991 (p. 6); B. Walsh, 1990 (p. 16).

35 Food Research and Action Center, *Community Childhood Hunger Identification Project: A Survey of Childhood Hunger in the United States*, March 1991 (p. vi).

36 J. Castillo, 1990 (p. 25).

37 U.S. General Accounting Office, *Food Stamp Program: A Demographic Analysis of Participation and Nonparticipation*, January 1990 (pp. 2-4); Food Research and Action Center, 1991 (Executive Summary).

38 *Descriptive Study of the Chapter 1 Migrant Education Program, Volume I: Study Findings and Conclusions*, prepared for the U.S. Department of Education by Research Triangle Institute, Research Triangle Park, North Carolina, January 1992 (p. A-46, Exhibit A.24.b).

39 B. White, 1988 (pp. 17, 32-33).

40 S. Morse, oral testimony before the National Commission on Migrant Education, Washington, D.C., March 1, 1992 (p. 44).

41 J. Pfannenstiel and D. Seltzer, "New Parents as Teachers: Evaluation of an Early Parent Education Program," *Early Childhood Research Quarterly*, Vol.4, 1989 (pp. 1-18); J. Palmer and M. Zalow, *Who Cares for America's Children?*, National Academy Press, Washington, D.C., 1990 (pp. 48-50).

42 J. Pfannenstiel and D. Seltzer, 1989 (p. 12).

43 National Commission on Infant Mortality, *Home Visiting: Opening Doors for America's Pregnant Women and Children*, Washington, D.C., 1990 (pp. 1, 5).

44 This figure represents center-based early childhood and care programs. E. Kisker, S. Hofferth, D. Phillips, and E. Farquhar, *A Profile of Child Care Settings: Early Education and Care in 1990, Volume I*, prepared for the Office of the Under Secretary, U.S. Department of Education by Mathematica Policy Research, Inc., 1991 (p. 23).

45 F. Fuentes, 1991 (p. 8).

46 U.S. Department of Education, *Proceedings of the National Conference on Early Childhood Issues: Policy Options in Support of Children and Families*, November 17-18, 1988 (pp. 18-19).

47 National Commission on Infant Mortality, 1989.

48 National Education Goals Panel, 1991 (p. 33).

49 N. Kowalkowski, oral testimony before the National Commission on Migrant Education, Watsonville, California, July 16, 1991 (p. 31).

50 U.S. General Accounting Office, *Early Childhood Education: What are the Costs of High-Quality Programs?* January 1990 (p. 17).

51 F. Fuentes, 1991 (p. 8).

52 B. Mainster, 1991 (p. 96).

53 S. Morse, 1992 (p. 56).

54 A. Henderson, J. Daft, and B. Gutmann, *A Summary of State Chapter 1 Migrant Education Program Participation and Achievement Information, 1989-90*, prepared for the Office of Policy and Planning, U.S. Department of Education by Westat, Inc., 1992 (p. 22, Table 2.1; p. 44, Table 2.12).

55 East Coast Migrant Head Start Project, *Migrant Head Start: The Unmet Need*, 1986 (p. 162).

56 G. O'Brien, phone conversation with National Commission on Migrant Education staff, August 12, 1992.

57 A. Henderson, et al., 1992 (p. B-15, Table B.9).

58 Ibid (p. 22, Table 2.1).

59 Ibid (p. 19).

60 Research-able, Inc., *Survey Research Findings: National Preschool Coordination Project*, prepared for the National Migrant Preschool Coordination Project, San Diego, California, September 1991.

61 B. Mainster, 1991 (pp. 69-70).

62 G. Richardson, "A Longitudinal Evaluation of Florida's Migrant Preschool Program," paper presented at the 1989 Conference of the Florida Education Research Association, November 16, 1989 (p. 5).

63 Ibid.

64 California State Department of Education, *Students in California Migrant Education Programs*, July 1990 (p. 6)..

Chapter 4
Migrant Children with Disablities

1 Interstate Migrant Education Council, *National Policy Workshop on Special Education Needs of Migrant Handicapped Students: Proceedings Report*, San Antonio, Texas, August 16-18, 1984 (pp. 11-12).

2 The term Special Education indicates specially designed instruction, at no cost to the parent, to meet the unique needs of a handicapped child, including instruction conducted in the classroom, in the home, in hospitals and institutions, and in other settings; and instruction in physical education, (P.L. 101-476).

3 For a complete review of all acts which cover individuals with disabilities, see: National Information Center for Children and Youth with Disabilities, *News Digest*, Vol.1, No.1, 1991.

4 Programs such as the Education of the Handicapped Act, renamed the Individuals with Disabilities Education Act (P.L. 101-476), provides comprehensive, Special Education services for infants, toddlers, preschoolers, children and youth. As a result of this law, any states which receive these federal funds must ensure that all children, regardless of the severity of their disability, will receive a free appropriate public education at public expense and under public supervision and direction. States must also demonstrate that children with disabilities are: assessed and evaluated in a non-biased manner (preferably using multiple measures); given an Individualized Education Program (IEP) or an Individualized Family Services Plan (IFSP) which specifically prescribe the unique services that they need; and, educated, to the maximum extent possible, in a regular classroom with children who do not have disabilities (i.e., the least restrictive environment).

5 34 CFR 300, Sections: 300.4; 300.346; 300.500-300.514; 300.532; and 300.550.

6 For a complete discussion of these provisions, see: R. Figueroa, S. Fradd, and V. Correa, "Bilingual Special Education and This Special Issue," *Exceptional Children*, Vol.56, No.2, The Council for Exceptional Children, 1989 (p. 175).

7 R. Figueroa, *The Education of Handicapped Migrant Students: A Preliminary Study of Current Practices and Policies*, prepared for the National Commission on Migrant Education, Division of Education, University of California at Davis, November 1, 1991; G. O'Brien, written testimony before the National Commission on Migrant Education, Buffalo, New York, April 29, 1991 (p. 4).

8 U.S. Department of Education, *To Assure The Free Appropriate Public Education Of All Children With Disabilities: Thirteenth Annual Report to Congress on the Implementation of The Individuals with Disabilities Education Act*, 1991 (pp. 3, A-33).

9 In the next report to Congress on the status of children with disabilities, however, there will be a separate section on migrant children.

10 Research Triangle Institute, *Volume I*, 1992 (p. A-67, Exhibit A.35).

11 According to the Commission's analysis of 1989-90 MEP State Performance Reports submitted to the U.S. Department of Education, the District of Columbia, Kansas, South Carolina, and Tennessee did not provide information on the number of participants. Texas and Washington did not provide the information either, but stated that such information would become available beginning the 1990-91 school year.

12 U.S. Department of Education, *Thirteenth Annual Report to Congress*, 1991 (p. A-50).

13 R. Figueroa, *The Education of Handicapped Migrant Students*, 1991 (p. 25); G. Muniz, oral testimony before the National Commission on Migrant Education, Bethesda, Maryland, September 22, 1991 (pp. 102-103).

14 Research Triangle Institute, *Volume I*, 1992 (p. A-17, Exhibit A.9.b).

15 F. Fuentes, correspondence with the National Commission on Migrant Education, unpublished data, July 2, 1991; G. Muniz, written testimony before the National Commission on Migrant Education, Bethesda, Maryland, September 22, 1991 (p. 9).

16 N. Acosta, written testimony before the National Commission on Migrant Education, McAllen, Texas, December 3, 1990 (p. 3); R. Figueroa, *The Education of Handicapped Migrant Students*, 1991 (p. 5).

17 F. Rivara, "Farm Injuries to Children in the United States," *Migrant Clinicians Network*, May-June 1990.

18 U.S. General Accounting Office, *Hired Farmworkers: Health and Well-Being at Risk*, February 1992 (p. 13).

19 B. Walsh, written testimony before the National Commission on Migrant Education, McAllen, Texas, December 3, 1990 (p. 11).

20 D. Velardi, written testimony before the National Commission on Migrant Education, McAllen, Texas, December 3, 1990 (p. 3).

21 A. Dever, "Migrant Health Status: Profile of a Population with Complex Health Problems," *Migrant Clinicians Network Monograph Series*, Austin, Texas, 1991; Also see: A. Dever, oral testimony before the National Commission on Migrant Education, Buffalo, New York, April 29, 1991 (pp. 243-250).

22 For a discussion of health problems and

how they may affect children's learning potential, see: L. Newman and S. Buka, *Every Child a Learner: Reducing Risks of Learning Impairment During Pregnancy and Infancy*, Education Commission of the States, Denver, Colorado, 1990.

23 N. Ruiz, R. Figueroa, R. Rueda, and C. Beaumont, *History and Status of Bilingual Special Education for Hispanic Handicapped Students*, California State Department of Education, 1991 (p. 3).

24 C. Coballes-Vega and S. Salend, "Guidelines for Assessing Migrant Handicapped Students," *Diagnostique*, Vol.13, 1988 (p. 67).

J. Cummins, "A Theoretical Framework for Bilingual Special Education," *Exceptional Children*, Vol.56, No.2, The Council for Exceptional Children, 1989 (pp. 111-119).

R. Figueroa, "Psychological Testing of Linguistic-Minority Students: Knowledge Gaps and Regulations," *Exceptional Children*, Vol.56, No.2, The Council for Exceptional Children, 1989 (pp. 147-48).

For example, simply translating an English assessment examination into Spanish without validating its comparability would yield misleading results. Likewise, the quality of interpreters used to translate during oral diagnosis can also yield questionable results if the interpreter is not properly trained. Tests developed in Mexico are not always appropriate because they are designed for monolingual Spanish-speaking children whereas some MEP children may have a certain level of English proficiency. Additionally, tests designed primarily for English-speaking children may not be culturally appropriate for some Hispanic children.

25 R. Figueroa, 1989 (p. 148); R. Rueda, "Defining Mild Disabilities with Language-Minority Students," *Exceptional Children*, Vol.56, No.2, The Council for Exceptional Children, 1989 (p. 122).

26 G. Muniz, written testimony, 1991 (p. 4).

27 Ibid (pp. 5-6).

28 The referral process begins when a teacher notices that a student is experiencing difficulties in the classroom. The teacher must first document interventions attempted in the classroom. Then the teacher discusses the referral with the principal who must approve it and forward it to the district's evaluation team. If an evaluation is warranted, the team contacts the parent, explains the procedure, and requests that the parent authorize the testing. A family history is taken, the child is tested, and a conference is held with the parent to discuss the test results. If intervention is recommended by the team and approved by the parent, the team and the parent create an education plan which will direct the intervention received by the child.

29 See for example: R. Figueroa, *The Education of Handicapped Migrant Students*, 1991 (p. 10); *Descriptive Study of the Chapter 1 Migrant Education Program. Volume II: Summary Reports of Intensive Case Studies*, prepared for the U.S. Department of Education by Research Triangle Institute, Research Triangle Park, North Carolina, January 1992 (p. 67).

30 For example, a Florida study found that in one school district, 13.2 percent of formerly migratory children were identified with disabilities, whereas only 2 percent of currently migratory children were so identified. Data presented at the National Migrant Education Conference, San Antonio, Texas, April 30-May 3, 1990; Also see: R. Figueroa, *The Education of Handicapped Migrant Students*, 1991 (pp. 5, 25-26); S. Salend, written testimony before the National Commission on Migrant Education, Bethesda, Maryland, September 22, 1991 (p. 1).

31 Research Triangle Institute, *Volume I*, 1992 (p. A-17, Exhibit A.9.a).

32 R. Rueda, 1989 (pp. 121-122); R. Guerra, oral testimony before the National Commission on Migrant Education, McAllen, Texas, December 3-4, 1990 (pp. 49-50); J. Scott, oral testimony before the National Commission on Migrant Education, Buffalo, New York, April 29, 1991 (p. 382).

33 R. Figueroa, 1989 (pp.145-150); G. Muniz, written testimony, 1991 (p. 3).

34 G. Muniz, written testimony, 1991 (pp. 1-4); R. Figueroa, *The Education of Handicapped Migrant Students*, 1991 (pp. 16, 20); S. Salend, 1991 (p. 9-10).

35 Such a program exists at the College of New Paltz, New York. For further information, contact Dr. Spencer Salend.

36 R. Figueroa, *The Education of Handicapped Migrant Students*, 1991 (p. 16).

37 W. Rollason, oral testimony before the National Commission on Migrant Education, Bethesda, Maryland, September 22, 1991 (p. 108).

38 Ibid.

39 Ibid.

40 M. Gomez-Palacio (former National Director of Special Education in Mexico) of the University of the Americas, Mexico City, Mexico, phone interview, June 26, 1992.

41 R. Guerra, 1990 (pp. 49-50).

42 Research Triangle Institute, *Volume I*, 1992 (p. A-17, Exhibit A.9.a). RTI found that the percentage of summer-term MEP children eligible for Special Education services was 2.4 for currently migratory children and 4.3 for formerly migratory children, compared to the 7.1 percent of currently migratory children and 7.3 of formerly migratory children who are identified with

disabilities during the regular school year.

43 R. Guerra, 1990 (p. 50).

44 R. Figueroa, *The Education of Handicapped Migrant Students*, 1991 (pp. 19-20).

45 Ibid (p. 9).

46 Ibid (p. 10); Research Triangle Institute, Volume II, 1992 (pp. 173, 179).

47 G. Muniz, written testimony, 1991 (p. 4).

48 Research Triangle Institute, Volume II, 1992 (p. 173).

49 L. Newman, *Hispanic Secondary School Students With Disabilities: How Are They Doing?*, SRI International, April 1992 (p. 17, Figure 5).

50 G. Muniz, written testimony, 1991 (p. 2).

51 S. Salend, 1991 (p. 4).

52 R. Figueroa, oral testimony before the National Commission on Migrant Education, Bethesda, Maryland, September 22, 1991 (p. 84).

53 G. Muniz, written testimony, 1991 (p. 5).

54 F. Martinez, written testimony before the National Commission on Migrant Education, McAllen, Texas, December 3-4, 1990 (p. 3).

Chapter 4
Gifted and Talented Migrant Children

1 It is commonly accepted that "gifted" refers to academic excellence and that "talented" generally refers to excellence in athletics and in the performing and creative arts; however, this report primarily discusses education of "gifted" and not education of the "talented."

2 J. VanTassel-Baska, J. Patton, and D. Prillaman, "Disadvantaged Gifted Learners At-Risk for Educational Attention," *Focus on Exceptional Children*, Vol.22, No.3, November 1989 (p. 1).

3 Some states do voluntarily report such data in their MEP state applications and performance reports, but it is not required.

4 1990 data reported. Council of State Directors of Programs for the Gifted, *State of the States*, Augusta, Maine, 1991 (p. 77).

5 Because of the size and nature of the sample, the standard error is large. Therefore, these figures should be considered with some level of caution. Furthermore, given the variability in criteria used to determine "giftedness" across states and schools, data across sites may not be comparable. *Descriptive Study of the Chapter 1 Migrant Education Program, Volume I: Study Findings and Conclusions*, prepared for the U.S. Department of Education by Research Triangle Institute, Research Triangle Park, North Carolina, January

1992 (p. 12).

6 J. VanTassel-Baska, J. Patton, and D. Prillaman, *Gifted Youth At-Risk: A Report of a National Study*, Council for Exceptional Children, Washington, D.C., 1991 (pp. 3-4).

7 J. Hamilton, "The Gifted Migrant Child: An Introduction," *Roeper Review*, Vol.6, No.3, 1984 (pp. 146-147).

8 J. VanTassel-Baska, et al., Gifted Youth at Risk, 1991 (pp. 12-16).

9 Ibid (pp. 12-14).

10 Ibid (p. 14).

11 J. VanTassel-Baska, et al., "Disadvantaged Gifted Learners," 1989 (p. 7).

12 L. Espinoza, "Report to the Commission: A Personal Perspective," submitted to the National Commission on Migrant Education, 1991 (p. 2).

13 Ibid (p. 2).

14 W. Durden, *Advancement of Talent Among Precollegiate Migrant Children and Youth*, Center for Talented Youth, Johns Hopkins University, November 1991 (p. 16).

15 S. Hatton, oral testimony before the National Commission on Migrant Education, McAllen, Texas, December 3, 1990 (p. 143).

16 W. Durden, *Advancement of Talent*, 1991 (p. iv).

17 I. Villalon, written testimony before the National Commission on Migrant Education, McAllen, Texas, December 3, 1990 (p. 1).

18 Ibid.

19 J. Hamilton, 1984 (p. 147).

20 W. Durden, Advancement of Talent, 1991 (p. 39).

21 D. Viadero, "Budget Cutters, School Reformers Taking Aim at Gifted Education," *Education Week*, Vol.11, No.26, April 18, 1992.

22 Council of State Directors of Programs for the Gifted, 1991 (p. 82).

23 P. O'Connell-Ross, U.S. Department of Education, phone interview, July 23, 1992.

24 For a discussion about this option, see: W. Durden, *Advancement of Talent*, 1991 (p. 43).

25 Ibid (pp. v, 38); A. Rodriguez, written testimony before the National Commission on Migrant Education, McAllen, Texas, December 4, 1990 (p. 72).

26 J. VanTassel-Baska, et al., *Gifted Youth at Risk*, 1991 (pp. 24-25).

27 W. Durden, *Advancement of Talent*, 1991 (pp. ix, 45).

28 S. Reis and J. Purcell, "An Analysis of the Impact of Curriculum Compacting on Classroom Practices," *Journal for the Education of the Gifted*, December 1991.

29 W. Durden, *Advancement of Talent*, 1991 (pp. 44-45).

30 S. Reis and J. Purcell, 1991; K. Westberg, et al., *The Classroom Practices Study*, National

Research Center on the Gifted and Talented, prepared for the U.S. Department of Education, 1992.

Chapter 4
Migrant Students
At-Risk

1 National Education Goals Panel, *The National Education Goals Panel Report: Building a Nation of Learners*, 1991 (p. 41).

2 "Child Poverty and Education," *Education Week*, May 20, 1992 (p. 3).

3 R. Lynch, oral testimony before the National Commission on Migrant Education, Bethesda, Maryland, September 23, 1991 (p. 190).

4 S. Morse, *Focus: Dropouts, An Interstate Forum on the Migrant Dropout*, prepared by Interstate Migrant Secondary Team Project, December 1986 (p. 5); National Association of State Directors of Migrant Education (NASDME), *Rethinking Migrant Education: A Response to the National Education Goals*, Migrant Education Task Force, March 1992 (p. 4).

5 M. Casserly, "Preliminary Technical Analysis of Dropout Statistics in Selected Great City Schools," The Great Council of Great City Schools, Washington, D.C., 1986 (pp. 18, 19).

The Council of Great City Schools found that there are six definitions of a dropout used throughout the United States. Each yields a different dropout rate.

■ Any person that leaves school prior to graduation or completion of a formal high school or equivalent education and who does not enter another program within 45 days.

■ Any entering freshman who does not graduate with his/her class.

■ Any senior high school student who leaves school before graduating because he/she is over-age, working full time, institutionalized, in the military, pregnant, married, excluded or not localized.

■ Any student who stops attending high school and has no intention of re-enrolling.

■ Any student who leaves school before completion of the twelfth grade for any reason other than transferring to another school district.

■ Any student registered in the ninth through twelfth grade or at a regular high school who leaves school and does not return or graduate between October 1 and June 30.

6 L. Selmser, conference call with the National Commission on Migrant Education, May 18, 1992 (p. 106).

7 P. Kaufman and M. Frase, *Dropout Rates in the United States: 1989*, National Center for Education Statistics, 1989 (Executive Summary).

8 *Descriptive Study of the Chapter 1 Migrant Education Program*, prepared for the U.S. Department of Education by Research Triangle Institute, Research Triangle Park, North Carolina, January 1992 (p. 8).

9 National Education Goals Panel, 1991 (p. 42).

10 Ibid.

11 See Chapter One of this report for a more complete discussion of the increased numbers of Hispanic immigrants in the migrant workforce.

12 *Migrant Attrition Project: Abstract of Findings*, Migrant Attrition Project, New York State University at Oneonta, August 1987 (p. 1).

13 *Evaluation of the Impact of ESEA Title I Programs for Migrant Children of Migrant Agricultural Workers*, Exotech Systems, Washington, D.C., 1975.

14 NASDME, 1992 (p. 12).

15 D. Helge, *Rural At-Risk Students— Directions for Policy and Intervention*, American Council on Rural Special Education (ACRES), Western Washington University, Bellingham, Washington, 1990 (p. 7).

16 D. Helge, oral testimony before the National Commission on Migrant Education, Bethesda, Maryland, September 23, 1991 (pp. 200-201).

17 Ibid.

18 For further discussion, see: R. Levy, *Grade Retention and Promotion: Considerations for Dropout Prevention*, Eastern Stream Center on Resources and Training (ESCORT), New York State University at Oneonta, 1989.

19 M. Mena, oral testimony before the National Commission on Migrant Education, McAllen, Texas, December 4, 1990 (pp. 92-93); M. Perez, oral testimony before the National Commission on Migrant Education, McAllen, Texas, December 4, 1990 (pp. 81-82).

20 Interstate Migrant Education Council (IMEC), *Migrant Education: A Consolidated View*, Denver, Colorado, July 1987 (pp. 6-7).

21 NASDME, 1992 (p. 15).

22 R. Guerra, oral testimony before the National Commission on Migrant Education, McAllen, Texas, December 3, 1990 (pp. 47-48).

23 F. Johnson, et al., *Migrant Students at the Secondary Level: Issues and Opportunities for Change*, Educational Resources Information Center (ERIC), Clearinghouse on Rural Education and Small Schools (CRESS), New Mexico State University, 1986 (pp. 19, 30).

24 Proud About Success Stories, Interstate PASS Committee on Migrant Education, 1990-91 (profiles of outstanding students in the Portable Assisted Study Sequence) (p. 22).

25 Information describing the PASS program

was taken from: B. Pessin, written testimony before the National Commission on Migrant Education, Bethesda, Maryland, September 23, 1991 (pp. 1-11).

26 In 1981 Arkansas and Washington started using PASS. By 1988 an additional 24 states were also using the program:

> Alaska, Arizona, California, Colorado, Florida, Georgia, Idaho, Illinois, Indiana, Maryland, Michigan, Minnesota, Montana, Nebraska, New Jersey, New York, Ohio, Oklahoma, Oregon, Pennsylvania, S.Dakota, Texas, Utah, and Wisconsin

27 Migrant Education Messages and Outlook, March/April 1992 (Vol. 10. No. 1 (p. 7).

28 B. Pessin, oral testimony before the National Commission on Migrant Education, Bethesda, Maryland, September 23, 1991 (pp. 219, 221).

29 E. Ogletree, *Status of Credit Transfer for Migrant Students in the United States*, Department of Curriculum and Instruction, Chicago State University, 1984 (p. 8).

30 Proud About Success Stories, 1990-91 (p. 24).

31 R. Lykes, briefing to the National Commission of Migrant Education.

32 R. Lyke, *CRS Issue Brief: High School Dropouts*, Education and Public Welfare Division, Congressional Research Service, Washington, D.C., October 1988 (p. 10).

33 A. Salerno and M. Fink, *Dropout Retrieval Report: Thoughts on Dropout Prevention and Retrieval*, Board of Cooperative Educational Services (BOCES), Geneseo, New York, 1989 (p. 1).

34 B. Pessin, oral testimony, 1991 (pp. 215, 225).

35 J. Prewit-Diaz, oral testimony before the National Commission on Migrant Education, Gettysburg, Pennsylvania, August 7, 1990 (p. 172).

36 Ibid.

37 R. Lynch, 1991 (p. 193).

38 R. Lynch, written testimony before the National Commission on Migrant Education, Bethesda, Maryland, September 23, 1991 (p. 5).

39 L. Velazquez, written testimony before the National Commission on Migrant Education, Bethesda, Maryland, September 23, 1991 (p. 1).

40 Honorable C. Pell, correspondence with the National Commission on Migrant Education staff, September 23, 1991.

41 The following table was taken from: IMEC, testimony in conjunction with HEP/CAMP Association and NASDME to the Subcommittee on Postsecondary Education, April 8, 1991 (p. 2):

Numbers of HEPs and Population Served by Them by Fiscal Year

FY	Numbers of HEPs	Numbers Numbers of Students Served
1984	20	2,800
1985	22	2,900
1986	20	2,675
1987	19	2,588
1988	22	3,226
1989	23	3,195
1990	23	3,090
1991	23	3,099

42 M. Kutner and L. Fink, *Descriptive Review of Data on the High School Equivalency Program (HEP) and the College Assistance Migrant Project (CAMP)*, Pelavin Associates, Washington, D.C., 1989.

43 H. Rincones, oral testimony before the National Commission on Migrant Education, McAllen, Texas, December 4, 1990 (p. 95).

44 G. Martinez, oral testimony before the National Commission on Migrant Education, Gettysburg, Pennsylvania, August 7, 1990 (p. 240).

45 G. Riley, *HEP/CAMP National Evaluation Project: A Comprehensive Analysis of the Impact of HEP/CAMP Program Participation*, California State University, Fresno, 1985 (p. 8).

46 J. Jensen, oral testimony before the National Commission on Migrant Education, Bethesda, Maryland, September 23, 1991 (p. 277).

47 L. Valezquez, "HEP Grad Becomes Community Leader," MEMO (Vol. 10, No. 2) May/June 1992 (p. 24).

48 S. Marks-Fife, written testimony before the National Commission on Migrant Education, Bethesda, Maryland, September 23, 1991 (p. 2).

49 R. Lyke, *The College Assistance Migrant Program and the Migrant High School Equivalency Program*, Education and Public Welfare Division, Congressional Research Service, Washington, D.C., June 1986 (p. 9). The cost per student is $40 which excludes institutional overhead charges.

50 Interstate Migrant Education Council, testimony in conjunction with HEP/CAMP Association and NASDME to the Subcommittee on Postsecondary Education, April 8, 1991 (p. 2).

51 "As the National Evaluation Project did not have a representative sample of all recent CAMP and HEP students, the data included... should be viewed as indicative of their characteristics, but not necessarily accurate estimates of them." R. Lyke, The College Assistance Migrant Program, 1986 (p. 5).

Chapter 5

1 M. Ruiz Scaperlanda, "CAMP: 20 years of changing lives," *Catholic Spirit Diocese of Austin*, Vol.10, No.5, May 1992.

2 W. Durden, *Advancement of Talent Among Precollegiate Migrant Children and Youth*, Center for Talented Youth, Johns Hopkins University, Baltimore, Maryland, November 1991 (p. iv).

3 L. Espinoza, CAMP Student (Intern to the Commission) Paper, 1991.

4 Interstate Migrant Education Council (IMEC), testimony in conjunction with HEP/CAMP Association and NASDME to the Subcommittee on Postsecondary Education, April 8, 1991 (p. i).

5 G. Riley, *HEP/CAMP National Evaluation Project: A Comprehensive Analysis of the Impact of HEP/CAMP Program Participation*, California State University, Fresno, 1985 (pp. 9-11).

6 See Chapter Four of this report for a detailed discussion of the High School Equivalency Program.

7 National Center for Education Statistics, U.S. Department of Education, *Digest of Education Statistics*, 1990 (Tables 34 and 281).

8 IMEC testimony before the U.S. Congress Sub-Committee on Postsecondary Education, 1991 (p. 2).

9 J. Jensen, written testimony before the National Commission on Migrant Education, Washington, D.C., September 23, 1991 (pp. 2-3).

10 Ibid (p. 5).

11 G. Riley, 1985 (pp. 75-77).

12 Migrant Education Messages and Outlook (MEMO), "Cal CAMPers Adopt Highway," Vol.10, No.2, May-June 1992 (p. 24).

13 M. Kutner and L. Fink, *Descriptive Review of Data on the High School Equivalency Program (HEP) and the College Assistance Migrant Program (CAMP)*, Pelavin Associates, Washington, D.C., 1989.

14 P. Hayes, communications with National Commission on Migrant Education staff, July 16, 1992.

15 J. Jensen, 1991 (pp. 13-14).

16 Ibid (p. 14).

17 R. Lyke, *The College Assistance Migrant Program and The Migrant High School Equivalency Program*, Education and Public Welfare Division, Congressional Research Service, Washington, D.C., June 1986 (p. 9).

18 IMEC testimony, 1991 (p. 2).

19 G. Riley, 1985 (p. 70).

20 J. Houghton, *The Efficacy of Migrant Higher Education: A Study of Graduates of CAMP at St. Edward's University*, HEP/CAMP Technical Assistance Conference for Central Stream, St. Edwards University, October 7 and 8, 1991 (p. 19).

21 G. Riley, 1985 (p. 77).

22 IMEC testimony, 1991 (p. 1).

23 G. Riley, 1985 (pp. 9-10).

24 J. VanTassel-Baska, J. Patton and D. Prillaman, *Gifted Youth At Risk: A Report of a National Study*, The Council for Exceptional Children, November 1991 (p. 21).

25 J. Hamilton, "The Gifted Migrant Child: An Introduction," *Roeper Review*, Vol.6, No.3, 1984 (pp. 146-147).

26 G. Riley, 1985 (p. 73).

27 Ibid.

28 Ibid.

29 Ibid (p. 72).

30 Ibid.

31 The following factors were found in successful CAMPs as identified by the HEP/CAMP National Evaluation Project:

■ Students who first attended a campus-based (or agency-based-school with strong links to an IHE) HEP and then CAMP, surpassed all other students in achieving long-term objectives with respect to education, employment, and income.

■ The programs with the highest numbers of students meeting program goals had clearly stated, measurable outcomes that had been communicated to and understood by both staff and students.

■ Programs that had operated continuously for more than 3 but less than 12 years were more effective as evidenced by student performance data as well as assessment of objectives and procedures. Programs in operation more than 12 years were only marginally more effective than newly-funded programs.

32 M. Kutner and L. Fink, 1989.

33 Ibid.

34 G. Riley, 1985 (p. 11).

35 J. Jensen, 1991 (p. 6).

36 G. Riley, 1985 (p. 11).

37 MEMO, "CAMPers Share in Scholarships," Vol.10, No.1, March-April 1992 (p. 24).

38 G. Riley, 1985 (p. 68).

39 M. Ruiz Scaperlanda, 1992.

40 G. Riley, 1985 (p. 57).

41 J. Jensen, 1991 (p. 4).

42 M. Ruiz Scaperlanda, 1992.

43 G. Riley, 1985 (p. 57).

44 M. Kutner and L. Fink, 1989.

45 IMEC testimony, 1991 (p. 4); G. Martinez, oral testimony before the National Commission on Migrant Education, Gettysburg, Pennsylvania, August 7, 1990 (pp. 242-243).

46 M. Kutner and L. Fink, 1989.

47 In 1987 a total of 2,588 students were served in 19 HEPs. Correspondence between John Perry (IMEC), John Jensen (HEP/CAMP Association) and Ronnie Glover (NASDME) and the Honorable William D. Ford, April 8, 1991.

48 J. Jensen, 1991 (p. 7).

49 R. Martino, "Migrant Group Turns Attention to College Participation," State

Education Leader, fall 1990.

50 J. Cabedo, oral testimony before the National Commission on Migrant Education, Watsonville, California, July 16, 1991 (p. 179).

51 IMEC testimony, 1991 (p. 4).

Chapter 6

1 Elementary and Secondary Education Act of 1966. See Chapter 1 of this report.

2 National Commission on Children, *Beyond Rhetoric: A New American Agenda for Children and Families*, 1991 (pp. 311-322).

3 Office of Migrant Education, U.S. Department of Education, *Directory of Services: Federal Agencies and Non-Federal Organizations Providing Services to Migrant and Seasonal Farmworkers and Their Families*, March 1991.

4 D. Martin and P. Martin, *Coordination of Migrant and Seasonal Farmworker Service Programs*, Administrative Conference of the United States, Washington, D.C., April 1992 (pp. 33-36).

5 All written testimony before the National Commission on Migrant Education, Buffalo, New York, April 29, 1991.

6 D. Martin and P. Martin, 1992 (pp. 52-53).

7 A review of FY 1991 MEP state applications reveals that there are at least 12 such state level committees in which state MEP providers participate. Also see: D. Martin and P. Martin, 1992 (pp. 30-32).

8 D. Martin and P. Martin, 1992 (p. 54).

9 B. Mainster, oral testimony before the National Commission on Migrant Education, Fort Myers, Florida, December 15, 1991 (p. 86).

10 J. Kimbrough and P. Hill, "Problems of Implementing Multiple Categorical Education Programs," September 1983 (pp. 20, 32).

11 L. Marsh, oral testimony before the National Commission on Migrant Education, Fort Myers, Florida, December 15, 1991 (pp. 65-66).

12 Research Triangle Institute, Volume I, 1992 (p. 16).

13 J. Kimbrough and P. Hill, 1983 (pp. 27-28).

14 M. Goertz, A. Milne and M. Gaffney, *School Districts' Allocation of Chapter 1 Resources*, prepared for the U.S. Department of Education by American Educational Research Association, Washington, D.C., April 1987; E. W. Strang and E. Carlson, *Providing Chapter 1 Services to Limited English-Proficient Students*, prepared for the U.S. Department of Education by Westat, Inc., 1991.

15 E. W. Strang and E. Carlson, 1991 (p. 55); R. de la Rosa, communication with National Commission on Migrant Education staff, January 31, 1992; F. Corrigan, communication with National Commission on Migrant Education staff,

March 4, 1992.

16 *U.S. Code Congressional Administrative News*, Vol.2 (p. 2739).

17 Pennsylvania MEP State Application FY 1991 (p. 3).

18 Massachusetts MEP State Application FY 1991 (p. 21).

19 Florida MEP State Application FY 1991 (p. 16).

20 R. de la Rosa, 1992; F. Corrigan, 1992.

21 Research Triangle Institute, *Volume I*, 1992 (pp. 17-18); E. W. Strang and E. Carlson, 1991 (pp. 53-54).

22 Research Triangle Institute, *Volume I*, 1992 (p. A-71, Exhibit A.37).

23 Research Triangle Institute, *Volume I*, 1992 (pp. 16-18).

24 U.S. General Accounting Office, *Immigrant Education: Information on the Emergency Immigration Education Act Program*, March 1991. Children who are eligible to participate in the program must have immigrated to this country within the last 3 years and must reside in a school district in which 500 children, or 3 percent of the total school participation, meets this eligibility criteria.

25 Research Triangle Institute, *Volume I*, 1992 (p. 60, Exhibit III.3; p. 61, Exhibit III.4).

26 Stafford-Hawkins Amendments of 1988, Section 1202(a)(2).

27 Research Triangle Institute, *Volume I*, 1992 (pp. 25-26).

28 P. Perez, oral testimony before the National Commission on Migrant Education, McAllen, Texas, December 3, 1990 (pp. 97-98).

29 Research Triangle Institute, *Volume I*, 1992 (pp. 13-16).

30 R. Zamora, oral testimony before the National Commission on Migrant Education, McAllen, Texas, December 3, 1990 (p. 117).

31 M. Berry, written testimony before the National Commission on Migrant Education, Fort Myers, Florida, December 15 (pp. 3-4).

32 T. Tobin, oral testimony before the National Commission on Migrant Education, McAllen, Texas, December 3, 1990 (p. 30).

33 A. Guzman, oral testimony before the National Commission on Migrant Education, McAllen, Texas, December 3, 1990 (p. 10).

34 A. Guzman, 1990 (p. 11); R. Luna, oral testimony before the National Commission on Migrant Education, McAllen, Texas, December 4, 1990 (p. 13).

35 E. Hernandez, oral testimony before the National Commission on Migrant Education, Watsonville, California, July 16, 1991 (p. 193).

36 H. Gloria, oral testimony before the National Commission on Migrant Education, McAllen, Texas, December 4, 1990 (p. 100).

37 J. Duran, correspondence with L.

Chavez, National Commission on Migrant Education, December 16, 1991.

38 For a complete statement, see: Education and Human Services Consortium, "New Partnerships: Education's Stake in the Family Support Act of 1988," Washington, D.C., 1990 (p. 13).

39 U.S. Department of Labor, unpublished National Agricultural Workforce Survey (NAWS) data, 1991.

40 J. Prewitt-Diaz, R. Trotter and V. Rivera, *The Effects of Migration on Children: An Ethnographic Study*, Centro de Estudios Sobre La Migracion, Pennsylvania State University, 1990 (p. 59).

41 J. Castillo, oral testimony before the National Commission on Migrant Education, McAllen, Texas, December 3, 1990 (p. 24).

42 J. Prewitt-Diaz, et al., 1990 (p. 59); J. Castillo, 1990 (p. 24); F. Fuentes, written testimony before the National Commission on Migrant Education, Buffalo, New York, April 29, 1991 (p. 7); D. Helge, written testimony before the National Commission on Migrant Education, Bethesda, Maryland, September 23, 1991 (pp. 2-3).

43 J. Castillo, 1990 (pp. 25-26); F. Fuentes, 1991 (p. 10).

44 D. Runyan and P. Morgan, *Nutrition and Migrant Health: Trends in Nutritional Services at Migrant Health Centers*, Georgetown University Child Development Center, 1987 (p. 18).

45 Oral testimonies of P. Gomez, N. Acosta, B. Walsh before the National Commission on Migrant Education, McAllen, Texas, December 3, 1990; N. Kowalkowski, oral testimony before the National Commission on Migrant Education, Watsonville, California, July 16, 1991 (p. 31).

46 National Association of Community Health Centers, *Medicaid and Migrant Farmworker Families: Analysis of Barriers and Recommendations for Change*, 1991; J. Castillo, 1990 (p. 25).

47 J. Shotland, D. Loonin and E. Haas, *Full Fields, Empty Cupboards: The Nutritional Status of Migrant Farmworkers in America*, Public Voice for Food and Health Policy, April 1989 (p. 81). A study on Food Stamp participation, for example, cited that many migrants are unaware of their eligibility for such benefits.

48 R. Mines, communication with the National Commission on Migrant Education staff, January 29, 1992.

49 B. Arnow, written testimony before the National Commission on Migrant Education, Buffalo, New York, April 29, 1991 (p. 2).

50 Ibid.

51 D. Martin and P. Martin, 1992.

52 S. Reig, written testimony before the National Commission on Migrant Education,

Buffalo, New York, April 29, 1991 (p. 9).

53 D. Martin and P. Martin, 1992 (p. 13).

54 Missouri MEP State Application FY 1991; North Dakota MEP State Application FY 1991.

55 B. Arnow, 1991 (pp. 3-4).

56 F. Fuentes, 1991 (pp. 12-15).

57 P. Coble, oral testimony before the National Commission on Migrant Education, Gettysburg, Pennsylvania, August 7, 1990 (pp. 1-4); Written testimonies of F. Fuentes, G. O'Brien, B. Arnow and D. Whittington before the National Commission on Migrant Education, Buffalo, New York, April 29, 1991.

58 D. Martin & P. Martin, ACUS, Coordination of Migrant Seasonal Farmworker Service Programs, April 1992 (p. iv).

Chapter 7

1 R. Levy, oral testimony before the National Commission on Migrant Education, Buffalo, New York, April 29, 1991 (p. 291).

2 P. Burton, R. Coley and M. Goertz, *The State of Inequality*, Policy Information Center, Educational Testing Service, Princeton, New Jersey, 1992 (p. 15). The Federal share for elementary secondary education rose until about 1980 where it reached a high of about 10 percent. Currently, it is estimated to be about 6 percent.

3 The estimates for migrant children were based upon the U.S. Department of Labor statistics on the numbers of agricultural workers. Estimates for children were calculated at .75 per worker.

4 Definition of an FTE: Assuming that a child who did not migrate resides in a state 360 days a year, MSRTS statistics are used to compile the amount of time each MEP child spends in a state over a calendar year. By adding the number of days each MEP child resides in a state, a full-time equivalency (FTE) for groups of MEP children can be calculated. These FTEs are computed by state as well as the nation as a whole to determine funding allocations until 1981. At that time, Federal funding no longer used the FTE for determining appropriations even though distribution of dollars to states continues to be based upon FTE.

5 Omnibus Budget Reconciliation Act of 1981, P.L. 97-35.

6 See Table 7.1 for actual statistics. The greatest increase was 328 percent after the first year of funding. Since this represented the difference between an initial program authorization and appropriations that were consistently made over the term of the program, this percentage was seen as not truly reflecting the pattern of changes in the national appropriation.

7 Constant dollars were calculated based upon the price index for the purchase of government goods and services. The index is anchored to a base year of 1982. These price indices produce estimates of dollar amount and change and should not be construed as actual dollars.

8 M. Colon and M. Portuondo, *Secondary Analysis of Selected Data on Migrant Education Programs, Fiscal Year 1990*, Department of Curriculum and Instruction, College of Education, Pennsylvania State University, March 1992 (p. 27).

9 Each state is allocated one percent of their total Chapter 1 monies for use in administration of both the LEA basic grant programs as well as the state administered programs.

10 C. Santa Ana, written testimony before the National Commission on Migrant Education, Bethesda, Maryland, February 14-15, 1991 (p. 4).

11 *Descriptive Study of the Chapter 1 Migrant Education Program, Volume I: Study Findings and Conclusions*, prepared for the U.S. Department of Education by Research Triangle Institute, Research Triangle Park, North Carolina, January 1992 (p. 122, Exhibit VI.I).

12 Ibid (p. A-123, Exhibit A.68).

13 Ibid.

14 R. Levy, 1991 (p. 291).

15 M. Goertz, A. Milne and M. Gaffney, *School Districts' Allocation of Chapter 1 Resources*, prepared for the U.S. Department of Education by American Educational Research Association, Washington, D.C., April 1987 (p. 189). This national study found that, except for one district, all sites responded to fiscal reductions by dropping support services, cutting instruction aides and reducing the number of students and/or schools served in order to maintain the intensity of their existing instruction program.

16 A. Henderson, J. Daft, and B. Gutmann, *A Summary of State Chapter 1 Migrant Education Program Participation and Achievement Information, 1989-90*, prepared for the Office of Policy and Planning, U.S. Department of Education by Westat, Inc., 1992 (pp. 20, 42).

17 Ibid (p. 34).

18 Research Triangle Institute, *Volume I*, 1992 (p. 126). Project costs per child were provided in *Volume II: Summary Report of Intensive Case Studies*.

Chapter 8

1 P. Barton and R. Coley, *America's Smallest School: The Family*, Policy Information Center, Educational Testing Service, Princeton, New Jersey, 1992 (p. 2).

2 G. Putka, "Some Schools Give Parents Crucial Roles in Educating Children," *Wall Street Journal*, December 30, 1991 (p. 45).

3 A. Salerno and M. Fink, *Home/School Partnerships: Migrant Parent Involvement Report*, prepared for the Office of Migrant Education, U.S. Department of Education by the Parental Resources for Involvement in Migrant Education Project, Geneseo, New York, 1992 (p. 1).

4 J. Soriano, Migrant and Bilingual Education Specialist, Delaware Department of Education, "Migrant Portraits, Migrant Choices," publication funded by the Migrant Education Interstate and Intrastate Coordination Program through the U.S. Department of Education.

5 N. Soriano, Migrant Education Instructional Specialist, "Migrant Portraits, Migrant Choices."

6 A. Salerno and M. Fink, *Home/School Partnerships*, 1992 (p. 2).

7 J. Prewitt-Diaz, *Factors That Affect the Achievement of Migrant Students* (Draft), Center for the Study of Migration, Division of Curriculum and Instruction, College of Education, Pennsylvania State University, August 1990 (pp. 38-40).

8 G. Putka, 1991 (p. 45A).

9 J. Prewitt-Diaz, *Factors*, 1990 (p. 47).

10 J. Prewitt Diaz, R. Trotter and V. Rivera, *The Effects of Migration on Children: An Ethnographic Study*, Division of Migrant Education, Pennsylvania Department of Education, 1989.

11 J. Prewitt-Diaz, *Factors*, 1990 (p. 46); Also see: J. Prewitt Diaz, oral testimony before the National Commission on Migrant Education, Gettysburg, Pennsylvania, August 7, 1990 (p. 170).

12 J. Prewitt-Diaz, *Factors*, 1990 (p. 47).

13 W. Rollason, letter to D. Garner, National Commission on Migrant Education, July 7, 1992; Also see: Fort Myers News-Press, July 14, 1991.

14 P. Barton and R. Coley, 1992 (p. 40).

15 A. Salerno and M. Fink, *Home/School Partnerships*, 1992 (p. 4).

16 Ibid (p. 2).

17 B. Lindner, *Drawing in the Family: Family Involvement in the Schools*, Education Commission of the States, Denver, Colorado, August 1988 (p. 5).

18 E. Clark and W. Ramsey, 1992 (p. 3).

19 W. Rollason, letter to D. Garner, National Commission on Migrant Education, July 7, 1992.

20 M. Velasquez, oral testimony before the National Commission on Migrant Education, Gettysburg, Pennsylvania, August 7, 1990 (p. 227).

21 A. Salerno and M. Fink, *Home/School Partnerships*, 1992 (p. 10).

22 J. Prewitt-Diaz, oral testimony, 1990 (pp.

188-189).

23 Migrant Education National Training Outreach (MENTOR), "The Family Support System: Education in its Broadest Context," *Harvesters*, Book 4, 1986 (pp. 10-11).

24 Statutory Requirements: Sections 1016 and 1202 (a)(4) of Chapter 1 of Title 1, ESEA; Regulatory Requirements: Sections 201.35 and 200.34 of the Chapter 1 LEA Program Regulations.

25 N. Pullum, written testimony before the National Commission on Migrant Education, Fort Myers, Florida, December 15, 1991 (p. 4).

26 E. Clark and W. Ramsey, 1992 (p. 5).

27 MENTOR, 1986 (p. 10).

28 M. Rivera, oral testimony before the National Commission on Migrant Education, Gettysburg, Pennsylvania, August 7, 1990 (pp. 225-226).

29 R. Cruz and V. Morales, oral testimony before the National Commission on Migrant Education, McAllen, Texas, December 4, 1990. (p. 30-35).

30 R. Cruz and V. Morales, *Project Even Start: Teaching Parents How To Teach Their Children at Home*, La Joya, Texas, June 1992 (pp. 1-3).

31 P. Poblete, *Home Tutorial Manual: A Guide To Set Up a Home Tutorial Program for Students Transitioning from Head Start into the Public Schools*, East Coast Migrant Head Start Project, Arlington, Virginia (pp. 1-34).

32 J. Epstein, "Paths to Partnership: What We Can Learn from Federal, State and District School Initiatives," *Phi Delta Kappan*, Vol.72, No.5, January 1991 (pp. 344-349).

33 C. Trevino, written testimony before the National Commission on Migrant Education, McAllen, Texas, December 4, 1990 (p. 11).

34 A. Salerno and M. Fink, *Home/School Partnerships*, 1992 (p. 7).

35 W. Rollason, letter to D. Garner, National Commission on Migrant Education, July 7, 1992.

36 A. Salerno and M. Fink, *Home/School Partnerships*, 1992 (p. 5).

37 Ibid (p. 9).

38 P. Perez, written testimony before the National Commission on Migrant Education, McAllen, Texas, December 3, 1990 (p. 5-6).

39 A. Salerno and M. Fink, *Home/School Partnerships*, 1992 (p. 6).

40 A. Salerno and M. Fink, *Promising Practices for Home/School Partnerships*, prepared for the Office of Migrant Education, U.S. Department of Education by the Parental Resources for Involvement in Migrant Education Project, Geneseo, New York, 1992 (p. 4).

41 Ibid (p. 19).

42 L. Ramirez, oral testimony before the National Commission on Migrant Education, McAllen, Texas, December 4, 1990 (p. 6).

43 Also see Chapter 4: Preschool.

44 L. Newman and S. Buka, *Every Child a Learner: Reducing Risks of Learning Impairment During Pregnancy and Infancy*, Education Commission of the States, Denver, Colorado, 1990.

45 B. Walsh, written testimony before the National Commission on Migrant Education, McAllen, Texas, December 3, 1990 (p. 10).

46 National Commission on Children, 1991 (p. 161). L. Sullivan, Secretary of the U.S. Department of Health and Human Services, testimony before the National Commission on Children, Washington, DC, July 2, 1990.

47 D. Garner, correspondence with National Commission on Migrant Education staff, July 16, 1992 (p. 88).

Additional Views of the Commissioners

 DIVERSIFIED RESEARCH, INC.
16 NORTH ASTOR STREET
IRVINGTON, N.Y. 10533
(914) 591-5440

August 27, 1992

Hon. Linda Chavez
Chairman
National Commission on Migrant Education
8120 Woodmont Avenue
Bethesda, MD 20814

Dear Madam Chairman:

You have provided the National Commission on Migrant Education with outstanding leadership for the past three years. I doubt whether we twelve, strong-minded, independent thinking individuals, with such diverse backgrounds and perspectives, could possibly have produced a consensus report without your guidance and direction.

It has been a rare privilege to serve on this commission. Even though ideological differences and conflicting opinions were manifest, we were always able to discuss issues honestly, openly and with respect for different points of view. I have a deep personal and professional admiration for my fellow commissioners.

I also want to commend and thank our able and dedicated staff. The same qualities which I hope made us good commissioners, undoubtedly made us a difficult group for whom to work. The staff has done an outstanding job attempting to satisfy so many masters.

Lastly, I would like to comment on the final report itself. Because we wanted to produce a consensus document, the report does not reflect any one commissioner's viewpoint or opinions. On most issues there was unanimous agreement; on some issues compromises were required and these are reflected in the report; on still other issues, the report represents majority opinion; and of course, some issues, considered to be relevant only by one or a few commissioners, are not touched upon in the report at all.

I am limiting my comments on the final report to four topical areas.

I.   My viewpoint has always been that the Commission interpreted its mission too narrowly. Congress mandated that the Commission address twelve specific questions. Ostensibly, answers to these questions would help Congress decide how to make the Migrant Education Program (M.E.P.) more effective. By limiting our work to answering only those questions specified by Congress, however, I believe we made the mistake of beginning our assignment somewhere in the middle of the project. We never critically examined the rationale for the M.E.P., as it was originally conceived and as it applies to the program's operation today.

My contention remains that all children have the right to the opportunity to be educated. If mobility causes problems related to proper grade placement, continuity of curriculum and credit transfer, for example, remedies should be developed for all children in this situation. If any children have educational deficiencies related to poverty, health needs, language, etc., they should be eligible for assistance. It seems to me that moving in search of agricultural employment, as opposed to moving to find employment in a factory or as a domestic, or not moving at all, is irrelevant vis-a-vis deserving educational opportunity.

If educational programs were simply based on educational need, many of the more controversial issues in migrant education would not be issues at all. For example, the argument whether or not currently migrant children should be served before formerly migrant children, would be moot. If the child has the educational need, regardless of when he moved, he should be served. If the child doesn't have the need, then he won't be served. If there is not enough money available to serve all children, those with the greatest needs, not the ones who have moved most recently, should be served first.

Similarly, the debate about the proper length of the "look-back" eligibility period for formerly migrant children also seems quite irrelevant. I can think of no good reason why someone with an educational need should be denied assistance by an education program, because he moved four years ago instead of two years ago?

Yet despite the this problem I have with the rationale for the program, I do believe that the M.E.P. is truly helping children who have profound educational, economic, health and other needs. Rather than eliminate the program, my preference would be to fold the M.E.P., as well as all other educational programs which presently serve selected students based on ascriptive characteristics, into open eligibility programs, designed to serve any child who needs and wants educational assistance.

II. There have always been and there will always be unequal levels
     of academic achievement. When unequal achievement is a func-
     tion of unequal opportunity, then a travesty has occurred and
     we as a democratic society have a responsibility to right this
     wrong. However, it is also true that children have different
     levels of ability and that some work harder than others. This
     difference will also lead to unequal levels of achievement.
     I make this point in connection with the M.E.P. for two
     reasons.

     First, with regard to eligibility for educational programs, I
     maintain that low achievement is not synonymous with educa-
     tional need, and should not be the single criterion for access
     to educational assistance. Funding should be directed toward
     children who are not achieving at their level of ability, at
     all levels of ability, not just at the low end.

     Secondly, with regard to the evaluation of educational pro-
     grams, I maintain that level of achievement, without regard to
     ability and various other factors, is not necessarily the most
     appropriate measure of the success or failure of a program.
     Specifically, the M.E.P. should not be judged to be performing
     poorly if participating migrant students have low levels of
     achievement. The program should more properly be judged on
     the basis of whether or not it is providing its constituents
     with opportunities for education which they would not other-
     wise have received. As a society we can only strive for equal
     opportunity; we cannot guarantee equal levels of educational
     achievement or economic success.

III. Another point of view I would like to have seen more strongly
     articulated concerns the role of the parent. In a very
     real sense all children are both victims and beneficiaries of
     their parents. Decisions and choices made by parents have a
     direct impact on their children. Over and over it is stated
     or implied in the report that migration has a deleterious im-
     pact on children. The report also acknowledges the primacy of
     the parents' role in the education of their children. But no-
     where do we make the very logical recommendation that migrant
     parents should be told that by taking their children with them
     when they migrate, they are hurting their children's chances
     of receiving a good education. We cannot on the one hand
     justify a whole program on the basis of the hardships assoc-
     iated with migrancy and then not come out in favor of trying
     to end the practice. If we believe migration is so detri-
     mental to the welfare of children, then M.E.P. parental
     involvement activities should include encouraging migrant
     parents to leave their children behind when and if they
     continue to migrate themselves. Ultimately, parents,
     including migrant parents, have to accept responsibility for
     their actions.

IV. Finally, I would like to state that my ideological orientation leads me to have very mixed feelings regarding the expenditure of public funds on research projects and studies, including the National Commission on Migrant Education. This being the case, I am committed to doing the best job we can possibly do, regardless of any awkwardness involved. In this spirit I wish that the Commission as a body had come out more strongly against the use of public monies, particularly migrant funds, for nonessential functions, especially travel and conferences. More specifically, I see no need for more than one national organization of migrant education officials. Since all states are represented by NASDME, there is simply no justification for IMEC which includes representation from only 16 states and whose $500,000 annual budget is used primarily for salaries and travel, with no direct services being provided to migrant children.

Despite my strong feelings on these four issues, I reiterate my position that the M.E.P. not only helps children with profound needs, but the migrant population's hard-work, self-help ethic makes them a most worthy and gratifying group to assist.

Respectfully yours,

Michael LaVelle

Michael LaVelle, Ph.D.

August 14, 1992

National Commission on Migrant Education
8120 Woodmont Avenue, 5th Floor
Bethesda, MD 20814

Dear Fellow Commissioners:

As you know, I have been a mainstream classroom teacher for twenty years. There was real wisdom shown when a public school teacher was appointed to this Commission because we teachers can often predict accurately the entire trend of our country several years before the federal government and all its many researchers can get an accurate grasp on developments. Why do we have this special ability? It is not because of any genius on our part, I assure you. We work so closely with the youth of tomorrow and their families that we can many times predict what the next generation will be like. We work with children when their parents are not around, and we get to see the children interact with their peers. We get to see on a personal level what is happening to the family structure. We do not have to wait to find out what is happening by watching the evening news; we often live it firsthand.

From my experience with many types of people, I can honestly say that there is not a worthier, more deserving group than the migrants of our country. Is there another group who moves around the country, travels in crowded conditions, lives in horrendous housing, and works by the sweat of their brows just so you and I can eat fresh fruits and vegetables? I admire their supreme work ethic and their dedication to the family unit. Their children are generally some of the most diligent, hard-working, and obedient children that we teachers have in our classes. For these last three years, it has been my joy to get to work with the other Commissioners and Staff in order to try to improve the lives and the education of these worthy migrants.

My chief concern on this Commission has been to try to develop recommendations which would have a positive impact on the entire migrant family structure. We must not allow our public policies to destroy the close family unit which most of our migrants enjoy. Our public policies should not be based on the premise that government should do whatever it wants to children unless clear evidence is presented to show that children are being harmed. Instead we should prohibit government from doing anything to children unless it can be convincingly shown that the children will benefit.

I was horrified when our Commission visited migrant day-care centers where <u>four-day old babies</u> were brought. One well-meaning health provider of a migrant day-care center said that frequently seven or eight such tots are transported in vans to the facility. My first thought was for the possible cranial damage which could occur in such tiny infants whose heads are not supported properly in transit, and my next question was why the migrant mothers were not being encouraged to breastfeed. We have heard very convincing testimony to the effect that the health of the migrant population is so poor that they qualify as a Third-World population. With migrant babies having such a high incidence of diarrhea, eye/ear/nose/throat infections, intestinal parasitic diseases, respiratory illnesses, obesity, allergy infections, and diabetes (For current information see NUTRITION THROUGH LACTATION, National Academy Press, 1991), surely our migrant women need to be properly supported by lactation specialists in order to give the babies the gift that only a mother can give. (I became even more concerned when I heard that WIC currently spends almost $500,000,000 a year on infant formula while spending only $8,000,000 on breastfeeding promotion. If infant formula were really better for children than breastmilk, then no amount of money would be too great; however, doesn't it seem ludicrous to spend $500,000,000 on infant formula while almost ignoring one of the greatest natural resources in our country?) I was also alarmed to learn that many migrant health centers spend as much as 80% of their budget toward treating dental caries in our migrant youngsters; such dental problems are caused largely by baby-bottle tooth decay. What about the physical and mental health of the migrant mothers themselves? Middle and upper-class women all over our country, after doing research on the subject of breastfeeding, generally agree that breastfeeding is healthier for them and their babies. Why, then, should our migrant women not have the same opportunity to stay home and nurse their babies? Don't they deserve the sense of empowerment and self-esteem which comes from being able to offer their babies the most perfectly designed baby nourishment that is known to man?

Then I also questioned a public policy which would facilitate a mother's leaving a four-day old baby in a public day-care center. The well-meaning people who thought up the welfare system for our country felt they were doing what was best, but we have all seen the destructive consequences which have arisen from that program. Are we doing the same thing by offering federally-funded day-care services which actually encourage a migrant mother to relinquish her tiny tot with his undeveloped immune system to the confines of a day-care center which is normally filled with sick children? There is a broad spectrum of research, including statements from the Centers for Disease Control, which indicates that large, licensed day-care facilities are major transmission centers for hepatitis, severe diarrhea, and other diseases. Studies show that the risk of infectious disease increases in direct proportion to the number of children who are kept in a day-care facility.

We classroom teachers must be concerned about the health and well-being of migrant babies because they will bring all their experiences with them when they come to school. Dr. Benjamin Spock, Dr. J. Burton White, Dr. Jay Belsky (one of the nation's leading defenders during the 1970's of full-time day care), and many other experts now agree that children who spend 20 hours a week or more in substitute care before they are one-year old do not establish secure parental bonds. J. Craig Perry, formerly Special Assistant for Child and Family Issues to the Chairman of the United States Senate Committee on Labor and Human Resources and a professor of human development at Brigham Young University, believes that public policy should require that warning signs be displayed in day-care establishments and should read:

> A child in day care is a child at risk. In day care, your child is likely to contract infectious diseases, is 300 percent more likely to require hospitalization, and is twice as likely to die from disease than are children at home. In day care, your child may be sexually or physically abused (potential abusers cannot be adequately screened out). Day care may make your child emotionally disturbed, insecure, belligerent, aggressive, more responsive to peers and less responsive to adults. If these effects of day care are not reversed through conscientious parenting, your child will be more likely to be delinquent in high school, use drugs, use alcohol, be morally permissive and sexually active, have an abortion, and later fail in marriage. When you put your child in day care, you assume some or all of these risks.

I agree with Robert Rector of the Heritage Foundation that government policy should not subsidize nonparental child care to the exclusion of parental care. I also think there is real merit in what Bill Mattox of the Family Research Council is proposing; let's grant non-discriminatory tax credits or vouchers in order to give the parents the choice of care-givers. For many of our low-income migrants, such a plan would actually add a positive amount to their incomes and would allow them the opportunity to keep their children at home. If the mother cannot stay home, then at least public policy should support other forms of family care for children. Maybe tax credits could be allowed for parents who want to house a grandparent or other relative who would take care of the children. This would at least keep the migrant infants out of the unhealthy environments of public day-care centers. Tax policies should be constructed in such a way that people pay lower taxes when they are in the child-rearing stages of life and more taxes when they do not have the responsibility of children. Surely a nation which has the capacity to invent a "smart" bomb can come up with a strategy which would promote and support the family structure.

Some other concerns which I have about the Migrant Education Program are as follows:

1. Only 17 of the 49 states (plus Puerto Rico, the District of Columbia, and Northern Mariana) participate in the migrant policy-making organization known as the Interstate Migrant Education Council. Because IMEC is supported by MEP funds, is the body that professes to promote interstate cooperation, and is studying the issue of mobility, then in order to follow basic, democratic principles, all states (not just 17) should be involved in this policy-making process. Since federal dollars are under tight constraint and there is already one MEP-funded organization on the national level (National Association of State Directors of Migrant Education) to which all states belong, I believe that a more appropriate plan would be for IMEC to be funded through state funding rather than through federal dollars. IMEC's budget of almost half a million dollars is larger than some states' entire MEP yearly allocations, and federal dollars need to be reserved for programs closer to the user level. Also, I have felt a deep concern over the fact that the chairman of IMEC is a Congressman; and the highest-paid employee of IMEC is a Senator. Is this practice not a potential conflict of interest since any increased MEP funding has to come of necessity through the appropriation process in Congress? That would be the same thing as my being a classroom teacher and also a member of the school board which votes teachers a raise.

2. I believe that a look-back window of two years (one year "currently" and two years "formerly") would be a more appropriate length of time for a child to qualify for MEP. The present six-year eligibility period goes beyond any reasonable expectations of the responsibility of the federal government. After a migrant child has lived in a school district for three years, the local school district should be prepared to pick up his needs.

3. The appropriate age span for MEP should be from age three through twelfth grade. It is impractical and logistically unrealistic to expect the schools to offer services through age 21 to students who are outside a states' compulsory school age. MEP should continue to offer referral services to migrants who are above the compulsory school age and should do everything possible to ensure that local and community services are made accessible to them.

4. Through the conscientious research of David Martin and Philip Martin, the Commission learned the probable reason why the children of migratory fishermen were added to the MEP eligibility definition in 1974. It had to do with the advocacy of a sister of a Congressman who introduced the new language in order to allow the continuation of a highly successful migrant program in Alabama which, upon investigation, was mistakenly serving the children of migratory fishermen. The expansion of the definition to migratory fishermen's children was probably meant to be helpful at the time; but through our site visits, I have observed that migratory fishermen's children do not truly fit the pattern of migrancy; and

I believe this group of people should be dropped from the definition.

I also do not feel that children of poultry workers should be included in the MEP eligibility definition. It seems to me that since poultry work is not seasonal and poultry workers do not exhibit the true pattern of agricultural migrancy that their children should be picked up by the local school districts who deal with normal mobility patterns.

5. By dropping fishing and poultry from the eligibility definition, by cutting back the look-back window from six to three years, by limiting MEP services from age three through twelfth grade, and by trying to conserve monies at the administrative and bureaucratic levels, additional MEP funds should become available. Therefore, I believe that MEP funding should stay at the current level with a renewed emphasis on funding accountability and fiscal responsibility.

I am thankful for the opportunity to have served on the National Commission on Migrant Education. I have come to respect and appreciate each Commissioner and Staff member and their tremendous dedication of time and energy to improve Migrant Education. I will watch with continued interest to see how the program progresses in the future years.

Sincerely,

Mrs. Donna Garner
Secondary Classroom Teacher

SIMMONS, OLSEN, EDIGER & SELZER, P.C.

Attorneys at Law

Professional & Business Center
P.O. Box 1949
Scottsbluff, Nebraska 69363-1949

Robert G. Simmons, Jr.
Howard P. Olsen, Jr.*
John F. Simmons
Rick L. Ediger
John A. Selzer
Steven W. Olsen

Jeffrey L. Hansen

* Also admitted in Wyoming

1502 Second Avenue
308-632-3811
Fax No. 308-635-0907

August 18, 1992

CONCURRING COMMENTS AND RECOMMENDATIONS
OF
COMMISSIONER ROBERT G. SIMMONS, JR.

"Change" is the political word for 1991. "Change" is what has happened to migrants since the Migrant Education Program was established in 1966. "Change (in significance) is not what happened to the Migrant Education Program since it was established in 1966. "Change" is needed in the Migrant Education Program. That "change" is not just the addition of more federal dollars.

A few observations of the present situation are relevant.

I.

It might be assumed that Congress, in establishing a migrant education program (MEP), had an objective of ending migrant labor as a way of life in this country. Such data as there is does not show a reduction in the estimated number of people who are in migrant labor compared to the estimated numbers who were in migrant labor when the MEP program started. The reason is not that MEP is not effective. The reason is that the services which migrants perform in and for the nation are still needed. When a person leaves migrancy, the need for the service is such that the leaving migrant's place in the migrant labor force is immediately taken by someone else. Significant numbers of the newer migrant laborers appear to come to this country from other nations. Their educational level starts out lower than that of the leaving migrant. Thus, the success of the MEP results in a lower educational level of the migrant labor force in this country.

The solution to the migrant education problem, therefore, must be a labor solution, rather than an education solution.

Until there is a change in that situation, there is unlikely to be a significant change for the nation resulting from the MEP, no matter how good MEP is or how much is spent on MEP.

Migrant laborers travel thousands of miles, many from other countries, under horrible living and travel conditions, to furnish needed services, when there are unemployed persons residing nearer and in the United States, capable of performing the same services. This is also a labor problem, rather than an education problem.

II.

The United States cannot educate all the children of mobile persons from all less prosperous countries, even if the labor of the parents is needed in the United States.

III.

There is not a valid objective distinction on educational needs between follow-the-crop-migrants (FTCM) and other students without a permanent, stable school home, who may, in fact, be mobile if not in a foreseeable migrant pattern. Perhaps MEP should be changed to mean "Mobile Students Educational Program".

From a need of education of children standpoint, there is no valid objective distinction of children whose parents' employment is subject to various protections offered by federal and state labor laws, and those children whose parents' employment does not have such protection; that nature of parents employment is not a valid distinction for defining beneficiaries of educational programs for the mobile.

IV.

The problems of migrant education for the individual student are not all caused solely by moving about from school to school. Great problems are caused by lack of attendance, lack of school records following the student (MSRTS was intended to assist this problem), lack of receiving credit for classes taken, lack of accruing credits for graduation, lack of educational planning and coordination, varying requirements for credits and graduation, etc. (many of which problems are discussed elsewhere in this report).

Probably a substantial reason for these problems and others is the fact that, aside from the parent, no one entity is responsible for the individual migrant student's educational program and progress. No one is responsible for seeing that the migrant student gets to school someplace, that the migrant student records get to the school where the migrant student may be, and that the migrant student gets credit for what the migrant student does there. There is no one responsible or available to plan and coordinate the migrant student's educational plans and programs. As to the non-migrant students, the school district in which the student resides has a direct interest, authority and responsibility in seeing that the student attends, and gets and education that is appropriate for that student, etc.

A migrant student who is a legal resident of a school district (herein called "Home Base District") is entitled to the same services and responsibility of that school district as the non-migrant students of that school district.

The Home Base School District now has no legal responsibility or authority to even be interested or sympathetic until the migrant student returns home.

Congress could change this.

Congress could authorize and require the state and/or the Home Base School District to be the district to plan the migrant students' educational program, to keep the records, to get the records to a school district where the student might be, to give the credits, to monitor progress, and to give a diploma when earned.

Congress could authorize and require the non-resident state and district to furnish education to that migrant student under the plan and direction of the Home Base District, and to report, etc., to the Home Base District as if the non-resident district was the agent of the Home Base District in furnishing the legal responsibilities of the Home Base District.

Federal MEP funds could be paid to the Home Base state or district for migrant students somewhere actually in a school in a non-resident district under the direction of the Home Base District. The Home Base District could be required to pay the non-resident district for the services rendered, under some equitable formula established by Congress.

As to migrant students from other nations, Congress could establish that the state in which the immigrant student's parents is first employed in the United States be the Home Base state (somewhat loco parentis) having responsibility for that immigrant student forthwith thereafter, and receive the federal MEP funds. The employer could be required to ascertain the relevant data on each potential migrant student of his employees and report that information to the state office designated in each to receive such report.

V.

It is not the Federal statutes and policies which create migrant labor and the problem of educating migrant children. It is the economic need of businesses (agricultural and otherwise) for seasonal labor that creates the migrant labor force. The cost of the migrant labor, including the cost of educating the children of migrant labor, is a cost of doing business for someone. I recommend that investigation occur as to a method of assessing the cost and responsibility of doing business to the states, communities and businesses benefited.

VI.

The function of MSRTS, as designated by Congress and as set out in Report, is to gather and transfer information. The process of gathering and transferring of information is not an educational function. The process of gathering and transferring of information is not unique or limited to any one type of governmental or private activity, and especially not unique to education. The process of gathering or transferring of information does not aid education, or any other activity, until the accurate information is received by someone who can use it. The process of transfer of information is not even a tool. The information when received becomes the tool. The educational use only begins then.

The use of education trained, experienced and motivated personnel in the function of the process of gathering and transferring information is a waste of their time and talents, which should be better used with children.

I recommend that the function of gathering and transferring of information be performed by contractors whose business is the gathering and transferring of information. I recommend that an entity in the business of transferring of information be invited to propose specifications for a contract. I recommend that these specifications be evaluated, modified and selected by an agency established by Congress, as described herein, and that such agency should award the contracts and oversee the performance thereof, and report to Congress and/or the President upon all of these matters.

It appears that much of the activity of MSRTS and use of MSRTS is designed and used for the purpose of pursuit of the federal dollar, rather than for the education of children. Since migrant education is a national problem, it is probably unrealistic to propose abandonment of the use of federal dollars to benefit migrant children, but it is not unrealistic to consider alternatives which reward actual education, instead of mere statistics. It is not unrealistic to consider the assignment of responsibility for migrant students to some entity which has a long-term interest in a particular student, rather than one which has only a temporary responsibility, changing with each move of that student.

I recommend that MSRTS records not be used as the basis of distribution of federal dollars.

VII.

Security and privacy are delightful ideas in the abstract. There are so many impediments now to the education of migrant students that, if transfer of information is made less speedy or efficient, difficult, burdensome or expensive (which I perceive that it would) by addition of security measures, the value of the speedy and accurate information will be damaged, perhaps to the extent of destruction. Security, if desired, should be imposed at the use-of-information level, not the transfer-of-information level.

VIII.

It was Congress which determined the need for a study, and it was Congress that determined that this study should be made by an agency independent of the United States Department of Education, in creating the National Commission on Migrant Education (NCME), as an independent agency to study and recommend to Congress.

It appears that Congress itself is the only body, etc., that cares enough about migrant, or mobile, student education over the whole nation, to carry out the recommendations set out in this Report, or to change the situation. I recommend that Congress establish an agency, independent of the Department of Education, reportable only to Congress and/or the President, to carry out the recommendations set out in this Report.

Respectfully submitted,

Robert G. Simmons, Jr.

RGS/jh

St. EDWARD'S
UNIVERSITY
A U S T I N · T E X A S

Office of the President

August 17, 1992

The Honorable Linda Chavez, Chairman
National Commission on Migrant Education
8120 Woodmont Avenue, 5th Floor
Bethesda, MD   20814

Dear Linda,

The National Commission on Migrant Education has been an ambitious,
cooperative effort among the Commissioners, the Commission staff,
hundreds of individuals who work in migrant education at all levels,
and the members of the migrant community themselves. We have
learned from one another and we have learned especially from the
members of the migrant community. Statistically, they may be the
most economically disadvantaged in our country, but they have a
real claim to be among the most gifted as well.

My only supplementary comment to the Commission's report would be to
focus on that giftedness. Early in the Commission's work we heard a
report from Dr. J. Prewitt-Diaz on the culture of migrancy. Dr.
Prewitt-Diaz distinguished the culture of migrancy from the culture
of poverty in very dramatic ways. Migrants are among the hardest
working in America and have proven their willingness and ability to
seize the opportunities that are given to them.

My personal experience confirms this description over and over.
Migrant students see the value of education and are determined to
take the opportunity to make life better for themselves and their
parents. They deal humbly with the educational gaps that need to be
filled in, and their primary response to success is gratitude.

In every study we have conducted at St. Edward's University, the
academic accomplishments of migrant students defy all expectations.
With support, they quickly become leaders within our campus community. Longitudinal studies show their academic and life successes
outdistance any expectations one would have of students from similar economic backgrounds. And studies of their earnings show that
they repay in taxes in one year more than any federal subsidy to the
educational program at the university.

3001 South Congress Ave.
Austin, Texas 78704-6489
512-448-8411

August 17, 1992
Page 2

I recite all of this because I think we need to understand federal
migrant programs as a critical, national investment and not just in
a humanitarian sense. "Investments" in any budgetary situation
ultimately increase the revenue side significantly faster than they
increase the expenditure side. The migrant population is a very
significant national resource that can be empowered and contribute
substantially to the future of this nation. Migrant education programs are a wise and productive national investment. I think it is
critically important that we maintain this perspective whenever we
look at migrant programs and migrant funding.

My own work on the Migrant Commission has been inspired by a large
number of heroic migrant students--Queta Cortez who is now finishing
her doctorate in chemistry at Texas A&M, Solomon Torres who is finishing his law degree at Columbia, Margarito Jimenez who is return-
ing to the Valley to become a teacher and counselor and help other
students the way one of his teachers helped him--and hundreds of
others. It has also been inspired by the clarity of vision and
commitment of national leaders like Congressman Bill Ford and
Congressman Bill Goodling. They have been tireless in keeping the
migrant population with its needs and giftedness in the national
eye.

My thanks to the members of the Commission staff and my fellow Commissioners for their good will and hard work.

Sincerely,

Patricia A. Hayes
President

PAH:cej

Redlands Christian Migrant Association

219 North First Street • Immokalee, Florida 33934 • (813) 657-3135

RCMA Education Effort For Rural Poverty Children

August 13, 1992

Honorable Linda Chavez, Chairman
National Commission on Migrant Education
8120 Woodmont Avenue, 5th Floor
Bethesda, Maryland 20814

Dear Linda,

A distinct highlight in my life's work with migrant children has been these last three years of collaboration with you and our colleagues on the Commission. Your sincere and committed leadership has been a major factor in the successful completion of our Congressional mandates. By any measure, the extraordinary calibre of our members, combined with the individual wide-ranging backgrounds of each of us as applied collectively resulted in a well-qualified commission. Yet that doesn't account for the chemistry that seems to have tied all of us together from the very first meeting.

Over the past 50 years I have been a member of more committees, councils and the like than I care to remember, yet not a one of those came close to meeting the high level of commitment, harmony, and respect for one another that was achieved on this Commission. Viewing the haphazard way we individually were chosen, some of this has to be attributed to luck, I suppose. But a goodly amount of the credit, I repeat, goes to your leadership, which tied us all together. And the migrant children have gained the benefits -- assuming that the Commission's recommendations are followed by Congress and the Administration.

In intending for this letter to be included with the individual comments by other commissioners, I would emphasize my total support of the consensus achieved in our deliberations as reflected in the body of our report. In no sense is my letter here a "minority" report.

I write to add emphasis to what the full Commission has said relative to the importance of parent involvement in migrant child education and to stress that much of what schools and administrators tout as parent involvement truly is not. Across the nation, with some marked exceptions acknowledged, schools on this vital issue are kidding themselves and neglecting the children.

This applies not to migrant children alone, but to the successful education of children from all groups of poor families -- rural and urban. In Florida, certainly, it is quite clear that our elementary schools are the greatest single barrier to poor children gaining a good education. And after quietly speaking one-on-one to parents and teachers in other parts of the nation where the Commission held hearings I learned that Florida is but one of the states where this charge may be leveled with ample justification.

The nationally prestigious Committee for Economic Development, in its 1987 report "Children in Need", states that parent involvement is the key (not a key, but the key) to children from disadvantaged homes achieving a good education. Yet, with few exceptions, school administrators steadfastly resist taking the initiatives necessary to make possible the meaningful involvement of poor parents in the education of their own children.

Now, I realize that virtually every elementary school has those cookie and kool-aid events once or twice a year (with yellow pads for parents to sign-in to "prove" the school has parent involvement). These are affairs during which the youngsters perform for parents, grandparents, aunts and uncles who happily and proudly come to watch the kids on display. That passes as parent involvement in a majority of school districts. Which, of course, it is not.

Achieving involvement of the parents requires conscientious and persistent effort by the schools. At a guess I would say 85 per cent of migrant parents feel that their children are not really wanted by the schools anywhere in the nation. And, unfortunately, they are about 50 per cent correct at the upper levels of all too many school districts.

Attitudes must be changed on both sides. But the first change has to come at the schools. Parents must be made to feel welcome. Schools must aggressively demonstrate that they want migrant children in their classrooms. Migrant Education is but a blip on the screen of most school systems. Its teachers are far down on the totem pole. It is the principal, the superintendent, and the school board members in whose hands rests the truly effective Migrant Education program at the local level.

At the appropriate federal and state levels there must be a firm determination to insist upon true parent involvement at the local family/school level.

Outreach to the homes is imperative, particularly in the home base states where migrant child school attendance is measured in months rather than weeks. Florida is such a state. In several county school districts our organization works in collaboration with school authorities to achieve together parent involvement. In one community over 200 families annually participate and have for seven years. Between 1,800 and 2,000 home visits are made in a single school year to those families. Average daily attendance has risen to 94 per cent. Over 90 per cent of the students show dramatic report card improvement. Behavioral problems have plummeted, while parent meetings -- held in Spanish -- have over flowing attendance. Parents now realize the importance of their involvement and the true significance of family commitment to their child's education on a day-to-day basis.

Student by student, family by family the goal of high school graduation then becomes a joint family/school challenge. On that basis a remarkable degree of success is being achieved. It is a formula that can work anywhere.

There is no substitute for true parent involvement. And no short cuts to achieving it.

Sincerely,

Wendell N. Rollason, executive vice president
Redlands Christian Migrant Association

Schedule of Meetings, Hearings, Site Visits and Witnesses

September 27, 1989
Business Session Meeting
Washington, D.C.

November 4, 1989
Business Session Meeting
Philadelphia, Pennsylvania

February 5, 1990
Business Session Meeting
Washington, D.C.

May 6 & 7, 1990
Site Visit & Commission Hearing
Little Rock, Arkansas

August 6 & 7, 1990
Site Visit & Commission Hearing
Gettysburg, Pennsylvania

October 1, 1990
Business Session Meeting
Washington, D.C.

December 3 & 4, 1990
Site Visit & Commission Hearing
McAllen, Texas

February 14 & 15, 1991
Commission Hearing
Washington, D.C.

April 28 & 29, 1991
Commission Hearing
Buffalo, New York

July 16, 1991
Site Visit & Commission Hearing
Watsonville, California

July 31, 1991
Business Session Meeting
Washington, D.C.

September 22 & 23, 1991
Commission Hearing
Washington, D.C.

December 15 & 16, 1991
Site Visit & Commission Hearing
Ft. Myers, Florida

March 1 & 2, 1992
Business Session & Commission Meeting
Washington, D.C.

March 27, 1992
Business Session Meeting
Bethesda, Maryland
(Conference Call)

April 20, 1992
Business Session Meeting
Bethesda, Maryland
(Conference Call)

May 22, 1992
Business Session Meeting
Bethesda, Maryland
(Conference Call)

June 22, 1992
Business Session Meeting
Bethesda, Maryland

July 16, 1992
Business Session Meeting
Bethesda, Maryland
(Conference Call)

July 28, 1992
Business Session Meeting
Bethesda, Maryland
(Conference Call)

August 24, 1992
Business Session Meeting
Bethesda, Maryland
(Conference Call)

September 23, 1992
Final Meeting/Report Release
Washington, D.C.

Migrant Student Record Transfer System (MSRTS)

Little Rock, Arkansas
May 6 & 7, 1990

Site Visit:
MSRTS Headquarters Facilities Tour

MSRTS Presenters:

Troy Rinker
Director, MSRTS
Arkansas Department of Education
Little Rock, Arkansas

Dr. James Hardage
Assistant Director, MSRTS
Arkansas Department of Education
Little Rock, Arkansas

Rick Johnson
Senior Project Leader, MSRTS
Arkansas Department of Education
Little Rock, Arkansas

Glenn Sheets
Senior User Services Consultant,
MSRTS
Arkansas Department of Education
Little Rock, Arkansas

Kay Love
Senior User Services Consultant,
MSRTS
Arkansas Department of Education
Little Rock, Arkansas

Nolan McMurray
Eastern Stream Manager, MSRTS
Arkansas Department of Education
Little Rock, Arkansas

Basil Julian
Eastern Stream Manager, MSRTS
Arkansas Department of Education
Little Rock, Arkansas

Bill Woolly
Western Stream Manager, MSRTS
Arkansas Department of Education
Little Rock, Arkansas

Migrant System Record Transfer System (MSRTS), Interstate/Interagency Coordination, Culture of Migrancy, & Parental Involvement

Gettysburg, Pennsylvania
August 6 & 7, 1990

Site Visits:
Adams-Cumberland Migrant Child Development Center
Bendersville, Pennsylvania

Adams-Cumberland & Eastern Franklin Counties Summer Programs
Arendtsville, Pennsylvania

Adams-Cumberland & Eastern Franklin Counties Career Education Programs
Gettysburg, Pennsylvania

Orchard and Camp Tour

Hearing Witnesses:

MSRTS Utilization

Tammy Dubbs
MSRTS Controller
Lincoln Intermediate Unit
Gettysburg, Pennsylvania

Marcia Kile
Program Consultant
Migrant Child Development Program
Gettysburg, Pennsylvania

Sharon Kraner
Elementary School Teacher
Gettysburg, Pennsylvania

Marian Benchoff
Jr. High School Guidance Counselor
Gettysburg, Pennsylvania

Elizabeth Miller
Program Nurse Practitioner
Gettysburg, Pennsylvania

Interstate/Interagency Coordination

Patricia Williams
Director
Pennsylvania Site Migrant Education Program
Clarks Summit, Pennsylvania

Teckla Decker
Florida Interstate Coordination Consultant
Ft. Myers, Florida

Larry Elworth
Program Coordinator
Pennsylvania Apple Marketing Program
Harrisburg, Pennsylvania

Parker Coble
Program Director
Migrant Child Development Program
Gettysburg, Pennsylvania

Suzanne Benchoff
Program Consultant
Recruitment & Support Services
Gettysburg, Pennsylvania

Dr. Edward Zuroweste
Medical Director
Keystone Migrant Health
Chambersburg, Pennsylvania

Donna Frederickson
Executive Director
ACCESS, Inc.
Gettysburg, Pennsylvania

Kay Brown
State Director for Rural Opportunities
Gettysburg, Pennsylvania

Reverend Joseph Hilbert
Christo Rey Catholic Apostolate
Bendersville, Pennsylvania

Parental Involvement

Dr. J. Prewitt-Diaz
Associate Professor
Penn State University
University Park, Pennsylvania

Kathy Doak
Dairy Worker Parent
Middleburg, Pennsylvania

Lenette Robinson
Eastern Stream Parent
Kent, New York

Annetta Hardy
Interstate Parent
York Springs, Pennsylvania

Patricia Lyons
Parent
Avon Park, Florida

Mr. & Mrs. Miguel Rodriguez
Interstate Parents
Gardeners, Pennsylvania

Dianna Rarig
Immigration Specialist
Agricultural Human Resource Management Association
Biglerville, Pennsylvania

Miguel Rivera, Jr.
College Senior
Aspers, Pennsylvania

Interagency Coordination, Migrant System Record Transfer System (MSRTS) Coordination, School Programs, and Parental Involvement

McAllen, Texas
December 3 and 4, 1990

Site Visits:
McAllen Independent School District
McAllen, Texas

Pan Am University
Higher Education Program
Edinburg, Texas

Hearing Witnesses:

Interagency Coordination Panel

Isabel Cordova
Women, Infant, and Children Program
Donna, Texas

Norma Acosta
Hidalgo County Women, Infant, and
Children Director
Edinburg, Texas

Juanita Castillo
Parent
Donna, Texas

Rafael Guerra
Education Director
Texas Migrant Head Start Council
McAllen, Texas

Paula Gomez
Executive Director
Brownsville Community Health Center
Staff Member
Brownsville, Texas

Deana Velardi
Brownsville Community Health Center
Staff Member
Brownsville, Texas

Dr. Bridget Walsh
Hidalgo County Health Care Physician
Edcouch, Texas

Aurora Valdez
Valley InterFaith Leader
Weslaco, Texas

Dr. Gilberto Pulido
D.D.S.
McAllen, Texas

MSRTS Coordination Panel

Alba Tinsman
Migrant School Nurse
McAllen, Texas

Lupita Garza
Migrant School Nurse
McAllen, Texas

Carlos Cantu
High School Counselor
McAllen, Texas

Delina Salinas
Recruiter
Independent School District
McAllen, Texas

Yolanda Molina
Mercedes Independent School District
MSRTS Clerk
Mercedes, Texas

Linda Diaz
LaJoya Independent School District
MSRTS Clerk
LaJoya, Texas

Jack Hall
Federal Program Coordinator
San Benito, Texas

Leroy Jackson
Director
Migrant Education Program
Edinburg, Texas

School Programs Panel

Frank Contreras
State Director
Migrant Education Program
Austin, Texas

Dr. Pablo Perez
Superintendent
McAllen Independent School District
McAllen, Texas

Dr. Roberto Zamora
Superintendent
LaJoya Independent School District
LaJoya, Texas

Francisco Martinez
Community Service Specialist
Advocacy, Inc.
Pharr, Texas

Eduardo Hernandez
Community Service Specialist
Advocacy, Inc.
Pharr, Texas

Irma Villalon
Gifted & Talented Program Teacher
LaJoya Independent School District
LaJoya, Texas

Sylvia Hatton
Assistant Superintendent for
Instruction
LaJoya Independent School District
LaJoya, Texas

Elena Mycue
Migrant Coordinator
McAllen Independent School District
McAllen, Texas

Carmen Bazan
Migrant Teacher
McAllen Independent School District
McAllen, Texas

Kyle Brashear
Teacher
McAllen Independent School District
McAllen, Texas

Parental Involvement Panel

Alicia Flores
Parent
Mercedes, Texas

Lydia Ramirez
Home and School Community Aide
Migrant Education Office
McAllen Independent School District
McAllen, Texas

Ellen Gonzales
Director of Specially-Funded Programs
LaJoya Independent School District
LaJoya, Texas

Carlos Trevino
Director
Tri-State Even Start
Washington State Migrant Council
Grandview, Washington

Roman Cruz
Facilitator/Coordinator
Tri-State Even Start Project
Washington State Migrant Council
Grandview, Washington

Victoria Morales
Facilitator
Tri-State Even Start Project
Washington State Migrant Council
Grandview, Washington

Guadalupe Figueroa
Parent
Weslaco, Texas

Edna Chita Puente
Texas State Parent Advisory Council
President
Weslaco, Texas

Consuelo Vasquez
Parent
McAllen, Texas

Arsenia Diaz
Student
McAllen, Texas

Dominga De La Rosa
Parent
McAllen, Texas

Abelina Juarez
Parent
McAllen, Texas

Veronica Sanchez
Student
McAllen, Texas

Jose Razo
Student
McAllen, Texas

Ruben Zamora
Parent
McAllen, Texas

Hilario Rincones
Director of Special Programs
University of Texas - Pan Am
Edinburg, Texas

Arnoldo Rodriguez
Principal
Sam Houston Elementary School
McAllen, Texas

Maria Perez Ramires
Former High School Equivalency
Program/College Assistance Migrant
Program Student
LaVilla, Texas

Martin Cortez
Former High School Equivalency
Program Student
Alamo, Texas

Nancy Zamora
Current High School Equivalency
Program Student
Weslaco, Texas

Mary Mena
Current High School Equivalency
Program Student
Elsa, Texas

Edna Tamayo
Parental Involvement Coordinator
Harlingen Consolidate Independent
School District
Harlingen, Texas

Ignacio Garcia
Federal Program Director
Harlingen, Texas

Hilda Gloria
Parent
Harlingen, Texas

Marciano Gloria
Parent
Harlingen, Texas

Tony Tobin
Migrant High School Counselor
Brownsville Independent School
District
Brownsville, Texas

Francisco Villareal
Parent
Brownsville, Texas

Josefina Angeles
Parent
Brownsville, Texas

Rual Luna
Student
Brownsville, Texas

Maria Edith Salinas
Student
Brownsville, Texas

Alberto Guzman
Student
Brownsville, Texas

Esmeralda Martinez
Parent
San Juan, Texas

Adelina Pena
Parent
San Juan, Texas

Natalia Rodriguez
Parent
San Juan, Texas

Flor Estela Rodriguez
Parent
Pharr, Texas

Julia Martinez
Parent
Pharr, Texas

Eudelia Resendez
Parent
Pharr, Texas

Migrant Education Program State Directors

Washington, D.C.
February 14 and 15, 1991

Hearing Witnesses:

National Association of State Directors of Migrant Education (NASDME) Panel

Ronnie Glover
President
NASDME
Louisiana Department of Education
Baton Rouge, Louisiana

Raul de la Rosa
Director
Supplementary Education Program
Washington Department of Education
Olympia, Washington

Frank Contreras
Director
Division of Special Programs
Texas Education Agency
Austin, Texas

Home Base States Panel

Thomas Lugo
Manager
Migrant Education Office
California Department of Education
Sacramento, California

Lou Marsh
Director
Florida Department of Education
Tallahassee, Florida

Receiving States Panel

Dr. Betty Hinkle
General Manager
Special Projects
Migrant Education Program
Colorado Department of Education
Denver, Colorado

Dr. David Pimentel
Director
Migrant Education Program
Colorado Department of Education
Denver, Colorado

Dr. Manuel Recio
Director
Migrant Education Program
Pennsylvania Department of Education
Harrisburg, Pennsylvania

Unique States Panel

Dr. Elizabeth Twomey
Associate Commissioner
Massachusetts Department of Education
Brookline, Massachusetts

Alexander T. Goniprow
Director
Migrant Education Program
Massachusetts Migrant Education Operating Agency
Brookline, Massachusetts

William M. Smith
Manager
Office of Migrant Education Program
New Jersey Department of Education
Trenton, New Jersey

U.S. Department of Education Panel

Dr. John T. MacDonald
Assistant Secretary
Elementary and Secondary Education
United States Department of Education
Washington, D.C.

Dr. Francis V. Corrigan
Director
Office of Migrant Education
United States Department of Education
Washington, DC

Interagency and Intrastate Coordination

Buffalo, New York
April 28 & 29, 1991

Hearing Witnesses:

Federal Initiatives Panel

Sonia M. Leon Reig
Associate Bureau Director for Program Development
Bureau of Health Care and Delivery Assistance
U.S. Department of Health & Human Services
Rockville, Maryland

John Florez
Deputy Assistant Secretary
U.S. Department of Labor
Washington, D.C.

Frank Fuentes
Chief
Migrant Programs Branch
Administration for Children, Youth, and Families
U.S. Department of Health & Human Services
Washington, D.C.

Beth Arnow
Coordinator
Migrant and Language Minority Programs
Georgia Department of Education
Atlanta, Georgia

Roberta Ryder
Executive Director
National Migrant Resource Program, Inc.
Austin, Texas

David Duran
Chairperson
National Advisory Council on Migrant Health
Department of Economic Support
Madison, Wisconsin

Diane Mull
Executive Director
Association of Farm Worker Opportunity Programs
Washington, D.C.

Sister Geraldine O'Brien
Executive Director
East Coast Migrant Head Start Project
Arlington, Virginia

State and Local Models Panel

Joe Velarde
Director
National Adult Migrant Farmworker Education Project
Elk Grove, California

Darlene Slaby
DirectorMigrant Education Program
Florida Department of Education
Indianapolis, Indiana

Rogelio Ramos
Director
Migrant Education Program
Princeville Grade School
Princeville, Illinois

Dr. DeWayne Whittington
Superintendent
Somerset County Public Schools
Princess Anne, Maryland

Health and Nutrition Panel

Dr. Alan Dever
Professor
Mercer University School of Medicine
Macon, Georgia

Dean Mason
Division of Immunization
Center for Disease Control
Atlanta, Georgia

Regina Tart
Nursing Supervisor
Tricounty Community Health Center
Newton Grove, North Carolina

Robert Mulvey
Chief
Program Operations
Food & Nutrition Service
United States Department of Agriculture
Boston, Massachusetts

Program Coordination Centers Panel

Robert Levy
Director
ESCORT Project
Eastern Stream Program Coordination Center
State University of New York
Oneonta, New York

Tadeo Reyna
Director
Central Stream Program Coordination Center
Texas A&I University
Kingsville, Texas

Nilda Garcia Simms
Project Director
Interface Migrant Education
Beaverton, Oregon

Projects and Studies Panel

Senator John Perry
Senior Project Consultant
Interstate Migrant Education Council
Denver, Colorado

Dr. Jim Gonzales
Senior Policy Analyst
Interstate Migrant Education Council
Albuquerque, New Mexico

Frank Contreras
Director
Division of Special Programs
Texas Education Agency
Austin, Texas

Barbara Wyman
Coordinator
Summer Program Academic Resources Coordination Center
State University of New York at Cortland
Cortland, New York

Local Administration of Migrant Education Program

Watsonville, California
July 16, 1991

Site Visits:

Cabrillo College

Aptos High School

Buena Vista Camp & Preschool

Allianza Elementary School

Migrant Education District Office

Hearing Witnesses:

Program Administration Overview

Janis Duran
Assistant Superintendent
Pajaro Valley Unified School District
Watsonville, California

Vic Marani
President
Board of Trustees
Pajaro Valley Unified School District
Corralitos, California

Thomas Lugo
Director
Migrant Education Office
California Department of Education
Sacramento, California

Dr. Paul Nava
Migrant Program Director
Pajaro Valley Unified School District
Watsonville, California

Recruiters

Georginia Hernandez
Recruiter
Pajaro Valley Unified School District
Watsonville, California

Jennie Gomez
Support Services Assistant
Pajaro Valley Unified School District
Watsonville, California

Educators

Norb Kowalkowski
Preschool Program Coordinator
Pajaro Valley School District
Watsonville, California

Lisa Massey
Migrant Middle School Counselor
Pajaro Valley Unified School District
Watsonville, California

Maria Marquez
Elementary School Teacher
Watsonville, California

Susan Griffin
Migrant Elementary School Teacher
Aptos, California

Secondary School Issues

Michael Sullivan
High School Counselor
Watsonville High School
Watsonville, California

Bob Gomez
Migrant High School Supplementary Instructional Teacher
Watsonville High School
Watsonville, California

Diana Young
Migrant Counselor
Watsonville High School
Watsonville, California

Roger Mock
Principal
Watsonville High School
Watsonville, California

Migrant Health Coordinators

Elaine Rohlfes
Migrant Health Coordinator
Pajaro Valley Unified School District
Watsonville, California

Barbara Garcia
Executive Director
Salue Para Gente Clinic
Watsonville, California

Other Local Community Programs

Jesse Camacho
Director
Mini-Corp
Sacramento, California

Florence Wyckoff
Migration and Adaption in the Americas
Watsonville, California

Todd McFarren
Mayor
Watsonville, California

Parent Education & Involvement

Lucy Portele-Castano
Parent Coordinator
Pajaro Valley Unified School District
Watsonville, California

Anastacio Andrade
Parent Advisory Council
President
Watsonville, California

Juan Rosillo
Parent Advisory Council
State Representative
Watsonville, California

Student Testimony

Lourdes Ramirez
Watsonville, California

Leticia Rocha
Freedom, California

Erendira Fabian
Watsonville, California

Handicapped, "At-Risk," and Gifted and Talented Migrant Students, Demographics, High School Equivalency Programs, & College Assistance Migrant Programs

Washington, D.C.
September 22 & 23, 1991

Hearing Witnesses:

Demographics Panel

Dr. William O'Hare
Director
Population & Policy Analysis
University of Louisville
Louisville, Kentucky

Handicapped Panel

Dr. Richard Figueroa
Professor of Education
University of California
Davis, California

Dr. Spencer Salend
Professor of Educational Studies
State University of New York
New Paltz, New York

Gloria Muniz
Specialist
Migrant/Bilingual Education
Oregon Department of Education
Salem, Oregon

"At-Risk" Population Panel

Dr. Robert Lynch
Director
BOCES Geneseo Migrant Center
Geneseo, New York

Dr. Doris Helge
Director
National World Development Institute
Western Washington University
Bellingham, Washington

Brenda Pessin
Coordinator
Migrant Education Resource Project
Illinois Migrant Council
Chicago, Illinois

High School Equivalency Program (HEP) & College Assistance Migrant Program (CAMP) Panel

Dr. John Jensen
Director
HEP/CAMP
Boise State University
Boise, Idaho

Steve Marks-Fife
Director
High School Equivalency Program
University of Oregon
Eugene, Oregon

Loida Velazquez
Associate Director
HEP
University of Tennessee
Knoxville, Tennessee

Gifted & Talented Panel

Dr. William Durden
Director
Center for Talented Youth
Johns Hopkins University
Baltimore, Maryland

Dr. Joyce VanTassel-Baska
Director
Gifted & Talented Education
College of William and Mary
Williamsburg, Virginia

Student Testimony

Rafael Gonzalez, Jr.
Cambridge, Massachusetts

Local Administration of Migrant Education Programs (MEP)

Ft. Myers, Florida
December 15 & 16, 1991

Site Visits:

Bethune Pre-School

Village Oaks Elementary School

Immokalee Middle School

Immokalee Child Development Center

Presentation:

Administrative Conference of the United States

Dr. Phil Martin
Professor
Department of Agricultural Economics
University of California at Davis
Davis, California

Dr. David Martin
Professor
School of Law
University of Virginia
Charlottesville, Virginia

Hearing Witnesses:

Barbara Mainster
Executive Director
Redlands Christian Migrant Association
Ft. Myers, Florida

Marjorie Berry
Coordinator
Chapter 1 Migrant Education
Lee County School Board
Ft. Myers, Florida

Frank Campano
Coordinator
Florida Migrant Education Summer Institute
Hillboro County Schools
Tampa, Florida

Nancy Pullum
Director
Palm Beach County Public Schools
Department of Federal Programs
Palm Beach, Florida

Early Childhood Development/Chapter 1

**Washington, D.C.
March 1 & 2, 1992**

Migrant Early Childhood Education

Dr. James Gonzales
Senior Policy Analyst
Interstate Migrant Education Council
Albuquerque, New Mexico

Chapter 1 Migrant Funding

Ms. Susan Morse
National Preschool Coordination Project
San Diego, California

Legislative Information

Summary of Legislative History*
of the Migrant Education Program

This section summarizes the legislative history of the Migrant Education Program (MEP) authorized under Chapter 1 of Title I of the Elementary and Secondary Education Act. Only statutory language is summarized; House and Senate committee reports, which are useful for explaining certain provisions, are not covered.

The legislative history focuses on provisions that explicitly apply to MEP; with several exceptions, provisions applying to Chapter 1 programs in general are omitted. The latter provisions, which are important for MEP, include requirements for fiscal accountability and controls (such as authority to carry over funds beyond a fiscal year), program evaluations, participation of the territories, and authority for the Secretary of Education to by-pass state agencies.

As is the case with any legislative summary, readers should refer to the actual statutory language for details.

ELEMENTARY AND SECONDARY EDUCATION AMENDMENTS OF 1966 (P.L. 89-750), November 3, 1966

This legislation created MEP as part of Title I of the Elementary and Secondary Education Act. It established basic features of the program that remain today:

■ Federal grants were made available to State Educational Agencies (SEAs).

■ Eligibility for services was restricted (at that time) to currently migratory children of migratory agricultural workers.

*This section was prepared by Mr. Robert Lykes, Congressional Research Service, August 1992.

■ Allocations to states were based upon:
   ☐ the number of such migratory children ages 5-17 (estimated at that time from Department of Labor data on migrant workers), including both full-time residents and the full-time equivalent of part-time residents, and
   ☐ average per pupil expenditures (measured at that time nationally, not by state) multiplied by a constant percentage.
■ MEPs had to be:
   ☐ designed to meet migrant students' special educational needs;
   ☐ coordinated with MEPs in other states (including transfers of student records);
   ☐ coordinated with other Federal programs for migrants; and
   ☐ in compliance with other Title I requirements for program evaluations, annual reports, children in private schools, provisions regarding size, scope, and quality, etc.

ELEMENTARY AND SECONDARY EDUCATION AMENDMENTS OF 1967 (P.L. 90-247), January 2, 1968

■ Eligibility for services was extended to formerly migrant children for a period of up to 5 years, provided they live in a program area and their parents concur; however, they were not counted for funding.

■ Allocations to states were based on the greater of state or national average per pupil expenditures, multiplied by a constant percentage.

■ Funds for MEP and other Title I state agency programs would not be reduced if total Title I appropriations were insufficient to provide full funding (only Title I basic grants would be reduced).

1970 AMENDMENTS TO THE ELEMENTARY AND SECONDARY EDUCATION ACT (P.L. 91-230), APRIL 13, 1970

■ Allocations to states were to reflect the number of children to be served, not previous year data.

■ Funds in excess of a state's need could be allocated to other states.

EDUCATION AMENDMENTS OF 1972 (P.L. 92-318), June 23, 1972

■ Children who are currently migratory were given priority for services.

■ Preschool children could be served, provided this would not reduce program services; however, they were not counted for funding.

■ The Commissioner of Education was directed to study and evaluate MEP.

EDUCATION AMENDMENTS OF 1974 (P.L. 93-380), August 21, 1974

■ Eligibility for services was expanded to include currently and formerly migratory children of migratory fishers; they were also counted for funding.

■ In determining allocations to states:
   ☐ formerly migrant children eligible for services were included among children counted;
   ☐ numbers of currently or formerly migratory children ages 5-17 (both full-time and full-time equivalents) were based upon Migrant Student Record Transfer System (MSRTS) data; and

□ state average per pupil expenditures (multiplied by a constant percentage) were used for all states, though raised to 80 percent or lowered to 120 percent of the national average if outside that range.

■ Each Title I state agency was guaranteed at least 100 percent of the funding it received the prior fiscal year (technical amendments in 1976 changes this provision to apply to each State's MEP and other Title I State agency programs).

EDUCATION AMENDMENTS OF 1978 (P.L. 95-561), November 1, 1978

■ Allocations to States were to reflect the special needs and additional program costs of summer students.

■ Parent advisory councils were established at both State and local levels and had to be consulted for program planning and implementation

■ Separate funding for grants and contracts with State Educational Agencies was authorized for the MSRTS and other coordination activities (technical amendments in 1979 changed this provision to a set-aside for MEP funds).

■ The funding guarantee for each State's MEP was extended at 100 percent for four years and at 85 percent the fifth year (for other Title I State agency programs, 85 percent was used all five years).

OMNIBUS BUDGET RECONCILIATION ACT OF 1981 (P.L. 97-35), August 13, 1981

■ Chapter 1 of the Education Consolidation and Improvement Act (title V, subtitle D of P.L. 97-35) replaced Title I of the Elementary and Secondary Education Act.

■ Funds for MEP and other Chapter 1 State agency programs were limited for three years to 14.6 percent of the total Chapter 1 appropriations.

■ Changes were made in some of the other Chapter 1 requirements with which MEP programs had to comply, such as evaluation and fiscal accountability provisions.

TECHNICAL AMENDMENTS TO THE EDUCATION CONSOLIDATION AND IMPROVEMENT ACT OF 1981 (P.L. 98-211), December 8, 1983

■ Regulatory definitions for agricultural activity, fishing activity, and the currently migratory child must continue to be used; no additional definition of migratory agricultural worker or fisher may be applied.

■ State Educational Agencies were required to evaluate Chapter 1 programs at least every two years and collect demographic data on children served.

1984 AMENDMENTS TO VARIOUS EDUCATION ACTS (P.L. 98-312), June 12, 1984

■ Eligibility for services was expanded to include currently migratory and formerly migratory children of fishers who migrate 20 miles or more to temporary residences to engage in fishing activity (this provision applies only to school districts of more than 18,000 square miles); they were also to be counted for funding.

NATIONAL SCIENCE, ENGINEERING, AND MATHEMATICS AUTHORIZATION ACT OF 1986 (P.L. 99-159), November 22, 1985

■ The separate program of coordination activities may be funded only with contracts.

■ The MSRTS contract was to be awarded to the State Educational Agency that received the award the preceding year, unless a majority of States object.

■ MSRTS activities shall not be considered an information collection that is sponsored by a Federal agency.

AUGUSTUS F. HAWKINS - ROBERT T. STAFFORD ELEMENTARY AND SECONDARY SCHOOL IMPROVEMENT AMENDMENTS OF 1988 (P.L. 100-297), April 28, 1988

■ Chapter 1 programs were placed under Title I of the Elementary and Secondary Education Act.

■ Allocations to States were based on currently and formerly migratory children ages 3-21 rather than 5-17.

☐ Formerly migratory children no longer must reside in a program area to be counted.

■ Eligibility for services was expanded to include currently and formerly migratory children of migratory agricultural dairy workers; they were also counted for funding.

☐ Preschool currently migratory children were to be served before school age formerly migratory children.

■ The Secretary of Education must develop a national standard certification form for eligibility.

■ States were limited to a 5 percent error rate in determining numbers of eligible children.

■ Consultation with parent advisory councils was continued but required only for programs lasting a school year.

■ Evaluations were required to determine the effectiveness of MEP in achieving stated goals and whether gains for formerly migrant children are sustained.

■ Coordination was required with additional programs including the Individuals with Disabilities Education Act (IDEA), the Community Services Block Grant Act, Head Start, migrant health, and other appropriate programs under the Departments of Education, Labor, or Agriculture.

☐ Grants or contracts for a national system of credit accrual and exchange were required.

☐ Separate program coordination activities may be funded with either grants or contracts and only in consultation with and approval of the States.

■ Individualized education programs approved under IDEA were included in the MSRTS.

■ The Commission on Migrant Education was established to study the issues related to the education of migrant children and report their findings to Congress.

PUBLIC LAW 100-297— APR. 28, 1988 102 STAT. 193

"SEC.1439.NATIONAL COMMISSION ON MIGRANT EDUCATION.

"(a) ESTABLISHMENT.—There is established, as an independent agency within the executive branch, a National Commission on Migrant Education (referred to in this section as the Commission').

"(b) MEMBERSHIP.—

"(1) The Commission shall be composed of 12 members. Four of the members shall be appointed by the President. Four of the members shall be appointed by the Speaker of the House, including 2 Members of the House, 1 from each political party. Four of the members shall be appointed by the President pro tempore of the Senate, including 2 Members of the Senate, 1 from each political party.

"(2) The chairman shall be designated by the President from among the members appointed by the President. If the President has not appointed 4 members of the Commission and designated a chairman within 60 days of the enactment of this Act, the members of the Commission appointed by the Speaker of the House and the President pro tempore of the Senate shall elect a chairman who shall continue to serve for the duration of the Commission.

"(3) Any vacancy in the Commission shall be filled in the same manner as the original appointment.

"(c) STUDY.—The Commission shall make a study of the following issues:

"(1) What are the demographics of the children of migratory workers today compared with 10 years ago and how are the demographics expected to change over the next decade.

"(2) What are the individual roles of the Federal, State, and private sectors in migrant affairs; how has each sector enhanced migrant educational opportunities, including entry into all types of postsecondary education programs; and should Federal programs include incentives for private and State participation.

"(3) What is the number of unserved or underserved migrant students who are eligible for the programs under this chapter nationwide and on a State-by-State basis.

"(4) How can migrant education, migrant health, migrant Head Start, Job Training Partnership programs serving migrants, HEP/CAMP, and adult literacy programs be integrated and coordinated at both the Federal and State levels.

"(5) How many migrant students are identified as potential drop-outs; how might this issue be addressed at the national policy level; and what effect does the migrant mother have on her children's performance.

"(6) How do the migrant programs under this chapter vary from State to State; how do their administrative costs vary; how do parent involvement and services vary.

"(7) What role has the Migrant Student Record Transfer System performed in assisting the migrant population; to what degree is it utilized for enhancing the education program at the local level and by the classroom teacher; is it cost effective; and how well would such a system adapt to other mobile populations like those in the inner cities or those in the Department of Defense overseas schools.

"(8) How many prekindergarten programs are available to migratory children; what services are they provided; what is the degree of parent involvement with these programs; what is a typical profile of a student in such a program.

"(9) How well are migrant handicapped and gifted and talented students identified and served; and what improvements might be made in this area.

"(10) How many of the students being served are identified as currently migrant' and how many are formerly migrant'; what differences are there in their needs; and how do services provided differ between those of currently migrant' and those of formerly migrant'.

"(11) How does interstate and intrastate coordination occur at the State and local levels.

"(12) Is there a need to establish a National Center for Migrant Affairs and what are the options for funding such a Center.

"(d) REPORTS.—

"(1) The Commission shall prepare and submit reports and recommendations to the President and to the appropriate committees of the Congress on the studies required to be conducted under this section. The reports for the studies required shall be submitted as soon as practicable.

"(2) Any recommendations and reports submitted under this paragraph which contemplate changes in Federal legislation shall include draft

legislation to accomplish the recommendations.

"(e) SPECIAL STUDY ON THE MIGRANT STUDENT RECORDS TRANSFER SYSTEM.—

"(1) The Commission shall conduct a study of the function and the effectiveness of the Migrant Student Records Transfer System.

"(2) The Commission shall prepare and submit to the Secretary of Education and to the Congress, not later than 2 years after the first meeting of the Commission, a report on the study required by paragraph (1).

"(f) COMPENSATION.—

"(1) Members of the Commission who are officers or full-time employees of the United States shall serve without compensation in addition to that received for their services as officers or employees of the United States; but they may be allowed travel expenses, including per diem in lieu of subsistence, as authorized by section 5703 of title 5, United States Code, for persons in the Government service employed intermittently.

"(2) Members of the Commission who are not officers or full-time employees of the United States may each receive $150 per diem when engaged in the actual performance of duties vested in the Commission. In addition, they may be allowed travel expenses, including per diem in lieu of subsistence, as authorized by section 5703 of title 5, United States Code, for persons in the Government service employed intermittently.

"(f) STAFF.—Such personnel as the Commission deems necessary may be appointed by the Commission without regard to the provisions of title 5, United States Code, governing appointments in the competitive service, and may be paid

without regard to the provisions of chapter 51 and subtitle III of chapter 53 of such title relating to classification and General Schedule pay rates, but no individual so appointed shall be paid in excess of the rate authorized from GS-18 of the General Schedule.

"(g) ADMINISTRATION.—

"(1) The Commission or, on the authorization of the Commission, any committee thereof, may, for the purpose of carrying out the provisions of this section, hold such hearings and sit and act at such times and such places within the United States as the Commission or such committee may deem advisable.

"(2) In carrying out its duties under this section, the Commission shall consult with other Federal agencies, representatives of State and local governments, and private organizations to the extent feasible.

"(3) The Commission is authorized to secure directly from any executive department, bureau, agency, board, commission, office, independent establishment, or instrumentality, information, suggestions, estimates, and statistics for the purpose of this section, and each such department, bureau, agency, board, commission, office, establishment, or instrumentality is authorized and directed, to the extent permitted by law, to furnish such information, suggestions, estimates, and statistics directly to the Commission, upon request made by the Chairman.

"(4) For the purpose of securing the necessary data and information, the Commission may enter into contracts with universities, research institutions, foundations, and other competent public or private agencies.

For such purpose, the Commission is authorized to obtain the services of experts and consultants in accordance with section 3109 of title 5, United States Code.

"(5) The heads of all Federal agencies are, to the extent not prohibited by law, directed to cooperate with the Commission in carrying out this section.

"(6) The Commission is authorized to utilize, with their consent, the services, personnel, information, and facilities of other Federal, State, local, and private agencies with or without reimbursement.

"(7) The Commission shall have authority to accept in the name of the United States, grants, gifts, or bequests of money for immediate disbursement in furtherance of the functions of the Commission. Such grants, gifts, or bequests, after acceptance by the Commission, shall be paid by the donor or the donor's representative to the Treasurer of the United States whose receipts shall be their acquittance. The Treasurer of the United States shall enter them in a special account to the credit of the Commission for the purposes in each case specified.

"(8) Six members of the Commission shall constitute a quorum, but a lesser number of 2 or more may conduct hearings.

"(h) TERMINATION.—The Commission shall terminate 3 years after the date of its first meeting.

"(i) AUTHORIZATION OF APPROPRIATIONS.—Effective October 1, 1988, there is authorized to be appropriated $2,000,000 to carry out the provisions of this section, which shall remain available until expended or until the termination of the Commission, whichever occurs first.

Aspects of MEP Eligibility

Eligibility for MEP is based upon meeting criteria in three areas: age, occupation of the child or family member, and how recently the child migrated.

Age:

Children from birth to age 21 (without a terminal certificate such as a high school diploma) are eligible, but only ages 3 to 21 are counted when determining state fiscal allocations.[1]

Occupation:

Agriculture or **fishing** activity for commercial sale or as a principal means of personal subsistence are the two major occupational categories considered for MEP eligibility. (Although the 1988 legislation added dairy workers, this population is considered to be a part of the agricultural labor force.)

Agricultural activity, by regulation, is defined to include the production or processing of crops, dairy products, poultry, or livestock and the cultivation or harvesting of trees.

Fishing activity, by regulation, is defined to include the catching or processing of fish or shellfish.[2]

Migrant Status:

Currently migratory refers to children who have moved within the past 12 months to enable the child, the parent/guardian, or member of the family to obtain temporary or seasonal work in agriculture or fishing activities across school district boundaries, across administrative areas within one district (e.g., Puerto Rico), and a distance of 20 miles within an 18,000 square mile district (e.g., Alaska).

Currently migrant children are further identified by their pattern of migration. If they cross state geographical boundaries, their MEP status is *inter*state. If they travel within a state's borders, their MEP status is *intra*state.[3]

Formerly migratory refers to children who are not now migrating, but who were eligible as a currently migratory child within the past 5 years.[4]

Notes

1 Eligibility criteria was expanded with the Stafford-Hawkins Elementary Improvement Act of 1988.

2 34 CFR 201.

3 MSRTS gives distinct codes to the type of mobility of an MEP-eligible child. Status Codes 1 through 3 relate to migration across states; 2 and 4 relate to migration with a state; and 3 and 6 relate to children who no longer migrate.

4 34 CFR 201.

Commissioned Studies

Frank Pitelli, Ph.D.
Pitelli & Associates
Edgewater, Maryland
■ *A tehnical study of the Migrant Student Record Transfer System.*

William O'Hare, Ph.D.
Urban Research Institute
University of Louisville
Louisville, Kentucky
■ *A study of the available demographic data on migrant farmworkers.*

Richard Figueroa, Ph.D.
University of California
Davis, California
■ *A study of handicapped students and selected MEP sites serving these student.*

Maria Colon
Pennsylvania State University
University Park, Pennsylvania
■ *A analysis of participation data in the state MEP plans and state performance reports.*

William Durden, Ph.D.
Center for Talented Youth
Johns Hopkins University
Baltimore, Maryland
■ *A study of selected MEP sites and evaluation criteria used for identifying and serving gifted and talented migrant student.*

Philip Martin, Ph.D.
University of California
Davis, California
■ *An analysis of the demographic data available on migrant farmworkers and the options for future assessments.*

David Martin, J.D.
Philip Martin, Ph.D.
Administrative Conference of the United States
Washington, D.C.
■ *A study on barriers to coordinating Federal programs and options for providing maximum benefits to migrant farmworkers.*

Exhibits

Exhibit 2.1
FY 1992 Section 1203 Coordination Grants

Title	Allocation	Description
Migrant Stopover Site Service Center	$252,134	This project in Hope, Arkansas provides educational, health, recreation, and other services at this stopover center. It is used by families traveling up the central stream. The staff identify MEP children, inform them (and their families) of the educational services available near the locations to which they are planning to travel. College recruitment materials are available. The center also informs SEAs and LEAs that these children will be arriving.
National Secondary Credit Exchange and Accrual Project	$350,000	This 3-year project was designed to improve migrant students' opportunity to meet graduation requirements and receive their high school diplomas. Activities include establishing a comprehensive database on graduation requirements, statistics, and available programs; reviewing the Portable Assisted Study Sequence, assisting SEAs in granting credit exchange and accrual; and developing a model system for credit exchange and accrual for migrant high school students.
Small State Identification and Recruitment Priority	$1,200,000	This competitive grant process for states was announced in June 1992. Although projects have yet to be funded, the goal is to provide additional MEP dollars to states that require additional support to adequately recruit migratory children. By expanding recruitment and coordination with other states, funded projects will be able to capture more inter- and intrastate migratory children.

Exhibit 3.1
Number and Percent of Currently and Formerly MEP Children Identified in each State/Jurisdiction in 1991

State	Currently Migratory		Formerly Migratory		Total
	Number	Percent	Number	Percent	
Alabama	2,428	0.46	2,831	0.54	5,259
Alaska	9,836	0.62	6,025	0.38	15,861
Arkansas	11,522	0.66	5,975	0.34	17,497
Arizona	8,818	0.48	9,439	0.52	18,257
California	79,619	0.38	127,942	0.62	207,561
Colorado	4,113	0.67	2,040	0.33	6,153
Connecticut	910	0.26	2,630	0.74	3,540
Delaware	442	0.43	578	0.57	1,020
District of Columbia	58	0.24	182	0.76	240
Florida	33,833	0.59	23,057	0.41	56,890
Georgia	7,303	0.75	2,388	0.25	9,691
Iowa	1,216	0.88	168	0.12	1,384
Idaho	6,019	0.57	4,493	0.43	10,512
Illinois	1,658	0.53	1,445	0.47	3,103
Indiana	4,886	0.88	649	0.12	5,535
Kansas	4,136	0.39	6,551	0.61	10,687
Kentucky	3,752	0.49	3915	0.51	7,667
Louisiana	2,166	0.29	5,226	0.71	7,392
Massachusetts	1,341	0.21	4,990	0.79	6,331
Maryland	530	0.78	147	0.22	677
Maine	3,749	0.46	4,328	0.54	8,077
Michigan	17,085	0.68	8,080	0.32	25,165
Minnesota	5,092	0.91	520	0.09	5,612
Missouri	982	0.53	881	0.47	1,863
Mississippi	1,689	0.30	3,945	0.70	5,634
Montana	954	0.95	52	0.05	1,006
North Carolina	4,712	0.61	2,972	0.39	7,684
North Dakota	1,535	0.97	51	0.03	1,586
Nebraska	1,354	0.91	137	0.09	1,491
New Hampshire	54	0.37	91	0.63	145
New Jersey	816	0.34	1,592	0.66	2,408
New Mexico	1,594	0.41	2,288	0.59	3,882
Nevada	534	0.35	998	0.65	1,532
New York	4,724	0.45	5,731	0.55	10,455
Ohio	5,309	0.89	630	0.11	5,939
Oklahoma	1,557	0.53	1,384	0.47	2,941
Oregon	11,404	0.55	9,282	0.45	20,686
Pennsylvania	2,921	0.49	3,087	0.51	6,008
Puerto Rico	4,482	0.29	10,845	0.71	15,327
Rhode Island	74	0.24	239	0.76	313
South Carolina	1,123	0.96	51	0.04	1,174
South Dakota	254	0.62	156	0.38	410
Tennessee	362	0.63	216	0.37	578
Texas	60,511	0.52	55,873	0.48	116,384
Utah	780	0.46	902	0.54	1,682
Virginia	1,106	0.86	180	0.14	1,286
Vermont	530	0.37	916	0.63	1,446
Washington	15,154	0.52	13,964	0.48	29,118
Wisconsin	2,235	0.86	363	0.14	2,598
West Virginia	71	0.89	9	0.11	80
Wyoming	429	0.88	58	0.12	487
Total Across States	337,762	0.50	340,492	0.50	678,254
Total Across Nation	298,471	0.48	329,679	0.52	628,150

Total across states includes children counted in more than one state. The total across the nation is an unduplicated count of children counted only once over the year. Based upon MSRTS statistics Unique Count for the 1990-1991 year. March 31, 1992 computer run.

Exhibit 4.1

Programs that Serve Migrant Preschool Children

Program	Funding Agency	Target Population	Services	Special Features
Migrant Education Program (MEP)	Department of Education	Ages 3 to 21 for both currently and formerly migrant children and below 3 under special circumstances.	Educational and support services.	Currently migratory children receive priority. This is an entitlement program.
Migrant Head Start (MHS)	Department of Health and Human Services	Birth to Compulsory school age for families whose primary employment is agriculture and moved within a year.	Education, health, nutrition, and social services.	Family-centered requiring parental involvement. This is an entitlement program.
Migrant Even Start (MES)	Department of Education	Ages 1 to 7 of parents who qualify for MEP and Adult Basic Education	Provides for adult literacy training, day care, and support services.	Trains parents to support the education of their child and provides parent education. This is a discretionary grant operating in 9 sites.

Exhibit 7.1
Migrant Education Program Fiscal Year Appropriations
Actual versus Estimated Constant Dollars including Year to Year Change

Year	Appropriation	Percent Change in Year to Year Appropriations	Estimated Constant Dollars	Estimated % Change in Constant Dollars
1967	$9,737,847		40,406,004	
1968	41,692,425	328.15	160,974,614	298.39
1969	45,556,074	9.27	164,462,361	2.17
1970	51,014,319	11.98	169,482,787	3.05
1971	57,608,680	12.93	177,257,477	4.59
1972	64,822,926	12.52	186,809,585	5.39
1973	72,772,187	12.26	195,099,697	4.44
1974	78,331,436	7.64	196,812,653	0.88
1975	91,953,160	17.39	212,854,537	8.15
1976	97,090,478	5.59	204,832,232	-3.77
1977	130,909,832	34.83	252,234,744	23.14
1978	145,759,940	11.34	259,821,640	3.01
1979	173,548,829	19.06	290,701,556	11.89
1980	209,593,746	20.77	323,947,057	11.44
1981	245,000,000	16.89	348,506,401	7.58
1982	266,400,000	8.73	349,606,299	0.32
1983	255,744,000	-4.00	314,568,266	-10.02
1984	255,744,000	0.00	297,722,934	-5.36
1985	258,024,000	0.89	285,424,779	-4.13
1986	264,524,000	2.52	279,328,405	-2.14
1987	253,149,000	-4.30	255,706,061	-8.46
1988	264,524,000	4.49	255,578,744	-0.05
1989	269,029,000	1.70	249,794,800	-2.26
1990	271,700,000	0.99	242,589,286	-2.88
1991	282,444,000	3.95	241,818,493	-0.32
1992	294,596,000	4.30	245,088,186	1.35

Between 1966 an 1975 Congress appropriated dollars for the year in which MEP funds were used. Starting with 1976, a forward funding cycle was used. The appropriations listed in this table are represented for the year in which they were used and not for the year in which they were authorized (e.g., 1976 to the present). Calculations to account for inflation were based upon the price index for State and Local Purchases of Services, Fixed Weight Version Beginning with 1978. These dollars were anchored to 1982 as the base year.

Exhibit 7.2
Differences Between Allocations & Formula Generated Funding

Fiscal Year	FTE-Based Appropriations	Actual Appropriations	Percent Differences
1980-81[2]	255,802,686	245,000,000	95.78
1981-82	286,541,011	266,400,000	92.97
1982-83	336,183,521	255,744,000	76.08
1983-84	367,453,919	255,744,000	69.60
1984-85	428,850,219	258,024,000	60.17
1985-86	449,295,429	264,524,000	58.88
1986-87	476,549,363	253,149,000	53.13
1987-88	532,053,309	264,524,000	49.72
1988-89	596,150,980	269,029,000	45.13
1989-90	742,272,858	271,700,000	36.60
1990-91	845,243,256	282,444,000	33.41

1. The discrepancy between FTE-Based Appropriations and Actual Appropriations is a result of expanding populations resulting from definitional changes and does not necessarily reflect currently migrant children being underserved.
2. Program capped. Annual amount determined by appropriations.

Exhibit 7.3
State-by-State Migrant Education Fiscal Allocation
Fiscal Years 1989 through 1992

State	FY89	FY90	FY91	FY92
Alabama	1,820,613	1,915,186	1,966,556	1,936,925
Alaska	7,009,227	7,515,397	8,581,362	9,881,306
Arizona	6,771,445	7,041,283	6,906,387	6,836,515
Arkansas	4,063,678	4,235,900	3,608,291	3,528,499
California	87,102,827	93,155,567	100,340,195	105,631,328
Colorado	2,337,207	2,370,032	2,242,095	2,279,292
Connecticut	2,277,045	2,010,054	2,269,791	2,336,022
Delaware	677,863	585,558	596,319	498,108
D.C.	68,596	87,137	119,164	149,237
Florida	23,173,414	23,533,882	23,051,848	22,317,952
Georgia	2,644,781	2,435,322	3,124,393	3,565,431
Idaho	3,243,289	3,372,527	3,765,270	3,836,397
Illinois	1,912,170	1,949,448	1,881,838	1,702,362
Indiana	907,516	1,140,089	1,433,874	1,754,447
Iowa	88,250	218,799	291,124	271,102
Kansas	3,760,763	3,783,236	4,016,322	4,584,295
Kentucky	1,879,416	2,175,756	2,721,808	3,647,793
Louisiana	3,565,520	3,177,875	3,012,306	2,931,964
Maine	3,339,442	3,434,748	3,739,052	3,911,606
Maryland	397,647	376,447	331,403	288,723
Massachusetts	4,659,530	4,591,267	4,350,702	4,238,889
Michigan	9,151,135	10,499,948	11,724,452	11,970,069
Minnesota	1,904,751	2,057,837	1,886,050	1,811,388
Mississippi	1,942,689	1,914,299	1,962,333	1,970,849
Missouri	782,006	725,904	709,942	661,344
Montana	345,317	290,523	274,069	289,956
Nebraska	390,567	340,406	405,574	526,546
Nevada	586,673	630,836	593,854	591,943
New Hampshire	111,552	123,394	117,232	105,092
New Jersey	1,773,291	1,544,047	1,373,821	1,231,463
New Mexico	1,248,175	1,306,003	1,336,693	1,478,086
New York	5,768,547	6,349,210	6,821,658	6,832,354
North Carolina	2,483,648	2,781,691	3,238,372	4,058,157
North Dakota	605,667	525,885	472,734	377,746
Ohio	1,327,439	1,342,827	1,522,577	1,528,804
Oklahoma	992,102	976,989	992,993	1,022,164
Oregon	7,523,502	8,348,055	9,385,180	9,654,203
Pennsylvania	2,377,846	3,028,394	3,697,227	3,565,437
Puerto Rico	2,758,254	2,866,255	3,308,931	4,657,188
Rhode Island	129,012	157,506	170,006	181,367
South Carolina	278,401	252,391	240,969	244,106
South Dakota	59,437	60,953	77,607	142,479
Tennessee	176,447	185,375	175,538	180,583
Texas	45,151,695	43,296,784	41,617,465	40,233,925
Utah	658,032	849,971	836,883	903,859
Vermont	708,204	763,325	743,652	1,129,842
Virginia	370,730	414,508	420,696	423,572
Washington	11,483,768	12,180,915	12,033,865	12,183,684
West Virginia	41,190	41,734	25,142	21,183
Wisconsin	784,700	812,759	800,378	727,557
Wyoming	268,040	238,961	282,007	207,389

Exhibit 7.4
Percent of FY 1989 MEP Allocations Carried Over to FY 1990

State	Allocation	Carryover	Percent
Alabama	1,820,613	143,820	8
Alaska	7,009,227	120,000	2
Arizona	6,771,445	300,000	4
Arkansas	4,063,678	620,128	15
California	87,102,827	10,528,698	12
Colorado	2,337,207	185,000	8
Connecticut	2,227,045	397,250	18
Delaware	667,863	140,000	21
D.C.	68,596	0	0
Florida	23,173,414	2,000,000	9
Georgia	2,644,781	209,571	8
Idaho	3,243,289	Missing	-
Illinois	1,912,170	412,000	22
Indiana	907,516	32,300	4
Iowa	88,250	0	0
Kansas	3,760,763	Missing	-
Kentucky	1,879,416	100,000	5
Louisiana	3,565,520	400,000	11
Maine	3,339,442	350,000	10
Maryland	397,647	20,000	5
Mass.	4,659,530	500,000	11
Michigan	9,151,135	200,000	2
Minnesota	1,904,751	0	0
Mississippi	1,942,689	270,909	14
Missouri	782,006	162,000	21
Montana	345,317	60,000	17
Nebraska	390,567	0	0
Nevada	586,673	20,000	3
NewHamp.	111,522	35,000	31
NewJersey	1,773,291	135,000	8
NewMexico	1,248,175	100,000	8
NewYork	5,768,547	0	0
N.Carolina	2,483,648	370,000	15
N.Dakota	605,667	33,000	5
Ohio	1,327,439	200,000	15
Oklahoma	992,102	180,458	18
Oregon	7,523,502	500,000	7
Pennsylvania	2,377,846	122,514	5
PuertoRico	2,758,401	51,000	2
RhodeIsland	129,012	50,000	39
S.Carolina	278,401	50,000	18
S.Dakota	59,437	8,500	14
Tennessee	176,447	44,112	25
Texas	45,151,695	5,408,268	12
Utah	658,032	131,600	20
Vermont	708,204	Missing	-
Virginia	370,730	55,000	15
Washington	11,483,768	1,391,488	12
WestVirginia	41,190	6,000	15
Wisconsin	784,700	0	0
Wyoming	268,040	40,000	15

These fiscal allocations were based upon FY89 expenditures reported by the office of Management Support Division in the U. S. Department of Education and the budgeted carryover amounts listed in the states MEP grant application.

Goals and Expectations

Plans for National Education Goals Panel and "America 2000"

National Education Goals

By the year 2000:

1. All children in America will start school ready to learn.

2. The high school graduation rate will increase to at least 90 percent.

3. American students will leave grades four, eight, and twelve having demonstrated competency in challenging subject matter including English, mathematics, science, history, and geography (and leave school) prepared for responsible citizenship, further learning, and productive employment in our modern world.

4. U. S. students will be first in the world in science and mathematics achievement.

5. Every adult American will be literate and will possess the knowledge and skills necessary to compete in a global economy and exercise the rights and responsibilities of citizenship.

6. Every school in America will be free of drugs and violence and will offer a disciplined environment conducive to learning.

America 2000

In support of those goals, President Bush announced April 1991 a four-part strategy:

1. For Today's Students: Better and More Accountable Schools.

2. For Tomorrow's Students: A New Generation of American Schools.

3. For the Rest of Us (Yesterday's Students): A Nation of Students.

4. Communities Where Learning Can Happen.

The National Association of State Directors of Migrant Education

Expectations for the Education of Migrant Children and Youth are:

1. Migrant children should enter first grade fully prepared to learn and schools should be fully prepared to help them learn.

2. The cultural and language diversity represented by migrant students should be used positively and creatively within schools and communities.

3. Between 1992 and 2002, the number of migrant students graduating from high school should increase annually by 10 percent.

4. Migrant students should complete the elementary grades with mastery of critical skills in learning to read, write, compute, and think.

5. Migrant students should complete the middle school grades able to reason critically and understand the relevance to their lives the subject matter they are learning.

6. Migrant students entering high school should be able to complete their educations and graduate successfully.

7. Migrant students should be provided stimulating learning experiences in science, mathematics, and technology education as they proceed through their school years.

8. The academic achievement of migrant students should be at a level that will enable them upon graduation from high school, to be prepared for postsecondary education, employment or both.

9. Migrant students who do not choose college should be provided school-to-work transition experiences so they leave high school prepared with the skills necessary to participate productively in the world of work and with the foundation required to upgrade their skills and advance their employment and career opportunities.

10. Adults and out-of-school migrant youth should be provided quality experiences and opportunities to improve their literacy, basic education, and problem solving skills.

11. Migrant children should attend schools that are free of drugs and alcohol and where students are well nourished and healthy, feel safe, and learn in a supportive and caring environment.

12. Every state department of education should have a successful comprehensive strategy for migrant children and youth that provides a process to bring about quality, equity, and congruence in their education.

Photo credits

Cover photograph from Redlands Christian Migrant Association.
Inside front cover from Texas Education Agency
Inside back cover © J. Fossett/The Image Works
Pages v, viii, x, 12, 26, 34, 64, 69, 84, 89 from the Texas Education Agency
Pages vi, 16, 55, 77 © J. Fossett/The Image Works
Pages xiv, 7 © Moore/The Image Works
Page 23 Donna Hurst
Page 43 Al Wright
Page 97 from Redlands Christian Migrant Association